NATIONS OF THE MODERN WORLD

ARGENTINA
H. S. Ferns
Professor of Political Science,
University of Birmingham

AUSTRALIA
O. H. K. Spate
Director, Research School of Pacific Studies,
Australian National University, Canberra

AUSTRIA
Karl R. Stadler
Professor of Modern and Contemporary History,
University of Linz

BELGIUM
Vernon Mallinson
Professor of Comparative Education,
University of Reading

BURMA
F. S. V. Donnison
Formerly Chief Secretary to the Government of Burma
Historian, Cabinet Office, Historical Section 1949–66

CYPRUS
H. D. Purcell
Professor of English,
University of Libya, Benghazi

DENMARK
W. Glyn Jones
Reader in Danish, University College London

MODERN EGYPT
Tom Little
Former Managing Director and General Manager of
Regional News Services (Middle East), Ltd, London

ENGLAND
A Portrait
John Bowle
Formerly Professor of Political Theory, College d'Europe,
Bruges 1950–67

FINLAND
W. R. Mead
Professor of Geography, University College London

EAST
GERMANY
David Childs
Lecturer in Politics, University of Nottingham

PAKISTAN   Ian Stephens
Formerly Editor of The Statesman,
Calcutta and Delhi, 1942–51
Fellow, King's College, Cambridge, 1952–58

PERU   Sir Robert Marett
H.M. Ambassador in Lima, 1963–67

POLAND   Václav L. Beneš
Professor of Political Science,
Indiana University

Norman J. G. Pounds
Professor of History and Geography,
Indiana University

SOUTH AFRICA   John Cope
Formerly Editor-in-Chief of The Forum *and South*
Africa Correspondent of The Guardian

THE SOVIET
UNION   Elisabeth Koutaissoff
Professor of Russian,
Victoria University, Wellington

SPAIN   George Hills
Formerly Correspondent and Spanish Programme Organizer,
British Broadcasting Corporation

SWEDEN   Irene Scobbie
Senior Lecturer in Swedish,
University of Aberdeen

SYRIA   Tabitha Petran

TURKEY   Geoffrey Lewis
Senior Lecturer in Islamic Studies, Oxford

YUGOSLAVIA   Stevan K. Pavlowitch
Lecturer in Balkan History, University of
Southampton

SYRIA

SYRIA

by

TABITHA PETRAN

PRAEGER PUBLISHERS
NEW YORK · WASHINGTON

BOOKS THAT MATTER

Published in the United States of America in 1972
by Praeger Publishers, Inc., 111 Fourth Avenue,
New York, N.Y. 10003

Library of Congress Catalog Card Number: 72–88257

Printed in Great Britain

Preface

IN PREPARING THIS BOOK I have received help from many
Syrians and other Arabs—so many that it is impossible to name them.
To all I am deeply grateful and tender my thanks. None are respon-
sible for my interpretation of events. I wish also to express my
appreciation to the staff of Chatham House library and of Jafet
Library of the American University of Beirut, especially to Miss
Evelyn Zacharia Samir Hawi, and Mrs Melia Khayr for their
patient and unfailing assistance.

Uckfield,   T.P.
April 1972

Certain sounds in the Arabic lang   re not readily differentiated by the untrained ear. Exact transliteration requires diacritical
marks and letters without equivalent in European alphabets. All are
omitted with the exception of the medial *ayn* here denoted by '.
Familiar Arabic names—e.g., Nasser, Nuri Said, etc.—appear in the
accepted English form.

Contents

List of Illustrations

Maps

Acknowledgements

ACKNOWLEDGEMENT for kind permission to reproduce illustrations is made to the following, to whom the copyright of the illustrations belongs:

W. H. Bartlett: 1, 2
Camera Press, London: 8, 14, 15, 16, 20, 21, 23
The *Daily Star*, Beirut: 9, 10, 11, 12
The Imperial War Museum, London: 3, 4, 5, 6, 7
Syrian Arab News Agency: 13, 17, 19, 22
UNRWA (photograph by Vartan Sarkissian): 18

List of Abbreviations

ACSP	Arab Collective Security Pact
ALM	Arab Liberation Movement
ANM	Arab National Movement
ASP	Arab Socialist Party
AUB	American University of Beirut
BSL	Banque de Syrie et du Liban
CIA	Central Intelligence Agency
CUP	Committee of Union and Progress
FAR	Federation of Arab Republics
ICATU	International Confederation of Arab Trade Unions
ILO	International Labour Office
IPC	Iraq Petroleum Company
MAC	Mixed Armistice Commission
MEJ	*Middle East Journal*
NCRC	National Council of the Revolutionary Command
NRC	National Revolutionary Council
PFLP	Popular Front for the Liberation of Palestine
PLA	Palestine Liberation Army
PLO	Palestine Liberation Organization
PMC	Permanent Mandates Commission (League of Nations)
SAR	Syrian Arab Republic
SNP	Syrian National Party
SSNP	Syrian Social Nationalist Party
UAR	United Arab Republic
UN	United Nations
UNRWA	United Nations Relief and Works Agency
UNTSO	United Nations Truce Supervision Organization

Chapter 1

Unrealized Nation

THE NAME SYRIA, first used by the Greeks, designated in history the geographic region lying at the eastern end of the Mediterranean between Egypt and Anatolia and, at times, also political or administrative divisions within it. The Arabs who conquered this region in the seventh century called it *Bilad Al-Sham*, 'the country on the left' or north of Mecca, Islam's holiest city. So it remained until this century when the Western Powers carved out of the region the states of Syria, Lebanon, Jordan, and Israel and gave parts of it to Turkey. In its contemporary form Syria did not exist before 1920. Neither its history nor its geography can be isolated from that of the region as a whole. In this and the next two chapters the term Syria applies to this region. Modern Syria will be referred to in these chapters as the Syrian Arab Republic.

The Syrian region is a geographic entity with marked natural boundaries – the Taurus mountains to the north; the Sinai peninsula and Arabia to the south; the Mediterranean to the west; and the desert to the east. No single, indigenous power has ever been able to assert political control over the whole region. Its original political organization was that of independent and often rival city kingdoms. From earliest times these cities – they are among the oldest continuously inhabited cities in the world – each acquired a particularist socio-political character which has persisted to the present day. For Syria's position at the pivot of the three historic continents and its character as a marchland between neighbouring empires made it a bridge and a battleground of external powers. Through much of its history it experienced political unity as a part of larger empires but relapsed into a greater or lesser degree of fragmentation when stronger powers contested for its control and when in rare moments it was left alone. The diversity of its internal configuration and the nature of its water resources (this is an area where water is more precious than land) contributed to its political fragmentation.

INTERNAL DIVERSITY

Syria, which lies mainly on the northern slope of the vast and

17

geologically ancient Arabian platform extending north-east across the Euphrates, is divided into two strikingly contrasted zones. To the west a double chain of mountains separated by a deep rift valley stretches from Turkey to Sinai. This double mountain barrier, a region of great variety and complexity about 60 miles wide, forms a façade for the vast steppeland-desert plateau of internal Syria.

Mediterranean Syria

A discontinuous maritime plain is wedged between the mountains and the rocky, almost straight, Mediterranean coast. This narrow plain widens in front of the Nusayriyah range below Latakia and is most extensive in the south in Palestine. Formed of alluvions washed down from the mountains and in the south also by sediment from the Nile, it is very fertile and intensively cultivated. The coast offers no good natural harbours for modern ships, but its sheltered coves sufficed for sailing vessels of the past. Since ancient times a string of port cities–Latakia, Tripoli, Byblos, Beirut, Tyre, Sidon, Acre, Jaffa, and Gaza–opened Syria to the Mediterranean world, but in antiquity many of these cities were isolated from each other by impassable mountain canyons.

A succession of river gorges and plains cuts the coastal mountain range into separate blocks (see map, pp. 268–9). The broken character of the northernmost sector, allowing corridors into the interior, made this area throughout history the principal passageway between Europe and Asia. Southward, where the Nusayriyah and Lebanon ranges hinder east–west movement, there are only two easy routes inland: the Tripoli–Homs gap between the Nusayriyah and Lebanon ranges and the Esdraelon plain at the southern end of the Lebanon range. The chief invasion and trade route from Egypt and the coast led through the Megiddo (Armageddon) pass in the Carmel range across this plain to the Jordan and on through the Yarmuk valley to inland Syria. The isolated valleys and ravines of the Nusayriyah and Lebanon ranges have always offered a refuge to the heterodox.

The eastern mountain chain, lower and more extensive than the coastal range, forms in the north the rolling uplands of the Kurd Dagh which fall east to the Euphrates. The Anti-Lebanon, the highest range in the eastern chain, begins below the Homs and Hama plateau and extends more than 130 miles south-west to Mount Hermon (*Jebel Al-Shaikh*, the grey-haired mountain) whose highest peak is over 9,000 feet. The only corridor through the Anti-Lebanon is the Zabdani depression which separates Hermon from the rest of the range. Above this depression, the Anti-Lebanon is composed of a parched and barren main ridge and the naked, white Qalamun ridges which fan north-east into the desert. Mount Hermon subsides southward to the plateaux of Golan and Hawran. The Hawran, studded with volcanic mounds, rises in the east to become the Jebel Druze with peaks of 5–6,000 feet.

The rift valley between the mountain ranges reaches its highest elevation–3,600 feet above sea-level–at the watershed in the Biqa plain between the Lebanon and Anti-Lebanon mountains; its lowest point is on the floor of the Dead Sea, 2,598 feet below sea-level. A succession of rivers flow through this valley. The Orontes moves north from one side of the watershed near Baalbek (hence its Arabic name, *Al-Asi*, the Rebel) to turn eventually into the Mediterranean at Antioch. Close by, from the other side of the watershed, the Litani (ancient Leontes) starts south to break away to the west, cutting through the Lebanon range to the Mediterranean at Tyre. The Jordan, whose headwaters drain the slopes of Mount Hermon, flows down through the Jordan valley to the Dead Sea. The rift valley rising again to sea-level extends south-east to the Aqaba Gulf. Parts of the valley, notably the Biqa plain and the broad plain between Homs and Hama, are very fertile. Other parts, where drainage is blocked, become swampland in winter. The Ghab, until recently a marshland created by a basalt sill blocking the Orontes, is today drained and reclaimed. The river now flows in part of this section through two irrigation channels.

Internal Syria

A great semicircle of grassland stretches from the south-east corner of the Mediterranean around the northern end of the Arabian desert to the Persian Gulf. The American historian James Henry Breasted christened this arc the Fertile Crescent. The western arm of the Fertile Crescent, lying in Syria, consists of the cultivable fringes of the desert at the base of the eastern mountain chain. These are, from south to north, the Hawran plain, the Damascus oasis, the plains of Homs, Hama, and Aleppo. (In the north-east section of the Crescent is the Jazira [Island] lying between the Euphrates and the Tigris. Geographically, the Jazira is part of Mesopotamia. Culturally, it has always been Syrian. It is included in the present-day Syrian Arab Republic, of which it forms the north-east corner.)

The western arm of the Fertile Crescent connects Egypt and Mesopotamia and so has always had great strategic as well as economic importance. In this desert fringe a line of cities–Aleppo, Hama, Homs, Damascus, and Amman–gave access to the desert and, by routes around and across it, to lands beyond. These 'desert ports'

are not more than 75 miles from the Mediterranean, but they are
separated from the line of seaport cities to which they lie parallel by
two mountain ranges and a rift valley. No one of these cities on either
side of the mountain ranges could constitute a natural centre of
gravity for the Syrian region.

The Syrian desert, or *Badiyat Al-Sham*, is a triangularly shaped
plateau forming the northern part of the Arabian desert. The top of
the triangle, whose apex reaches into the Fertile Crescent near
Aleppo, is known as *Shamiya* to the Arabs and as the Little Desert to
Europeans. Oases, natural springs, and wells make it something less
than a desert in the usual sense of the term and allowed it to become
throughout history the most frequently travelled highway between
east and west. Perennial shrubs, thistles, and scanty grasses also
provide summer pasture for the flocks of nomadic and semi-nomadic
tribes which winter in Arabia. The bottom of the triangle, called
Al-Samawa by the Arabs and the Great Desert by Europeans, is a
barren, waterless, stony plateau. Even here, however, meagre winter
rain leaves on the outskirts and in depressions a brief aftermath of
grass on which the nomad's camels may feed. The western section of
the desert is called the Hamad; the eastern, the Widian (from its
many wadis).

Rainfall

Sea and desert influence the climate of Syria from opposite directions. Rainfall, often torrential, occurs only in winter months. The
maritime plain and the western slopes of the coastal mountains have
a temperate, typically Mediterranean climate, with an annual rainfall of 20–30 inches on the coastal strip and 40 or more on the
mountains. The coastal mountain chain cuts off the rest of Syria from
the tempering influences and rainclouds of the Mediterranean except
where these pass inland over the low mountains in the north and
through the Tripoli-Homs and Esdraelon corridors to water respectively the plains of Aleppo, Homs, and the Hawran. A central semi-
arid zone stretches from the great rift valley over the internal plateau
within a rainbelt of 20–10 inches a year. In this typically 'Syrian'
climate, the long, luminous, almost cloudless summers are very hot
and the winters relatively cold. In the arid desert zone to the east,
where torrid summers last ten months and more, rainfall is less than
8 inches and diminishes towards the interior.

Rainfall is very badly distributed and decreases progressively from
north to south away from the mountains of Turkey and from west to
east away from the coastal range. It also varies greatly from year
to year and from month to month. The 'seven lean years' of drought

and famine recorded in the Bible have reoccurred through millennia and indicate that the fertility of the Crescent is highly relative. Sixty per cent of the land area of the present-day Syrian Arab Republic receives less than 10 inches of rain and only 10 per cent receives sufficient rainfall (20 to 40 inches) to assure relatively stable non-irrigated cultivation. Another 30 per cent with 10 to 20 inches supports dry farming subject to good rainfall. The water problem is complicated by the high rate of evaporation and the erosion caused by torrential rains, which do not assist vegetation.

Population Distribution

Population distribution follows climate, soil, and, above all, the availability of water and is therefore very uneven. Population is most dense in the coastal regions and on the lower mountain slopes, less so in the rift valley and central plains, and thins out rapidly eastward of the eastern mountain chain. The Little Desert, where the line between pasture and cultivation fluctuates with the rainfall, is the summer home of semi-nomadic and nomadic tribes. The Great Desert is the domain of the camel and camel-rearing nomads.

FRAGMENTING INFLUENCES

Syria has no economic backbone such as the Nile gave to Egypt or the Tigris–Euphrates to Iraq. Its rivers are not navigable, and many of them dry up in summer. The tenth-century Arab geographer Maqdisi remarked that 'In the whole country of Syria there is not a river carrying boats aside from the ferry'. The Euphrates, an international river, which runs 420 miles through the present-day Syrian Arab Republic, has swift currents which make it navigable only downstream. Syria's rivers have acted, not as arteries of communication and commerce, but as barriers to political unity. These rivers, moreover, do not lend themselves to use for irrigation on any significant scale and so have not evoked the collective effort, discipline, and ultimate political unity required to harness the potential of the Nile. Until very recently, waters of Syrian rivers have been used only locally along the banks. To raise water from the deep river beds is very difficult. Since Roman times all-wooden water-wheels or *norias*, powered by the current of the river, have lifted water along the central section of the Orontes to irrigate fields between Homs and Hama and gardens and orchards between Hama and Cheizar. The biggest are 80 feet in diameter. The oldest *norias* still turning today date from the Mamluk period (1260–1517). The monotonous moaning of the *norias* on the Orontes, however, will soon be stilled.

Construction of the Rastan dam has so lowered water-levels that some *norias* have already stopped turning and others will follow. *Norias* (but not the unique all-wooden type of Hama) have also been used on the Euphrates and the Khabur. Within the past generation motor pumps have arrived by the thousand along the banks of these rivers. Irrigation of this type, involving only a local effort, gives no impetus to political integration beyond the immediate vicinity. The great dam now being built on the middle course of the Euphrates near Tabqa is the first attempt since antiquity to exploit a river on a national scale.

In the semi-arid steppeland between the mountains and the desert only the most ingenious use of meagre water supplies has made cultivation possible, but the methods used do not constitute a unifying force here either. An intricate irrigation system begun in ancient times on the Barada River created the oasis of Damascus. The Barada is one of a number of small rivers which rise at the foot of the eastern range to flow eastward and expire in the desert. It breaks from a mountain ravine onto the Damascus plain at an elevation of nearly 3,000 feet. Six main artificial channels called *Nahr* (River) carry the water over the sloping plain; they are divided and subdivided by diversion dams of earth, stones, and branches which direct the water down to new channels and sub-channels below. Each plot receives its share of water through sluices which are opened for fixed periods and at fixed intervals according to complex arrangements established by tradition. Other springs, rivers, and streams of the Qalamoun ridges and Mount Hermon are exploited by similar primitive irrigation systems.

Poor in rainfall and surface water, Syria has been relatively rich in subterranean water owing to the porous rock of which much of the country is formed. Permeable rock–especially the limestone tops and cores of many of the mountains and the volcanic rock spread widely over the interior–quickly absorbs rainfall and so preserves it from evaporation. Rain and snow accumulate as subterranean water to reappear in springs at the base of mountains and plateaux and wherever the water meets an impermeable rock layer. The long depression between the mountain ranges is watered by springs which give birth to rivers and sometimes swampland.

For millennia subterranean water has been exploited by wells and by *qanawat* (singular: *qanat*), also called *foggaras*. Water is lifted from wells, often by a chain of buckets moved by an animal-turned wheel. Motor pumps are now more frequent. Their extensive use has already critically reduced water-levels in some areas. *Qanawat*, requiring a sloping land surface, are in effect 'horizontal wells': subterranean channels are dug upslope into water-bearing strata in order to bring water to the surface downslope by gravity flow. This system, introduced by the Persians more than 2,000 years ago, requires expert calculation of the levels of underground water seepage. *Qanawat* may extend for several miles. They were used extensively in the past in parts of central Syria, the Aleppo and Damascus plains, and the eastern slopes of the eastern mountain chain. After cleaning and repair, some are now back in use.

CARAVAN TRAILS, A UNIFYING INFLUENCE

Syria's central position in the old world made it a great junction for overland and sea routes from Further Asia and India to the Mediterranean, Africa, and Europe as well as for exchanges between its neighbours, Mesopotamia, Egypt, and Anatolia. Some of the trails developed in prehistoric times. By 3,000 B.C. caravan trade was so well established that its methods were standardized and commercial exchanges regularized.[1] Desert routes could not have been used before the domestication of the camel towards the end of the second millennium B.C. and the arrival in the Syrian desert early in the first millennium B.C. of the single-humped camel and the swifter single-humped dromedary from Arabia.

Numerous passageways between Syria and Arabia reflected the always intimate relations between these regions. From Mesopotamia, caravan trails ran along the Euphrates or Tigris river banks, where vegetation and water were available, to connect across or around the desert with the various cities of Syria. The most common link between Egypt and Syria was by sea to the Phoenician ports and thence through mountain corridors to inland cities. The overland trail from Egypt followed the Sinai coast to the Esdraelon corridor and on to Damascus.

Both Aleppo and Damascus became great caravan junctions. At Aleppo, halfway between the Mediterranean and the western bend of the Euphrates, converged routes from Europe (through the northern gateway to Syria), from India and the Persian Gulf (by way of the Euphrates and the Little Desert), from China, Central Asia, and Persia (through the Caspian and Zagros Gates), and from Damascus, Homs, and Hama (along the inland slopes of the eastern mountain range). Damascus, situated on the highway crossing Syria from north to south, was linked by the legendary spice road to Arabian cities and ports and so to India and Africa. It was also a staging post on the route linking the Nile to the Euphrates. From Damascus a trail followed the Qalamoun ridge, where wells provided water, to the Palmyra oasis and thence to the Euphrates.

Caravan trails used in one period were often abandoned in another. Wars put some routes out of action. The choice of route for the eastern trade was a subject of recurring dispute and itself sometimes provoked wars and determined the fate of empires. Shifts in international routes condemned some cities to die while others prospered. The Nabatean city of Petra, situated at a key junction of the spice road with various highways to the market towns of the Mediterranean, flourished as the middleman of this trade from about the end of the fourth century B.C. and became the capital of a caravan kingdom. This kingdom developed its own characteristic Nabatean civilization before a change in trade routes doomed it to eclipse during the second century A.D. As Petra declined, the oasis of Palmyra, a halt on transdesert crossroads between the Mediterranean and the Euphrates, expanded into a wealthy caravan empire with a cosmopolitan Syrian-Greek-Persian culture. Conquest by the Romans and a shift in the Damascus–Euphrates route ended Palmyra's grandeur at the end of the third century A.D.

If caravan trade made Syrian cities commercial rivals, it had a far greater unifying influence. For caravan routes linked the internal cities with each other as well as with the outside world and so facilitated the development of a common language and common ways of life.

THE PEOPLE

Throughout historical times peoples of many different origins and tongues entered Syria. But the strongest immigration and the most persistent infiltration has been semitic. The provenance of the semitic-speaking peoples is uncertain. The theory that they originated in the Arabian peninsula is disputed since evidence is lacking and, as already noted, long-range nomadism was impossible before the domestication of the camel. Another theory holds that, if they came from the desert, it could only have been from the desert outskirts as semi-nomadic pastoralists engaged in sheep-rearing, perhaps on the semi-desert steppelands along the inner fringes of the Fertile Crescent.

Syria's earliest inhabitants spoke a non-semitic language, but semitic-speaking peoples were already present about 3,000 B.C. Thereafter semitic migration flowed into Syria at roughly thousand-year intervals. During the third millennium B.C. the Amorites arrived in north Syria and another branch of this migration, sometimes called the Canaanites, came to the Syrian coastlands. The Arameans and the Hebrews arrived during the second millennium B.C. and the Nabateans (an Arab people) about a millennium later. The Arabs, who infiltrated from Arabia almost continuously from the latter half of the first millennium B.C., arrived as conquerors in the seventh century A.D. and continued to infiltrate thereafter.

Many foreign invaders conquered and ruled Syria. Hittites and Hurrians, Hyksos and Egyptians, Assyrians and Babylonians, Persians and Philistines, Greeks and Romans, Arabs, European Crusaders, Mongols, and Turks at one time or another established themselves in all or part of Syria, some for many centuries. Yet, apart from the Arabs, few of these ethnic and cultural elements left a permanent mark. The fusion of the Arabs with the already settled population, also in the main semitic, made for a substantially homogeneous people with a specific Syrian character.

This people–fractured by clan, socio-cultural and religious parochialisms–retained a particularist bent. Much of the population had entered Syria as small independent tribes which 'fitted the little shelves and corners of Syria so that Syria was tribal both by her form and by the character of her population'.[2] Each of these regions developed its own customs, folklore, manners, costumes, and even pronunciation. The primacy of kinship ties extending from the family, the basic social unit, through clan and tribe reinforced local particularisms. Even today the sense of belonging, of identification, often does not reach beyond the family or the tribal collectivity. Rival tribal allegiances have often divided the Syrian people. The antagonism between the Qays and the Yaman–according to folklore the former were north Arabian and the latter south Arabian tribes–appeared in Syria when the Qays immigrated there after the Arab conquest.[3] For centuries this antagonism split the population into rival and often warring factions, although its basis became ever more obscure. As late as the nineteenth century, the Qays-Yaman conflict erupted in bloody, if petty, wars.

The main socio-cultural division was that between townsmen, nomads, and villagers. These groups have shared a common economy but on very unequal terms. The villager supplied the city with food, raw materials, and tax revenues; from it he received little, if anything, beyond occasional protection against nomad depredations. The villager traded his grain and flour for the nomad's meat, wool, and animal dung; in times of scarcity the nomad pillaged his cultivated land. The city, primarily a centre of commerce and exchange, depended on the nomad for animal products and for the camels, guides, and protection required by its caravan trade.

Foreign rule widened the social fissure between city and countryside since foreign rulers occupied only the cities. Cultural, social, and political influences from many civilizations flowed into the cities. The countryside, largely untouched by these influences beyond experiencing a greater or lesser degree of exploitation as a result of foreign conquest, remained a world apart. Townsmen and nomads despised the villagers, the majority of the population.

The modes of life of the three communities have been very different. Until recently they developed in isolation from each other. Yet all outside the mountain areas have been more or less influenced by the desert heritage and a tribal ethos. The villager was himself often a former nomad. And in some cities, even in this century, houses were still arranged in tribal groupings. Today the division remains, but changes since the Second World War—improvement of communications, progressive sedentarization of the beduin, migration of villagers to the cities, and provision of some government services, however inadequate, to the countryside, have very slowly begun to erode traditional barriers.

Differing religious loyalties produced diversity within Syria's overall cultural unity. The self-administered religious community as the basis of social organization goes far back in Syrian history. Islam reinforced this institution. Since Islamic law, the *Shari'a*, which until the last century regulated every aspect of Muslim life, does not apply to non-Muslims, Islam from the beginning allowed Christian and Jewish authorities to manage the affairs of their own communities, in effect granting them autonomy in the legal, religious, administrative, social, and educational fields. These religious communities often acquired a political, national consciousness and under the Ottoman system tended to become states within a state. The entanglement of politics with religious differences produced factionalism and conflict between communities. It also created veritable sacerdotal theocracies which made politics an affair of clan chieftains and prevented the individual from acquiring political rights and fulfilling a political function. Specialization of economic function along religious lines strengthened the particularist identity and tendencies of each community.

Syria was the cradle not only of great religions but also—in particular during the Byzantine period and the social ferment of the early centuries of Islam—of a profusion of heresies, schisms, and jealous sects. Some of these sects survived, especially in mountain fastnesses and isolated rural areas.

In the tenth and eleventh centuries Shi'a Muslim sects found in Syria a favourable terrain. Shi'ism derived from the split that developed over the succession to Muhammad soon after his death. Shi'a means partisan or follower and came to denote the 'partisans of Ali', Muhammad's cousin and son-in-law. The Shi'a claimed the succession for Ali and his line by divine right in opposition to the main body of Muslims, the Sunnis (followers of the *Sunna* or traditions) who held that the Muslim community must elect the Caliph (*Khalifah*: successor) from the members of Muhammad's tribe, the Quraysh. The Shi'a schism in part expressed social tensions and the discontent of the down-trodden. Shi'a movements often raised the banner of socio-religious revolt. As Shi'ite beliefs merged with local cults and creeds, Shi'ism split into a number of sects, but all had in common a belief in Ali and his line either as *imams*–divinely inspired Messiahs–or as incarnations of the deity. The last *imam* (literally 'one who leads the caravan'), who was still in hiding, would return to earth as the *Mahdi*, the 'God-guided one', to restore justice in the world. The most revolutionary of the Shi'a movements was the Isma'ili.

Three esoteric offshoots of the Isma'ili movement survived in the mountains of Syria and developed distinctive social and cultural traditions. They are the Isma'ilis, the remnants of a neo-Isma'ili movement (the Assassins) which terrorized the rulers of Syria in the twelfth and thirteenth centuries from its strongholds in the Nusayriyah mountains; the Nusayris or, as they are commonly known today, the Alawis (because they worship Ali); and the Druzes.

In the Syrian Arab Republic today the Isma'ilis (whose main centres are in India and Pakistan) are a tiny minority. In the nineteenth century most of them moved to the Salamiyah district near Hama, where the Ottoman Sultan Abdul Hamid II granted them land. (Salamiyah was a great Isma'ili centre during the movement's early centuries.) Isma'ilis in the Salamiyah district advanced economically and socially after the Second World War, while those still in the Nusayriyah mountains remained poor and backward.

The Alawis are descendants of the old indigenous inhabitants of the Nusayriyah mountains where Shi'ite doctrine fused with earlier pagan nature worship of sacred springs and trees. The Alawi religion, in which women have no part, divides its followers into an initiated élite and an uninitiated majority. Reflecting the persecution it has suffered, this religion–like the Druze–permits religious dissimulation (*taqiyah*). Alawi society is still tribal, organized in five confederations embracing tribes and sub-tribes. Tribal chieftains and notables, who are often at the same time religious leaders, have traditionally exercised great power.

The dismemberment of Syria after the First World War left the largest Alawi concentration in what is now Latakia province of the Syrian Arab Republic. Alawi peasants, however, have been driven by rural overpopulation to seek work in the plains of Homs, Hama, and Aleppo. Many Alawis fled from Alexandretta when it was annexed by Turkey in the late 1930s to join their co-religionists in the Nusayriyah mountains. Non-Alawis, mainly Sunni Muslims and Greek Orthodox Christians, have until very recently dominated the city of Latakia and the towns of the coastal plains. The economic and social position of the largely rural Alawi population has been that of a subjected minority, although it constitutes the bulk of the population of Latakia province. The Alawis are the Syrian Arab Republic's largest minority, numbering between 600,000 and 700,000 or about 11 per cent of the population. Traditionally they have been the poorest, most backward, and oppressed section of Syrian society.

The Druze sect originated early in the eleventh century when the Fatimid Caliph of Egypt, Al-Hakim, claimed to be the incarnation of the deity and a Persian, Isma'il Al-Darazi, converted mountaineers of southern Lebanon to this belief. Bloody Qays-Yaman conflicts among the Druzes early in the eighteenth century and conflicts with the Maronite Christians in the mid-nineteenth century provoked waves of Druze migration to the Hawran. The Jebel Hawran then came to be known as the Jebel Druze. In the Druze religion, in which God's will is revealed only to a few, a religious hierarchy is based on the degree of initiation into the secrets of the doctrine, of which the majority remain in ignorance.

Today the Druze account for 90 per cent of the population of the Jebel Druze and about 3 per cent of the total population of the Syrian Arab Republic. Druze society is traditionally organized around ruling families or clans, but it does not have a hierarchy of families or chieftains. Many Druzes are mountain peasants with smallholdings. The Druzes have played an important role in modern Syrian political and cultural life.

Of about ten Christian sects in the Syrian Arab Republic some date from the Byzantine period, some from the sixteenth and seventeenth centuries when certain elements of the Eastern Christian Churches became affiliated with Rome, and some arrived as refugees in the inter-war period. More than 70 per cent of Christians are Arabic-speaking. These are the Greek Orthodox, Greek Catholics, Syrian Orthodox, Syrian Catholics, Maronites, Roman Catholics, and some Protestants. Non-Arabic-speaking Christians include the Armenians (Orthodox and Catholic) and the Assyrians (Nestorians), both groups having arrived between the wars. The Greek Orthodox community is by far the largest, comprising more than a third of all Christians and more than half of those who speak Arabic. In general this community has been closer and more sympathetic to the Muslim majority than have the other Christian sects. Christians, mainly engaged in non-agricultural pursuits, are scattered in cities and towns all over the Syrian Arab Republic. The fact that they have been better educated than Muslims and in closer contact with the West has contributed to Christian–Muslim tension. Owing to a lower birthrate and in recent years considerable emigration, especially of Armenians, the proportion of Christians in the population is decreasing and is today no more than 8 per cent.

Ethno-linguistic minorities are less important than religious-cultural minorities, and their numbers can only be estimated. The largest ethno-linguistic minority, the Kurds, may total around 300,000. The Kurds, who boast an ancient history, are indigenous to Kurdistan, the mountainous region of eastern Turkey, north-west Iran, and northern Iraq. They have been an integral part of Syrian life for centuries. Most are Sunni Muslims. Many are Arabized and completely assimilated. In the inter-war period, Turkish repression provoked a wave of Kurdish immigration into French-mandated Syria and Lebanon. In the Syrian Arab Republic today, Kurds live in the Jazira; the Kurd Dagh mountains north-west of Aleppo where the population is entirely Kurdish; the Jarablus area north-east of Aleppo; and the Salhiya quarter of Damascus where they have been settled since the twelfth century and the days of Salah Al-Din (Saladin), a great Arab hero but himself a Kurd.

Circassian refugees from Russian conquests in the Caucasus arrived in the Jazira in the 1860s and 1870s. After the Russo-Turkish War of 1877–78, the Ottoman Sultan Abdul Hamid II settled Circassians as agricultural colonists on the fringes of the desert to serve as a bulwark against the beduin and the Druzes. Qunaytra in the Golan is sometimes called the 'Circassian capital'. Still largely tribal, the Sunni Muslim Circassians, numbering 50–60,000, are beginning to intermarry with Arabs and adopt the Arabic language.

Other minorities existing in the present-day Syrian Arab Republic are Armenians, most of whom arrived as refugees from the Turks after the First World War, Assyrian refugees from Iraq, Turcomens (descendants of Turkish-speaking tribes from Central Asia), and Jews. Numbering about 30,000 before the creation of Israel, the Jews have since been reduced by emigration to about 5,000 living mainly in Damascus and Aleppo.

Structurally, the Syrian population appears relatively homogeneous. Estimated linguistic minorities today constitute no more than 10 per cent of the total. Even this group is in the main bilingual and at least partially Arabized. More than 90 per cent of the population are Muslims, and roughly three-fourths are Sunni Muslims. The Arabic language is a great unifying factor. But the description of Syria as a 'mosaic of minorities' fits its social dynamism. The unequal and differentiated contribution of the Sunni majority and the many minorities may help to explain the important role played by elements from the minorities. For they reflected, even if in a deformed way, the aspirations not only of their own groups but also of a large part of the whole population.

[1] Christina P. Grant: *The Syrian Desert*, London, 1937, p. 50.

[2] George Adam Smith: *The Historical Geography of the Holy Land,* London, 1897, 4th ed., p. 10.

[3] These tensions did not reflect racial differences but, says G. E. von Grunebaum, 'the consequence of transferring primitive pre-Islamic concepts of the state and judiciary customs to the government of a world empire', *Classical Islam,* London, 1970, pp. 69–70.

Chapter 2

Agent of Civilization

As a land bridge linking three continents and a fertile oasis between sea and desert, Syria throughout history attracted migrating peoples and conquering armies. Struggle for possession of Syria provided the dynamic of the ancient Near East and remained a central theme in Syrian history. The nomad and the settled contested for this fertile land through millennia until the auto and the airplane decided the issue in this century. Opposing pressures of peoples making inroads into the Fertile Crescent have shaped the Near East since ancient times, and down to the present day powers based in Egypt, Mesopotamia, and Anatolia have periodically resumed their efforts to dominate Syria and so achieve regional supremacy. These struggles made Syria not only a battleground but a meeting-place of the most varied cultural influences. Ideas and techniques also moved along the trade routes of which Syria for so long was a central junction. Assuming the role of middlemen in these exchanges, Syrians absorbed and moulded these civilizing influences to stimulate some of mankind's most significant intellectual and spiritual achievements.

THE ANCIENT WORLD

Already on the eve of history, Egypt and Mesopotamia, both lacking wood, a precious commodity in the ancient world, were drawn to the Syrian coastland by the cedar, cypress, and pine forests of the Ammanus and Lebanon ranges. Egyptian contacts with the Syrian coast developed towards the end of the fourth millennium. Sumerian cities during the third millennium, and perhaps earlier, acquired cedar from the Ammanus and silver and gold from Cilicia across northern Syria. Byblos (Gubla) emerged in the third millennium as the chief trading port of the Syrian coast, dealing with Egypt, to which it exported timber and resin (used for mummification), with Mesopotamia, from which it got seals and jars (probably re-exported to Egypt), and Anatolia, from which it received silver and obsidian. Byblos and other city kingdoms of Syria—as intermediaries in the growing commercial and cultural traffic between

31

Egypt, Mesopotamia, Anatolia, and the Aegean–became highly civilized and wealthy. The war booty seized by Pharaoh Thutmose III after he defeated '330 princes each with his army' at the Battle of Megiddo (1479 B.C.) reveals the advanced development of the crafts of the Syrian city kingdoms, the prosperity of their agriculture, and the wide extent of their trade relations. By this time Syria's principal cities–Damascus (Dimesheq), Aleppo (Khalaba), Hama (Hamath), Byblos (Gubla), Jaffa (Joppa), Homs, Gaza, Tyre (Sur), and Sidon–stood in place. Some had already been there for centuries, even millennia.

Syria's most significant contribution to civilization, the invention of the alphabet, was made during the second millennium B.C. The alphabet, the process of a long evolution, appeared when the written symbol was disassociated from the syllable and related to sound. The earliest known form of a true alphabet dates back to the fourteenth century B.C. in Ugarit (Ras Shamra). The thirty letters of this alphabet appeared in a cuneiform writing in Ugaritic, a semitic language rather similar to Arabic with which it had many words in common. The Phoenicians developed the alphabet, passing it on to the Arameans and other semitic peoples and to the Greeks who added vowel signs not used in semitic languages.

Incursions of 'sea peoples' and land peoples in the latter part of the second millennium compelled the two empires then occupying Syria–the Hittites in the north and the Egyptians in the south–to withdraw. In the interval of several centuries before the expansion of Assyrian power, the peoples of Syria asserted their independence and created civilizations which left an enduring influence.

The Arameans and Hebrews had settled in Syria by the end of the thirteenth century. Biblical accounts of the Hebrew infiltration into Palestine reveal that the Hebrews took over an already advanced civilization. Around 1000 B.C., David established a Hebrew kingdom in the hills of Samaria and Judaea. At its zenith early in the tenth century, this kingdom, whose population was neither exclusively nor 'even mainly Hebrew',[1] embraced Transjordan and Palestine except for the coastal plain which was occupied by the Philistines. Under David's son, Solomon, the kingdom contracted and, after Solomon's death around 925 B.C., split into the tiny kingdoms of Judaea and Israel. The Arameans founded city kingdoms in the Mesopotamian–Syrian corridor in the north and, towards the end of the eleventh century, the kingdom we know as the Aram or Syria of the Bible, which stretched from the Yarmuk to the Euphrates. Arameans, controlling the overland routes to the East, became the middlemen of the trade of south-west Asia. Their principal city, Damascus, capital of Aram, achieved commercial hegemony and great wealth. Aram proved strong enough to hold off the Assyrians for several centuries. In this period, too, the Phoenician city states, with Tyre in the lead, won a new lease of life and planted colonies at Carthage and other trading posts along the Mediterranean coasts.

Phoenicians, Hebrews, and Arameans all made a significant contribution to man's cultural heritage. The Phoenicians assumed a pioneering role in the use of iron in tools and shipbuilding, and opened the horizons of the ancient world by their discovery of the Atlantic Ocean. The Hebrews developed the idea of the oneness of God, a single and sublime moral power, when in exile their tribal cult of Yahweh evolved into a movement with a universal message. Although the Hebrew religion reverted to national exclusiveness, this universalist concept became the heritage of Christianity and Islam. The Arameans, the first to adopt the Phoenician alphabet, carried their more simply written language, Aramaic, along the trade routes of the ancient world. By the middle of the first millennium B.C. Aramaic had become the language of commerce and culture of south-west Asia, the vernacular of its people, and the *lingua franca* of the Persian Empire. Aramaic language and culture influenced the Arab states which arose in eastern Syria in the latter part of the first millennium B.C. Aramaic also displaced Hebrew and was spoken by Christ. It remained the vernacular of the Syrian countryside for almost a thousand years; its Syriac dialect survived even longer as the language of the Christian Churches of Syria and Mesopotamia. Aramaic also became the language through which Greek culture was originally transmitted to Islam.

The independent Syrian states, weakened by frequent conflicts, succumbed to the Assyrian Empire in the eighth century B.C., the Babylonian in the seventh, and the Persian in the sixth. For all but a few hundred of the 2,500 years since, Syria remained a part of larger empires. In these empires, as in the Persian, Syria was often to experience local autonomy. Unifying semitic and other peoples in one of the greatest empires of antiquity, the Indo-European Persians inaugurated a millennium of non-semitic dominion and prepared the way for a new era. With the fall of the Persian Empire to Alexander in 333 B.C., the ancient Near East passed into history.

FRONTIER BETWEEN EAST AND WEST 333 B.C.–A.D. 636

Syria's inclusion in the Seleucid kingdom (301–64 B.C.), in the Roman Empire (64 B.C.–A.D. 395), and in the Byzantine Empire (A.D. 395–636) made it for a thousand years the frontier between East and West and its people the mediators in East-West cultural exchanges. A century-long influx of Greek settlers followed establish-

ment of the Seleucid 'Kingdom of Syria', which at its greatest extent
reached from the Aegean to India and Turkistan. The Greek settlers
became the ruling class of Syria. Their improvement of communications promoted a great expansion of Syrian trade with Arabia, India,
the Far East, and Europe, and also stimulated the growth of Syrian
manufactures and agriculture. New Greek cities, and Syrian cities
colonized by the Greeks, became the principal centres for the
diffusion of Greek culture. The synthesis of Greek and oriental
civilization produced Near Eastern Hellenism, which prevailed in
varying degrees in the cities of Syria till the Arab conquest. The
Syrian contribution to this hybrid Greek-Roman-Syrian culture was
most notable in philosophy and jurisprudence. Antioch, Tyre,
Beirut, and Apamea became important centres of Hellenistic culture.
The combination of Greek mathematics with Syrian techniques
stimulated scientific advance, especially in the application of rotary
motion.[2]

Under the Romans Syria prospered. Cities, irrigation works, and
communications were constructed. Syrians in great numbers invaded
the West carrying their goods, ideas, gods, manners, and enterprising
spirit to the farthest reaches of the empire. Syrian manufactures—
blown glass, linen fabrics, dyed wool and silk, metal, leatherwares,
and jewellery–then among the most advanced in the world, captured
Mediterranean and West European markets; some Syrian products
were carried as far as China and England. Syrian entrepreneurs—
dominating the caravan trade between the Far East, India, and
Europe and the banking system that financed it–pushed outwards
the economic frontiers of the Roman world. Businessmen and
artisans from Syria settled and worked in Italy, Gaul, Spain, along
the Rhine and the Danube, and even in England. Profits from
industry and commerce supported the brilliant civilization of Syrian
cities where Greek and Roman settlers and Syrian merchants and
landlords enjoyed great wealth, while most of the population in both
towns and villages subsisted in miserable poverty.

The Roman colonial administration employed many Syrians.
Syrians more than once ascended the throne of the Caesars. The
popularity of Syrian entertainers–mimes, musicians, jesters, jugglers
–who travelled through Europe provoked Juvenal's famous complaint: 'The Syrian Orontes has long since poured its water into the
Tiber, bringing with it its lingo and manners, its flutes and its
slanting harp strings'.[3] Syrian mystery cults and divinities spread
throughout the Mediterranean world where, with the development
of communications and travel, numerous local deities were giving
way to more universal gods.

Christianity–in part a fusion of elements in oriental cults, Greek philosophies, and Judaism–was born during the Roman period in Syria, and until the seventh century Syria remained the principal centre of the new religion. As Rome declined, Christianity and Hellenism united in the culture of Byzantium and in a theocratic Byzantine empire. Byzantine theocracy increased the alienation of the common people from Hellenism, which had always been an urban culture of the educated classes. Popular disaffection with the oppression of Byzantine rulers found expression in revolt against the official religion. Schisms and heresies, the founding of separate Syriac-speaking Christian Churches, teaching of Syriac in monasteries, and translation into Syriac of Greek philosophy and science–all were part of an Aramaic linguistic and literary renaissance which developed in opposition to the Greek language and the Greek-speaking religious and political ruling class. Through this renaissance and relentless Byzantine persecution of the Syrian Churches, a Syrian national consciousness and a distinctive Syrian culture (in painting, sculpture, architecture) began to take form.[4]

Throughout the entire period of Greek, Roman, and Byzantine rule, Arab infiltration into Syria was almost continuous, and from the second century B.C. Arab principalities, including the Nabatean kingdom and Zenobia's 'Syrian Kingdom' based on Palmyra, ruled in eastern Syria. Numerous south Arabian tribes settled in Syria in the early Christian centuries, embraced Christianity, and adopted Syrian ways of life. These Syro-Arabs living among the Aramaic-speaking people of Syria spoke a mixture of Arabic and Aramaic. Through them, Syrian cultural influences reached the Arabs of Arabia and contributed to the rise of Islam. Through the Aramaic renaissance and the growing Arab element, Syria had already on the eve of the Arab conquest recovered its semitic heritage.

To most Syrians, the Arab conquest in A.D. 636 came as a liberation from persecution by alien Byzantines. Their refusal to resist the Arab advance contributed to the defeat of the numerically superior forces of a more civilized Byzantium and to the establishment of Muslim rule in all Syria by 640. So ended nearly a thousand years of Western supremacy. The Arab occupation of Iraq and the conquest of Egypt followed.

THE ARAB KINGDOM

The Muslim Arabs established themselves as a warrior aristocracy in cities on the edge of the desert. Since the Syrian population was already partially Arab and the new religion seemed to a society riven by disputatious sects just another Christian heresy, the newly arrived Arabs did not appear wholly alien. Christians and Jews were left in possession of their homes, lands, and places of worship and in charge of their religious and community affairs, but they were subjected to a poll tax and heavy tribute. The old Byzantine administration and its Christian personnel continued to serve the new rulers.

Damascus, the 'beauty spot of the world' in nomad eyes, in time became a Muslim holy city because of its associations with the prophets. In 661, Mu'awiyah, the able and powerful Governor of Syria who came from the Umayya branch of the old pagan aristocracy of Mecca, secured election as Caliph and made Damascus the seat of the Caliphate. His selection of Damascus, rather than the earlier governmental centres, Mecca or Kufah (in Iraq), as his capital reflected a shift of leadership away from the beduin tribes of the conquest to the Christianized Syro-Arab tribes long established in Syria. Mu'awiyah transformed the theocratic Caliphate into a secular hereditary monarchy.

During the ninety-year rule of the Umayyads Syria became the heartland of an empire larger than that of the Romans. At its greatest extent early in the eighth century, the Umayyad empire stretched from the Atlantic and the Pyrenees to the Himalayas and the marches of China and from the Aral Sea to the first cataract of the Nile. This Islamic empire often appeared to be Syrian owing to the prominent role played by Syrians in its administration, armies, navy, and economic expansion. But Syria itself became ever more Arab. Within half a century of the conquest, Arabic became the official language and by the ninth century had succeeded its kindred tongue, Aramaic, as the vernacular of Syria. Arabization reinforced the cultural unity of Syria which survived all challenges for the next millennium and more. Islamization at first proceeded gradually. In the early eighth century only a small fraction of the Syrian population was Muslim. But within a few centuries continuing Arab infiltration from Arabia and conversions made Islam the religion of the majority.

Unlike the Byzantine rulers who drained money and wealth out of Syria to Constantinople, the Muslim Arabs spent the tribute they collected within the country. The expansion of the empire and the abolition of old frontiers throughout its vast extent provided Syrian artisanry with new markets and gave great impetus to the development of worldwide commerce. Within Syria, construction of roads and irrigation works, colonization of agricultural land, and the flow of slaves and war booty into Damascus generated great wealth. (Yet epidemics and famine were common.) Multiplying contacts within the empire and beyond brought new cultural and technical influences to Syria, enriched the quality of Syrian life, and broadened its scope. The Umayyad century was Syria's 'golden age'. The meeting of Syria's ancient civilization with the vigorous and inquiring spirit of the Arabs brought to flower the Islamic culture that was to lead the world for the next five centuries.

In the first half of the eighth century, the empire's centre of gravity started moving eastward with the restoration of Byzantine supremacy in the Mediterranean and a shift in trade routes that made the irrigated Tigris-Euphrates valley rather than Syria their principal junction. The overthrow of the Umayyads by the Abbasids (lineage of Abbas, uncle of the Prophet) in 750 and the transfer of the Caliphate to Iraq confirmed this change. Syria was reduced to provincial status. Over the next two centuries Syrians asserted their national identity in repeated revolts under the white banner of the Umayyads and around leaders claiming to be the messiah returned to deliver Syria from Abbasid oppression and to restore its former glory.

On the other hand, Syrians also contributed significantly to the great intellectual renaissance inspired by Abbasid Baghdad in the century after 750. Earlier Syrian translations of Greek works into Syriac provided the groundwork of this renaissance. Translations of the main works of Greek science, now begun in Baghdad's House of Wisdom, were made most frequently from the Syriac and often by Syrian Christians. The organized translation into Arabic of Greek, Persian, and Indian learning made available the scientific and philosophical heritage of the ancient world and lighted the fires of one of the most significant movements in the history of ideas. The fusion of Greek and Eastern wisdom, made in Arabic by scholars and thinkers of the Islamic empire, eventually returned to Europe to stimulate its awakening. The heritage of the ancients and the secularist and rationalist approach developed by Islamic science precipitated within Islam a centuries-long struggle between rationalist and traditionalist dogmatic currents.

MANY-SIDED STRUGGLE FOR SYRIA

The Abbasid Caliphate endured until 1258 when it fell to the Mongols advancing from Central Asia. Already in the late ninth century, however, it began to fragment, and in the next three centuries the struggle for Syria achieved an unparalleled intensity. A bewildering number of ephemeral rulers, rival contenders, and shifting alliances marked this struggle in which Syria was splintered into petty states. During much of this period, southern Syria lay in the Egyptian sphere of influence and northern Syria in that of Iraq, but the powers based in these countries changed, and their hold on Syria was often so faltering that local petty authorities prevailed.

In a time of social crisis throughout the empire, Shi'ism evoking a response among Abbasid-hating Syrians became a principal contender in the struggle for Syria. An extreme Shi'a sect, the Isma'ili, offered the common people deliverance from social oppression, while its philosophy, impregnated with Greek, Indian, and Persian thought, attracted leading intellectuals and scholars. From its centre at Salamiyah in central Syria the Isma'ili movement during the tenth and eleventh centuries carried on agitation throughout Syria and even at times set up territorial principalities.

Arab tribes from the Syrian desert, taking advantage of dwindling Abbasid power, moved into settled areas of Syria, captured cities, and even succeeded in establishing beduin dynasties. The most important, the Hamdanid dynasty, ruled northern Syria from Aleppo during the tenth century. The struggle for Syria took a new turn when in 969 the Fatimid Caliphate (established earlier in the century in Tunis by the Isma'ili movement) occupied Egypt, built a new capital, Al Kahira (Cairo), and with its Berber armies won a precarious hold over Syria. Fatimid Cairo, Abbasid Baghdad (itself now dominated by Turkish and Persian mercenaries), and Christian Byzantium as well as Isma'ilis and invading Turcomen tribes fought over Syria throughout much of the eleventh century.

In the latter part of the eleventh century, the Seljuk Turks from Central Asia, the Crusaders from Europe, and an underground Isma'ili movement, which had its headquarters in Alamut, an inaccessible mountain fortress in northern Persia, entered Syria. The Seljuks, converts to Islam who had set themselves up in Baghdad as Sultans and made puppets of the Caliphs, pushed back the Byzantines and occupied much of Syria, but Seljuk power split into rival kingdoms. The Crusader states, established in the main along the coast, fought with each other and with Muslim princes to extend their control. This struggle cut across religious lines. The neo-Isma'ili movement, the Assassins (from *hashishiya*, hashish-smoker), became a powerful political force in Syria and throughout the twelfth century waged war against orthodox Islam and somewhat less energetically against Christian infidels.

The unification of Muslim Syria was achieved in the twelfth century by a Seljuk slave, Zangi of Mosul, and his son Nur Al-Din. On Nur Al-Din's death, his representative in Cairo, Salah Al-Din (Saladin), who had made himself effective ruler of Egypt, terminated the Fatimid Caliphate, absorbed Nur Al-Din's Syrian kingdom, and created a united Syrian-Egyptian state. Towards the end of the twelfth century he pushed the Crusaders out of all but a narrow coastal strip of Syria. Saladin's Ayyubid successors ruled Syria and Egypt until the mid-thirteenth century when Turkish-speaking Mamluk (slave) warriors of the Ayyubids seized power in Egypt and in 1260 defeated in Palestine Mongol armies which had swept across Syria. The Mamluks then expelled the last of the Crusaders, tamed the Assassins, already weakened by Mongol destruction of Alamut, and brought Syria into their kingdom.

These centuries of anarchy and confusion proved to be a turning-point in Syrian civilization. The Crusades were but an episode which had little influence beyond convincing Syrians of the inferiority of Western civilization. However, in the course of the Muslim struggle to oust the Crusaders, reunify Syria, and root out neo-Isma'ili subversion, the country was transformed from a stronghold of Shi'ism into a bulwark of Sunni orthodoxy. Among other reasons, the Kurdish and Turkish princes who led this struggle were zealous defenders of orthodoxy. Remnants of the harassed and persecuted Shi'a sects now sought refuge in isolated mountain areas where they remained fiercely dissident.

In this period of almost unceasing petty warfare cities nonetheless prospered and developed culturally. The brilliant court of the Hamdanids in Aleppo patronized and sheltered some of the greatest figures in Islamic culture; Ayyubid Aleppo became the thriving hub of a prosperous state. Damascus experienced a cultural renaissance under Nur Al-Din and developed under the Ayyubids as a great religious, cultural, and economic centre. But the changes that took place in the physical structure of the cities in this period reveal the insecurity that prevailed. Houses turned their backs to the streets to bar direct access. Cities broke up into self-contained quarters, each self-sufficient and enclosed by walls and gates; each religious community became segregated in its own quarter.

During these centuries the Islamic empire itself was undergoing profound changes, of which the instability in Syria was a partial reflection. From the ninth century onwards Abbasid power became increasingly dependent on mercenary armies of foreigners, mainly Turkish slaves, and the Arab warrior aristocracy lost its function. At the same time, owing to European expansion in the Mediterranean and nomadic movements in Central Asia, the empire's overland and maritime trade both declined. With insufficient revenue to pay its officers and officials, the state granted them concessions to collect taxes on specified lands subject to performance of military and other services. This system was not properly speaking feudal since the concession was not to the land but to a source of revenue, implied no vassalage, was not hereditary, and was always revocable.[5] Moreover, the holders of the concession lived in the cities and owed no responsibility to the land or the cultivator.

But, as mercantile economy slowly gave way to a rural-based economy and as central authority weakened, quasi-feudal trends appeared. Concessions sometimes in practice became hereditary and sometimes included the right to administer the area as well as collect taxes. Cultivators could not leave the land until all taxes had been paid. Such trends appeared in Syria under the Seljuk Turks and were further developed under the Ayyubids. The appearance of these trends more or less coincided with the rise of an alien military caste and political disintegration. Migration into the empire in the late tenth century of nomadic Seljuk Turkish tribes had accelerated its fragmentation. The Turkish slave caste and the incoming Seljuks, both converted to Islam, seized power in one locality after another and in time achieved political and military supremacy. Thus, the vast horizons of an empire with worldwide trade connections gradually contracted to the bounds of local military and quasi-feudal authorities. Arabs were relegated to a secondary role. The Turkish military caste, indoctrinated from the beginning to serve as the defender of orthodoxy, became in a time of social polarization a bulwark of the existing order upon which orthodoxy rested.

Fear of innovation and relentless persecution of nonconformism further narrowed social and intellectual horizons. Arab science began to decline with the undermining of the once powerful merchant class, the patron of learning and science, and with the rise of alien military rulers. The long struggle within Islam over acceptance or rejection of rationalism and the scientific spirit ended with the triumph of dogmatism and the disappearance of intellectual freedom. The common people, condemned to submission to an absolutist authority and a fatalism inculcated by religious teaching, found refuge from social afflictions in mystery cults and magic, when their frustration and misery did not erupt in desperate insurrections.

THE LONG STAGNATION

When Syria came under the rule of the Egyptian Mamluks in 1260, its civilization, although still among the first in the world, was thus already waning. Through the greater part of the 257-year rule of the Mamluks, Syrian cities remained the home of an advanced civilization, enhanced by Mamluk-built mosques, *madrasas* (religious colleges), fountains, and Mamluk-encouraged applied arts. But the creative impulse was disappearing; the underlying processes of decline were soon accelerated; Syrian civilization lost the ability to respond to new challenges.

A series of calamities in the fourteenth and fifteenth centuries—plague, locusts, famine, earthquake, and flood—reduced the population. Mongol invasions in 1299–1303 and 1400–01 partially destroyed Damascus and Aleppo and left much devastation. Frequent civil wars among the Mamluk emirs, drawing in rival factions of the population, were even more destructive.[6]

Depopulation and excessive taxation progressively diminished the output of agricultural products and manufactures. Syria, moreover, no longer held its once central position in international trade. Italian cities controlled the carrying trade of the Mediterranean; Egyptian ports had become the emporia of international maritime trade; certain caravan routes shifted away from Syria. Yet Damascus, producing luxury wares and weapons for the Mamluk élite, remained a great cultural and industrial city until 1401, when Tamerlane's mass deportation of its scholars and artisans paralyzed its cultural life and crippled its artisan industry. Venetian wares then made inroads into Syrian markets. At the same time, however, a shift in the silk route between Persia and Europe made Aleppo the centre of this trade, and it again became prosperous.

Late fifteenth-century geographical discoveries contributed to Syria's decline. The route to India around the Cape of Good Hope opened by the Portuguese proved easier and much cheaper than the land and sea routes commanded by the Arabs, and in time robbed Syria and Egypt of their role as middlemen in the trade between Asia and Europe. Discovery of the Americas shifted the world's commercial centre from the eastern Mediterranean to the Atlantic and left Syria remote and isolated from the new focal points of civilization. And there it stagnated.

The Ottoman Empire

In the Ottoman conquest of 1516 Syria passed from the hands of one Turkish master to another and became part of a powerful and wealthy world empire. The Ottomans respected Arabic as the language of Islam, made no attempt to colonize or Turkify the Arab provinces, and became the defenders of the faith. So the Arabs did not for the greater part of the Ottomans' 400-year rule regard them or their empire as alien.[7] Incorporation into the empire brought Syria an empire-wide market and made it the main communication link between the Eastern empire and Europe. Aleppo developed as the Levant's chief market city where European merchants established their trading stations and consulates. Damascus flourished as the principal staging-post for the annual *Haj* (pilgrimage) to Mecca, for which it supplied the provisions and transport.

In the decentralized Ottoman system of government, the authority of the Turkish Pasha (Governor) of the province was supported by Turkish military forces but seldom extended beyond the garrison towns. Elsewhere local lords and chieftains were granted almost complete internal autonomy and entrusted with tax collection and maintenance of security. This system worked more or less effectively until the latter part of the seventeenth century.

The Ottoman defeat before Vienna in 1683 marked the beginning of the empire's long retreat. A continuing inflow of cheap silver from the New World produced throughout the sixteenth and seventeenth centuries a steep price inflation and repeated currency devaluations. Most classes were impoverished, while a few speculators and traders became very wealthy. Ruinous inflation made corruption the norm throughout the government administration at a time when the Sultans had become ineffectual and traditional local power centres in Syria, as elsewhere, began to extend their authority.

For Syria, the period of Ottoman decline was one of social regression during which economic development was arrested and then reversed and the transformation of the country into a market for the industrializing West began. The principal instrument in this process was the treaty of 'capitulations' (chapters of concessions). These trading concessions limited Ottoman customs duties on imports from the states to which the concessions were granted and accorded various extra-territorial privileges. Treaties of Capitulation were signed with France and Britain in the sixteenth century and eventually with virtually all European states. As the balance of power between the empire and the West shifted, the European powers dictated the terms of these treaties and widened European privileges. Under the Capitulations, France extended its 'right' to protect European Catholics resident in the empire to all Catholic Ottoman subjects, and Russia claimed a similar 'right' over the Greek Orthodox. The Capitulations thus opened the empire wide to European economic penetration and European political interference.

Under the Capitulations, European goods paid a very low customs duty on entry into the empire, while Syrian and other Ottoman goods seeking to enter Europe were subject to prohibitive duties or barred outright. European goods were exempted from all Ottoman duties and local levies within the empire, but indigenous goods were heavily taxed and subject also to bribes and extortions. Syrian exports to Europe dwindled. European finished goods and agricultural products from European colonies began to capture some of Syria's traditional markets, undermined a number of its artisan industries, drained out gold, and so contributed to inflation and impoverishment. The inequality between foreign and indigenous enterprise, enforced by the Capitulations and by superior Western power, inhibited the accumulation of capital and so blocked capitalist development. The indigenous mercantile bourgeoisie which developed as the broker and agent of European trade was almost exclusively

Christian and Jewish, and enjoyed virtually the same extra-territorial privileges as did foreigners.

In these circumstances, the Syrian provinces became increasingly dependent on agriculture, but the prevailing tax-farming system (a chain of farmers and sub-farmers extended from the Pasha down to the lowest local notable) had become ruinous. For there was no administrative supervision, taxes were extortionate, the cultivator was always in debt, and usury 'carried to the most crying excess . . . the greatest scourge of the Syrian countryside'.[8] Among Syrian peasants, a spirit of rebellion was not lacking: tax collection required military expeditions and in the mountains and other areas beyond the reach of the government or local troops peasants refused to pay taxes and retained a certain independence.

By the eighteenth century, Syria was completely decadent. The population had fallen from about 4 million in the fourteenth century to no more than one and a half million. The Ottoman government could no longer maintain security. The Shammar and Anaza tribes moving into the Syrian desert from Arabia in the seventeenth and eighteenth centuries successfully challenged its control. Devastating beduin raids carried off harvests, laid waste the cultivated fields, and pushed back the frontiers of cultivation. Trade and pilgrimage caravans, towns and villages were also plundered or required to pay tribute. Military forces mutinied and, making local alliances, fought each other for power. Pashas, petty lords, and local chieftains in constant strife with the central authority intrigued and clashed among themselves in innumerable petty wars. Qays-Yaman conflicts and internal dissensions divided the people. Extortion, official and unofficial confiscation, violence, and factionalism were the order of the day.

The Syrian provinces had a special importance to the Ottoman government since they controlled the routes between Istanbul and Mecca and contained the holy cities, Jerusalem and Damascus, the 'Gate to Mecca'. Although Ottoman rule was apt to be stronger in Syria than in other Arab provinces, local dynasties won virtual independence in the Lebanon in the sixteenth century, and in southern Syria in the late seventeenth and early eighteenth centuries. By the first half of the eighteenth century, a number of Pashas–some of local origin like the Azm family of Damascus–were able to maintain practically independent rule.

In the latter part of the century, however, Egypt, seeking to throw off the Ottoman yoke, began to contest with Istanbul for control of Syria. The ensuing struggle for Syria involved not only Cairo, Istanbul, and a number of local Syrian rulers, but also St Petersburg, London, and Paris. An Egyptian expeditionary force to

Palestine was defeated in the 1770s. In 1799, the plague and the British fleet compelled Napoleon to abandon his attempted conquest of Syria. But another expedition from Egypt was soon to usher Syria into modern times.

[1] Neville Barbour: *Nisi Dominus*, Beirut, 1969, p. 11.

[2] J. D. Bernal: *Science and History*, London, 1965, pp. 115, 158–9.

[3] Philip K. Hitti: *History of Syria*, London, 1951, p. 302.

[4] H. Lammens: *La Syrie Précis Historique*, Beirut, 1921, Vol. I, 13–17.

[5] Claude Cahen: 'Ikta', *Encyclopedia of Islam*, London, 1970.

[6] Ira Lapidus: *Muslim Cities in the Later Middle Ages*, Cambridge, Mass., 1967, p. 27.

[7] Zeine N. Zeine: *Arab-Turkish Relations and the Emergence of Arab Nationalism*, Beirut, 1958, pp. 13–17.

[8] C. F. C. Volney: *Travels Through Syria and Egypt*, London, 1787, Vol. II, 265.

Chapter 3

Leaven of Change

NAPOLEON'S OCCUPATION OF EGYPT in 1798 moved the 'Eastern Question'–competition for dominance in the Ottoman Empire and inheritance of its possessions–to the centre of European power politics. Forces set in train by this development–Egypt's occupation of Syria from 1831 to 1840, Ottoman reforms, and growing European encroachment throughout the century–brought about the disintegration of Syria's millennial society. By the end of the century a Syrian effort to reintegrate society on a new basis to meet the challenge of a new age was just beginning.

THE EGYPTIAN OCCUPATION

Ibrahim, son of Muhammad Ali Pasha, Viceroy of Egypt, commanded the Egyptian expeditionary force that succeeded in expelling the Turks from Syria in 1831. Deeply resentful of the Europeanizing reforms of the Ottoman Sultan Mahmoud II, Syrians welcomed the Egyptians as 'liberators' from the 'infidel Sultan'. But they were soon disillusioned, for Ibrahim's reforms proved more far-reaching than the Sultan's and more offensive to Syrian sensibilities. Ibrahim aimed at developing Syria as a source for raw materials and manpower. (He wanted cedar wood for his fleet, among other things.) Accordingly, he unified the country under a strong central administration, its first in centuries, and ended the dominion of quasi-feudal lords and military and religious chieftains. He disarmed their private armies, replaced tax-farming by direct taxes collected by salaried government officials, appointed his own representative as the sole authority in each town, secularized the judicial administration, and created administrative councils to aid district governors. In these councils merchants played a major role and Christians and Jews were for the first time represented.

The resulting security and order permitted expansion of agricultural and raw-material production. The Egyptians drained marshes, brought abandoned land under cultivation, introduced new agricultural methods, planted mulberry and olive trees, encouraged peasants and nomads to reclaim the land, and improved roads.

During the occupation cotton production doubled. Cotton, timber, coal, iron, silk, wool, and hides were exported to Egypt.

But the occupation coincided with a swelling inflow of European goods into Syria which had started with the end of the Napoleonic Wars. The competition of cheap British cotton and other goods threw thousands out of work–in 1833 ten thousand in Damascus and Aleppo alone. And by 1840 the population of these two cities had measurably declined. At the same time Ibrahim facilitated European intervention in Syrian affairs by encouraging foreign missions, schools, and consulates to establish themselves in the hinterland, even in the holy cities of Jerusalem and Damascus.

While European economic encroachment weakened Syria's traditional economy, penetration of European influences strained its social fabric. Ibrahim's expedition was tacitly supported by France; in a sense he was extending French influence in Syria. The fact that Syrian Christians were already under the protection of the European powers, especially France, meant that Ibrahim would rely upon and co-operate with Christians. In fact, he gave his administration a most secular style. His efforts to remove the disabilities under which Christians and Jews laboured troubled the Muslim majority. For, after the early period of Islam, Muslim toleration of self-administered non-Muslim religious communities had been conditioned in practice on non-Muslim acceptance of virtual second-class citizenship. Ibrahim, however, not only enforced equality of status; he was even pro-Christian. He employed many Christians in his administration, rearmed the Christians of the Lebanon, and used Christian troops to suppress Druze and Nusayri rebellions. These measures alarmed and angered Muslims, particularly because special relations tied the non-Muslim communities to the Christian European powers which had assumed their 'protection'.

Muslims also hated military conscription, which put them in the Egyptian army for a minimum of fifteen years. (Christians were exempted from conscription.) All Syrians resented subjection to forced labour on fortifications and an ever growing burden of taxation. Many of the resources of the Egyptian army were expended in repressing uprisings against conscription and in confiscating arms. The British exploited this disaffection when they decided to compel Egyptian withdrawal from Syria. Anti-Egyptian revolts instigated by British and Ottoman agents, particularly in the Lebanon, assisted Anglo-Austrian forces to oust the Egyptians in 1840 and restore Ottoman rule.

THE PERIOD OF REFORMS 1839–76

In Syria, the *Tanzimat* (Reorganization) reforms of the restored Ottoman government were directed mainly at bringing the country under centralized Ottoman control and, as demanded by the European powers, at removing restrictions on Christians and Jews. But the Ottoman government was too weak to enforce these reforms. With the Egyptian departure, the old ruling class of quasi-feudal lords, chieftains, and town notables assumed control of the revived provincial administration and resumed tax-farming.

Restoration of Ottoman rule with European aid opened Syria to almost unlimited European economic intervention. The commercial treaties signed by Ottoman rulers in 1838 were now applied to Syria and further reinforced the already great advantages enjoyed by foreign goods and merchants under the Capitulations. An enormous increase in imports of cheap European finished goods, combined with adoption of European clothing and styles of living, caused a decline in Syrian manufactures. Import of European cotton yarn and other semi-finished goods made Syrian manufacturers dependent on the European industrial system. European economic domination undermined the class that had been the backbone of the Syrian economy, artisan manufacturers and traders who handled their goods. Under the pressure of European demand, subsistence agriculture partially gave way to commercial agriculture specializing in a few cash crops for export, but agricultural exports could not keep pace with the rapidly rising import bill. The trade deficit widened throughout the century; the outflow of gold to meet the deficit contributed to rising prices and impoverishment.

Merchants and notables adversely affected by these changes turned to the land. Pressures grew for the establishment of private landownership. Under the Islamic system of landownership all land – except the built-on properties of towns and cities, which were considered absolute freehold and called *mulk*, and certain allodial estates – was considered the inalienable property of the Muslim community as a whole represented by the state. *Miri* (from *emir*: prince), land or state domain – and in Syria this was most agricultural land – was held by the occupier as a lessee of the state, subject to payment of a rent or tax. The 1858 land code was devised to ensure occupiers stability of holding and provide the basis for increased tax revenues.

The law, with its subsequent amendments, however, opened the door to private appropriation of land and the establishment of private latifundia. Tax-farmers, leaseholders, tribal chiefs, and city notables step by step tightened their control over the land to acquire *de facto* ownership. Most large private estates in Syria date from the period following application of the 1858 land law. (The rest were established during the French Mandate.) Titles to the land were often acquired by fraud. The law introduced compulsory registration of all *miri* land; it also prohibited registration in the name of a village or tribe. Village and tribal lands were registered in the names of influential persons or tribal shaikhs, who soon acquired complete possession. City notables took possession of lands cultivated by peasants, whose indebtedness increased with the development of commercial agriculture. Actual cultivators were transformed into sharecroppers and hired labourers, condemned to hardship and misery.

Large-scale entry of European capital into the empire began after the Crimean War. European loans on onerous terms created an ever growing state debt, requiring new loans to pay off the interest on the old, and ever higher taxes. Towards the end of the century, Istanbul was taking almost four-fifths of Syria's tax revenues.[1] France, holder of the greater part of the Ottoman state debt, won economic concessions in Syria. French investments–mainly in ports, railroads, and roads–facilitated foreign trade but did not serve the domestic economy and had little impact on it beyond introducing modern techniques on a limited scale. Development of communications, however, began to break down the isolation of some towns and villages. European influence led to the adoption of hygienic and sanitary measures in the cities. The population started to grow, but emigration commencing in the 1860s continued at an accelerating rate until 1914.

As Syria's economy was converted into a dependency of European capitalism, the European powers assumed a collective tutelage over the empire. Their representatives arrogated to themselves the functions of government and told the Pashas just what to do. European interference was nowhere more flagrant than in matters touching the religious minorities. Each power now had one or more religious community as its exclusive client. Maronites looked only to France and the Greek Orthodox and Armenians to Russia; Britain adopted the Druzes, the nascent Protestant community, and the Jews. With the religious communities embroiled in the rivalries of the Powers, sectarian conflicts intensified; the relations of these communities with the government and almost everybody else were compromised.

Ottoman decrees, issued under European pressure, proclaiming equality of status for Christians and Jews further aggravated religious antagonisms. Rumours of European and Christian plots, combined with the real European-Christian subversion of Ottoman authority, fed Muslim fears. The rash of anti-European and anti-Christian disturbances that erupted in Syria in the 1850s and early 1860s– Aleppo rebellion of 1850, Nablus riot of 1856, Maronite-Druze war in the Lebanon, and the Lebanese and Damascus massacres of 1860 – expressed Muslim hostility and frustration in the face of the painful changes and economic hardships brought about by Christian Europe's encroachment on almost every aspect of life. The 1860 massacres in the Lebanon provided a pretext for French military intervention and for a settlement imposed by the Powers. This made Mount Lebanon a special *sanjaq* (district), with a governor appointed by the Sultan in consultation with the Powers and directly responsible to him.

Europeanizing reforms culminated in the 1870s in a brief constitutional experiment. A constitution, modelled on the French constitution, was proclaimed by the new Sultan, Abdul Hamid II, in 1876. It preserved the autocratic powers of the Sultan, but it also contained a bill of rights, and provided for an elected chamber. The chamber survived only eleven months. In February 1878, following a disastrous war with Russia, the Sultan prorogued it indefinitely and shelved the constitution. Abdul Hamid's thirty-three-year rule was one of heavy-handed repression.

POLITICAL AWAKENING

Syrians entered the nineteenth century still without a political life or political consciousness. By the latter half of the century, under the conflicting influence of increasing European encroachment and Western political ideas, they began to experience a gradual political and intellectual awakening along with a defensive intensification of traditional and Islamic loyalties.

The first stimulus came from the Egyptian occupation. Its administrative councils gave Syrians their first opportunity in modern times to participate in the administration of their own affairs. The Egyptians also shook Syrians out of their intellectual lethargy by making available to a narrow élite the Arabic works on science, philosophy, and other subjects that were printed in Cairo after 1820 as well as Arabic translations of European works. These publications continued to enter Syria after the Egyptians departed. By 1870, Syrians had become the principal translators of European works.

The Europeanizing reforms and growing European economic and political pressures that followed the Ottoman restoration provoked Syrian doubts about their relations to the Turks, who, far from defending Islamic civilization, seemed to be assisting its subversion. European consular reports of the 1850s and after speak of Syrian restiveness under Turkish rule, even of Syrian hatred for the Turks. Secret societies demanding Arab autonomy were reported to be active in Beirut, Damascus, and Aleppo in the late 1870s and 1880s.

Education was gradually extended by the appearance of Ottoman state schools in the 1850s and by the increase soon after in the number of schools maintained by indigenous Christian communities and by foreign missions, especially in the Lebanon. Syria acquired more state schools than did other Arab provinces, but Ottoman expenditures on education in Syria were still very small—roughly a tenth of the military expenditures there.[2] Most people remained illiterate. Education, limited as it was, created an audience for the many Arabic publications then becoming available. Secular Arabic publishing was started in Beirut by Syrians in the 1850s. Arabic books, periodicals, and translations of many kinds appeared. Syrian Christians and Muslims developed Arabic journalism, founding newspapers in Beirut, Istanbul, and Cairo. Arabic publications and literary societies inspired an Arabic cultural revival. University education became available with the opening of the University of Istanbul in 1846, and the establishment later in the century of the Syrian Protestant College (later the American University of Beirut) and the Jesuit Université Saint-Joseph, also in Beirut.

New currents of thought flowed into Syria from Syrian exiles in Egypt, from contact with the Americas through emigration, from translation of European, especially French, works, which gradually gave currency to the ideas of the French Revolution and the rationalism of the Enlightenment, and from the New Ottoman movement, which promoted revitalization of Islam as well as the idea of an 'Ottoman nation' according equal rights to all. As the Western impact disrupted the old civilization, exposing its backwardness relative to the West, the rising class of intellectuals, teachers, professional people, and businessmen sought a new basis for integration and a means to overcome the humiliating disparity.

The response of Christians and Muslims to the new stimuli inevitably differed. Christians could more easily accept the new ideas from the West, among them the concept of secular nationalism. In Christian thought, this idea found different applications. Some put forward the idea of Ottoman brotherhood embracing all subjects of the empire without racial or religious discrimination. Others adopted the conception of Syria as a homeland to be shared by Muslim and non-Muslim Arabs. Still others came to think in terms of an Arab nationality. Not a few Christians, uprooted by the new influences, identified with one or another Western country. And it was the Christians who emigrated.

Leading Muslim thinkers sought to defend Islamic civilization by reforming Islam and by forging Muslim solidarity into an effective weapon against Western domination. Since they attributed the decadence of Islam to the corruption of primitive Islam, reformation involved the restoration of 'pure Islam', the Islam of the Arabs. The goal of restoring an Arab Caliphate won advocates, although most remained loyal to the Ottoman Caliphate. Pan-Islamists promoted the study of classical Arabic, stressing its religious mission and the glories of Arab civilization. A concept of Arab linguistic, cultural, and ethnic unity gradually emerged and with it one of Arab Islamic nationalism. Later on, secularist Muslim approaches developed, especially among Muslims studying abroad and the emerging urban élite. Muslim secularism, like Christian secularism, took different forms, contributing to the development of both Ottomanism and Arab nationalism.

Nationalist ideas, often ambiguous, whether Christian or Muslim, secular or religious, came together in a common consciousness of cultural and political rights. Christians and Muslims both demanded equal rights with the Turks within the empire and restoration of the 1876 Constitution and parliament. Thus, in the latter part of the century, the basis was gradually laid for co-operation in a common movement to secure political rights.

The majority of Syrians were untouched by these ideas. They were influenced rather by Abdul Hamid's promotion of a religious revival and his wooing of the Arabs, especially the Syrians. His appointment of Syrians to high position, endowment of religious institutions, construction of mosques and of railroads to link Syria more closely to Istanbul reinforced Syrian loyalty to the empire. The Hijaz railroad from Damascus to Medina, construction of which began at the turn of the century, was entirely financed by Muslim subscriptions. This railroad could restore to Damascus its former role as the principal staging-post for the pilgrimage, a role lost with the ending of the Damascus-Mecca caravan in mid-century.

BEGINNINGS OF THE ARAB NATIONAL MOVEMENT

The importance of mercantile activity in the cities of Syria and the intensive cultural action long carried on by the French and the Americans contributed to the development of a secular anti-despotic movement in Syria. This movement recruited its first activists from the intelligentsia, especially that part of it which participated in political life in Istanbul. This rising urban élite of professionals, journalists, intellectuals, government officials, and army officers— from the upper or upper-middle classes and families of city notables— was predominantly Muslim but included some Christians. It led Syria's fight, first, for political rights and then for independence.

The first significant political action of the Syrian intelligentsia was its participation in the Committee of Union and Progress (CUP),

organized by the Young Turks around the demand for restoration of
the 1876 Constitution. Restoration of the constitution following the
July 1908 revolution, however, did not bring Arab equality. The fact
that only candidates with a knowledge of Turkish were allowed to
stand for parliament spurred Arab demands for recognition of Arabic
as the official language of the Arab provinces and acceptance of its
use with Turkish in official business. The development of the Young
Turk movement on Turkish nationalist lines after 1909, and its
harsh Turkification policy, gave impetus to Arab nationalism. But
the Arab national movement still did not aim for more than autonomy
within the empire. This goal reflected both reluctance to break with
the established Islamic order consecrated in the Ottoman Empire
and the somewhat limited aims of the Arab urban élite which was
primarily interested in winning a share in rule.

The Syrian intelligentsia, Syrian notables, and their sons provided
the bulk of the membership of the Arab societies, open and secret,
that now proliferated in Istanbul and the principal Arab cities. The
Ottoman Decentralization Party, established in Cairo by eminent
Syrians, was the most influential. The most effective secret societies
were *Al-Ahd* (The Covenant), composed of Arab army officers,
mainly Iraqis, and *Al-Fatat* (Young Arab Society), founded in Paris
in 1911 by mainly Syrian students and refugees. *Fatat's* goal was a
bi-national empire, but the idea of Arab separatism was already
beginning to develop.

The Arab national effort in this period was, with the exception of
a notable contribution from Iraqi officers, predominantly a Syrian
affair, and for the most part its goals continued to be limited. The
Young Turks' rejection of Arab demands, however, provoked a
gradually widening current aiming at independence. Fear of European designs on the Arab provinces, enormously enhanced by the
Italian invasion of Libya and periodic appearances of British and
French cruisers off the Syrian coast, inhibited a more rapid development of this current. (Even after Turkey entered the war, *Fatat*
resolved to side with the Turks if European designs on the Arab
provinces materialized.)

Also active in this period were a number of semi-autonomous Arab
emirs in the Arabian peninsula. They hoped to take advantage of
Turkish difficulties in the Balkans and preoccupation with the
1911–12 Italian war to manoeuvre for greater independence. Among
them, the ruler of the Hijaz, Husain Ibn Ali, Sharif of Mecca,
cherished ambitions to become Caliph. In 1911, a group of deputies
in the Ottoman parliament wrote the Sharif that they were prepared
to recognize him as Caliph and join him in a revolt to liberate the
Arabs from Turkish 'tyranny and slavery'. This gesture was, in

effect, the first step in the process by which the more or less secular Arab national movement of the urban élite was placed under the leadership of Arab Islamic nationalism and of tribal chiefs of the desert. Early in 1914, the Sharif made discreet overtures to the British, seeking recognition of his independence from Istanbul.

ARAB-BRITISH NEGOTIATIONS

The outbreak of the First World War thus found Britain already in contact with the Sharif of Mecca. Ottoman alliance with Germany imposed on Britain a war strategy designed to open a breach between the Arabs and the Turks. The British idea was to offer the Arabs some kind of independent Muslim state in exchange for Arab revolt against the Turks. Since this concept had to be reconciled with France's 'special interests' in Syria and at the same time advance Britain's own ambitions in Arab territories, the project evolved somewhat ambiguously.

On 31 October 1914, Lord Kitchener, Secretary of State for War, in a message to the Sharif's second son, Abdullah, proposed that the 'Arab nation' assist England in the war, promising in return aid against aggression and hinting at the possibility of an Arab Caliphate. The British choice of the Sharif to lead the projected revolt gave dominance to the most backward element in the Arab movement—the religiously-oriented tribal chieftains of the desert. These chieftains, later transformed into kinglets, then became Britain's partner in the dynastic Arab national movement which was to provide the structure of British control in the Arab East throughout the inter-war period. But, whatever use Britain later made of the Sharif and his family, it was the (mainly Syrian) urban élite that spearheaded the Arab drive for independence. Even the most activist elements of this élite, however, felt it necessary to call in the religious tribal chiefs as their spokesmen. In spring 1915, *Ahd* and *Fatat* opened negotiations in Damascus with the Sharif's third son, Faisal. As a result, Faisal joined both societies, and the societies agreed to make the Sharif the spokesman for their programme. Thus, when the Sharif in July 1915 began his correspondence with Sir Henry McMahon, British High Commissioner in Egypt, he spoke for the Arab national movement and, following Kitchener, used the term 'Arab nation'.

The Husain-McMahon correspondence (July 1915 to January 1916) defined the terms under which the Arabs would undertake a revolt against the Turks. The Sharif, following the Damascus Protocol to the letter, demanded independence for Iraq, for the Arabian peninsula (with the exception of Aden), and for all geographic Syria. McMahon agreed, subject to certain crucial reservations which, however, were for the most part vaguely expressed. A. L. Tibawi's study of British Foreign Office Papers, which were made public in the late 1960s,[3] reveals that the imprecise British reservations were deliberate double-talk devised to deceive the Arabs. The British and French were concurrently dividing the Arab provinces among themselves. The agreement concluded in April 1916 by Mark Sykes and Georges Picot gave preponderance to France in Syria and to Britain in Iraq and Haifa. McMahon's reservations and his evasiveness in dealing with the Sharif left the door open to Anglo-French claims while inducing the Arabs to believe their demands would in the main be realized. Later British attempts to interpret McMahon's reservations as excluding 'the whole of Palestine west of Jordan River' from the area of Arab independence are contradicted by official British documents. Lord Curzon told the War Cabinet Eastern Committee on 5 December 1918:

> The Palestine position is this. If we deal with our commitments, there is first the general pledge to Hussein in October 1915, under which Palestine was included in the areas to which Britain pledged itself that they should be Arab and independent in the future.[4]

However naïve the Sharif may have been in his dealings with the British, the nationalists were very much alive to the possible danger of exchanging Turkish for European overlordship. The Balfour Declaration of 2 November 1917 promising 'establishment in Palestine of a national home for the Jewish people' and Trotsky's publication the same month of the hitherto secret Sykes-Picot Agreement confirmed their fears. Since the Turks were then trying to reach an accommodation with the Arabs, the British could hardly afford to ignore Arab alarm and so gave the Arabs a number of 'specific and unmistakable' promises of self-determination and independence.[5]

THE ARAB REVOLT

Although the national movement accepted the Sharif's leadership, its original plan had been to begin the revolt in Syria with the mutiny of Arab divisions stationed there. The British opposed this plan. It was, in any event, frustrated when Jamal Pasha, Commander-in-Chief of the Ottoman Fourth Army stationed in Syria, transferred these divisions to the Gallipoli front. Syrian nationalists were unable to make a direct contribution to the revolt which was launched by the Sharif in the Hijaz in June 1916. Jamal Pasha's rule in Syria was too oppressive. But Turkish repression also induced many Syrians, who might otherwise have remained emotionally attached to the empire, to support the national movement. When Jamal Pasha executed thirty-four eminent Syrian Muslims and Christians in 1915 and 1916, he deprived the movement of its foremost political leaders and gave it its first martyrs. Imprisonment, torture, or deportation to remote parts of the empire were the lot of many other Syrian nationalists. Common martyrdom of Muslim and Christian made for Muslim-Christian solidarity.

To the people, the war brought great suffering. British blockade, locust plagues, arbitrary Turkish requisition of food and animals, destruction of fruit and olive trees, and widespread corruption all but ruined the economy. Famine and disease claimed 200–300,000 lives.

The Arab revolt, carried out by tribal levies and a number of Syrian and Iraqi officers, contributed to the Allied victory in the First World War. The Arab army, under the command of Faisal, tied down large Turkish forces in the Hijaz, harassed Turkish communications, and protected General Allenby's right flank as he slowly advanced through Palestine. Following a decisive Turkish defeat at Megiddo in September 1918, all Syria fell to the Anglo-Arab armies. As the Turks withdrew, Arab banners were raised in the cities of Syria before the arrival of Anglo-Arab troops, and in Beirut an Arab administration was established. Early in October, a few days after his forces entered Damascus, Faisal proclaimed 'an absolutely independent government embracing all Syria'.

PROMISES BETRAYED

Anglo-French decisions about the administration of Syria, of which the Arabs had not been informed, came to light piecemeal. On 8 October, General Allenby replaced the Arab authority in Beirut with a French Military Governor, and wherever Arabs of the coastlands had taken control in the name of the Arab government he dislodged them. He then set up three military administrations in Syria: Occupied Enemy Territory (South) – Palestine – under a British officer; Occupied Enemy Territory (North) – Beirut, Mount Lebanon, and the northern coastland – under a French officer; and Occupied Enemy Territory (East) – internal Syria including Transjordan – under an Arab Military Governor. To outraged Syrian protest the British replied that these administrations were provisional, without political significance, and would not prejudice a future political settlement. They proved to be the first step in the dismemberment of Syria.

On the eve of the Versailles Peace Conference, Britain and France reached agreement on the disposal of the Ottoman Empire's Arab provinces and application of the mandate system. In return for confirmation of its 'rights' in Syria and Cilicia, France abandoned its claim to Mosul and accepted British control of Palestine. The only question still at issue was the fate of internal Syria, claimed by France but then under Faisal's administration. Sharp Anglo-French disagreement on this question in March 1919 led President Wilson to propose an international commission of inquiry 'to discover the desires of the population' of the regions concerned. Since France and Britain refused to participate, the investigation was made by an exclusively American commission composed of Dr Henry Churchill King and Charles Crane. The commission's observations merit attention, although they were ignored by the statesmen and published only in 1922.

The commission found Syria's 'economic, geographic, racial and language unity too manifest' to justify partition, urged that 'the unity of Syria be preserved in accordance with the earnest petition of the great majority of the people of Syria', and warned against 'the real danger of breaking Syria up into meaningless fragments'. There should be only one Mandatory Power and this for a 'limited term' only. This power should be the United States or Britain but, owing to the general aversion to French rule among all but certain Catholic groups in the Lebanon, in no case France. Originally sympathetic to Zionism, the commission came to the conclusion that the Zionist programme of unlimited Jewish immigration 'looking forward finally to making Palestine distinctly a Jewish State' needed 'serious modification'. For the Zionist programme involved 'a gross violation' of the principle of self-determination and 'of the people's rights' and could be imposed only by force. Palestine, the commission said, must be included in the united Syrian state.[6]

In September 1919, Britain agreed to the French claim to internal Syria and told Faisal he must come to terms with France; over a three-month period British troops in the coastal zone made way for French contingents; the Arabs held the interior. In a tentative understanding reached with Clemenceau, Faisal yielded on many points to the French rather than heed the popular demand in Syria to fight for independence. This understanding was never put into effect owing to the opposition of the French generals and the Syrian nationalists. In April 1920, the Allied Supreme Council meeting at San Remo awarded France the Mandate over Syria and Lebanon and Britain a Mandate over Palestine, into which the Balfour Declaration was incorporated, and over Transjordan. In July 1920, the French occupied Damascus, put an end to the Arab government, and exiled Faisal, its king. (The British later put Faisal on the throne of Iraq.)

THE NATIONAL ARAB GOVERNMENT
OCTOBER 1918–JULY 1920

From Faisal's arrival in Damascus in October 1918 until the French occupation of Damascus on 25 July 1920, a national Arab government exercised authority in internal Syria behind the façade of a military administration and inspired loyalty in other parts of Syria. This first Arab government was Syrian and secular, and largely the creation of the Syrian urban élite which aimed at establishing a modern state. Its higher officials were practically all Syrians who had been trained either in the Ottoman civil service or in the British administration in Egypt. District governors were usually local citizens. Most lower officials, also Syrians, were drawn from the Ottoman bureaucracy. The government and the leadership of the national movement seemed to recognize that sectarian rivalries served only the European powers and that elimination of religious discrimination was essential to attain unity and independence. Christians as well as Muslims held high positions in the government and took an active part in political work. The speeches of Faisal and other leaders emphasized Christian, Muslim, and Jewish unity in a common struggle. As it penetrated the masses, however, Syrian or Arab nationalism became Sunni Muslim nationalism and sometimes fanaticism. This was fanned by French attempts to exploit sectarian differences, the inflow of Armenian refugees from Turkey, and the general frustration that set in as Anglo-French intentions became clear.

The government took many steps to modernize the country. Schools were Arabized and special seminars were held to train teachers. Textbooks were translated into Arabic. A long-range plan to expand education was carefully studied and prepared. Twenty-four new schools were opened in Damascus (including ten for girls) and twelve in Aleppo. An agricultural school was established and another rebuilt. An educational journal appeared. The law school and medical college in Damascus reopened. The Arab Academy, founded in 1919, undertook to find Arabic terms for scientific and technological use. A beginning was made in setting up a rudimentary public health service. Military dispensaries were ordered to treat poor patients without payment. The government opened a national hospital, introduced free smallpox vaccination for children, and founded an Agricultural Bank to provide low-interest loans to farmers. Early in 1919, a committee began to study the needs of agriculture, including the development of water resources, co-operatives, and fertilizer requirements. Efforts were made to repair bridges and roads and plans were drawn up to encourage industrial development and to reform the tax system.[7]

The Arab Zone's brief experience in self-government took place in adverse circumstances. Cut off from its normal outlets on the Mediterranean and artificially divided from the rest of Syria, the Zone was disorganized by war. Dependence on Britain restricted the government's authority. The time was too short, and the government's resources too limited, to permit execution of all its reforms. Moreover, the government was not without its share of incompetence and venality. Yet self-government did call forth a national effort. It reached its climax in the Syrian National Congress.

The initiative for calling the Congress came from an offshoot of *Fatat*, the Arab Independence Party (*Hizb Al-Istiqlal Al-Arabi*). In the Arab Zone, Congress delegates were elected under pre-war Ottoman procedures, while those from Palestine and the coastland were picked by local notables because the British and French prohibited elections and meetings. Yet the Congress unquestionably reflected majority opinion. The King-Crane Commission found it truly representative. Its delegates were on the average young, and of those whose background is known, almost half were university graduates.[8]

On 2 July 1919, the Congress, meeting in Damascus, adopted a series of resolutions known as the Congress Programme. This was published throughout Syria and handed to the King-Crane Commission, which observed:[9]

> It is the most substantial document presented to the Commission and deserves to be treated with respect. The result of an extensive and arduous political process, it affords a basis on which Syrians can get together, and as firm a foundation for a Syrian national organization as can be obtained.

The programme called for Syria's complete independence within its natural frontiers and for a democratic constitutional monarchy with safeguards for the minorities. It rejected Zionist claims to Palestine, French claims to Lebanon, the mandate system, and any foreign political control, but agreed to accept technical and economic aid from the United States or Britain for a period of not more than twenty years. The programme upheld the principle of Arab unity in demanding economic union between Syria and an independent Iraq. Its main preoccupation, however, was the establishment of an independent and united Syria; the line between Syrian and Arab nationalism was not yet drawn.

Two parties formed within the Congress: the Progressive (*Hizb Al-Taqaddum*), consisting mainly of members of *Fatat* and *Ahd*, and the Democratic (*Hizb Al-Demoqrati*), made up largely of city notables dissatisfied with Faisal's policy of compromise. The former group tended towards more modern concepts and even won majority support for a clause in the draft constitution granting women civil and voting rights; in the end, however, this was omitted for fear of a conservative backlash.[10] (Only twenty-nine years later did Syria become the first Arab state to grant women's suffrage.) These political groupings and others represented the politically articulate élite of the urban well-to-do whose only avenue to the uneducated majority was through the Friday public meetings at the mosques, where shaikhs and political leaders tried to inculcate nationalist ideas and organized mass actions.

Throughout the autumn and winter of 1919, nationalist fervour mounted and defence committees formed in the principal towns. Provocations and counter-provocations produced frequent Syrian-French clashes. Sentiment grew for a Syrian alliance with Mustafa Kemal's Turkish forces, while in the north nationalists began to co-operate with the Kemalists. Violent street demonstrations in Damascus in December 1919 showed that Faisal's policy of compromise did not command the support of the people.

The Syrian National Congress adjourned in December at Faisal's request, but was reconvened in February 1920. Popular demonstrations throughout the country demanded an immediate declaration of independence. The Congress now took command and acted thereafter as a national assembly. On 8 March, it proclaimed the independence of all Syria, a constitutional monarchy with Faisal as king, and formation of a national government. (At the same time the Iraqi branch of *Ahd* declared Iraq independent under the Sharif's second son, Abdullah.) These decisions electrified the people in the Arab Zone, Palestine, and many parts of Lebanon. Angry popular protests against the San Remo mandate awards compelled formation of a more nationalist government under Hashim Al-Atasi, a great landowner of Homs. A draft constitution, prepared in this period, provided for the unity of all Syria in a federal system, an elected bicameral legislature, and a bill of rights. It was unanimously approved early in July.

The French at this time built up a strong military force on the coast and crushed with great harshness large-scale rebellions in the Nusayriyah mountains and among the Shi'a population of southern Lebanon. Even the Maronites of Lebanon became disaffected with French rule. Early in July 1920, the Maronite-dominated Administrative Council of the Lebanon, meeting secretly, decided to proclaim Lebanon's independence from French tutelage and its fraternal cooperation with Syria. French rule in the Levant was clearly threatened, and France acted swiftly. A French ultimatum to Faisal demanded in effect his unconditional acceptance of French authority throughout internal Syria. Faisal ultimately bowed to this demand and, when the National Congress refused to ratify his decision, he dissolved it.

As French forces advanced towards Damascus, furious demonstrations demanded resistance to the death; some hundred or more demonstrators were killed by Faisal's police. The poorly armed Arab forces decided to fight. Badly-equipped volunteers under the leadership of War Minister Yusuf Al-Azmah joined regular troops in an effort to hold the Maysalun pass near Damascus. This brave if hopeless resistance, in which Azmah was killed, held up the advance of overwhelmingly superior French forces for a few hours. For Syrians the resistance at Maysalun remains one of the great moments in their modern history and Al Azmah one of their most honoured national heroes.

Although the Arab government was short-lived, its efforts and those of the national movement provide an index to the potential available had it been allowed to develop. With all its limitations and shortcomings this government was probably the most popularly based that Syria had known in more than a thousand years. The idea of an independent and modern United Syrian Arab state as outlined in the programme of the Syrian National Congress did not disappear with the arrival of the French but continued to be a goal of the national movement in the period between the wars.

[1] Vital Cuinet: *Syrie, Liban et Palestine*, Paris, 1896, p. 383.
[2] H. Lammens, op. cit., Vol. II, 201.
[3] A. L. Tibawi: *A Modern History of Syria*, London, 1969, Chapters 8 and 9.
[4] Public Record Office Document CAB 27/24.
[5] The quote is from an American Commission of Inquiry, The King-Crane Commission, sent to the Near East in 1919. See below, p. 56.
[6] *Foreign Relations of the US: Paris Peace Conference 1919*, Vol. 12, 787–99.
[7] Angus Mundy: *The Arab Government in Syria*, AUB thesis, Beirut, 1965.
[8] R. Bayly Winder: 'Syrian Deputies and Cabinet Members 1919–1959', Part II, *MEJ*, Vol. 17, Winter-Spring 1963.
[9] King-Crane Commission, op. cit., p. 781.
[10] Hisham Nashabi: *The Political Parties of Syria 1918–1933*, AUB thesis, Beirut, 1952.

Chapter 4

A Truncated State

THE POST-WAR SETTLEMENTS broke geographic Syria into 'meaningless fragments' and placed them all under foreign occupation. In response to Zionist demands, Britain extended the borders of Palestine to include both banks of the Upper Jordan River, the eastern shores of Lake Huleh and Lake Tiberias, and a strip of land running into southern Lebanon which gave Palestine control of one source of the Jordan. British-mandated Transjordan became a separate emirate under the Sharif's second son, Abdullah. France ceded to Turkey the fertile wheatlands of Cilicia, the ancient Syrian cities of Aintab and Urfa (Edessa), the northern hill country, and the Baghdad Railroad running across north Syria. The railroad's southern edge became French-defined Syria's preposterous northern frontier. This settlement brought Turkey to within 30 miles of Aleppo and a few miles of Alexandretta; deprived Aleppo of its natural markets and its water supply (since much of the water of the Quwaik River was in 1926 diverted into Turkey); and drove tens of thousands of Armenian refugees from Cilicia into a Syria already suffering severe unemployment. These frontier settlements violated Article 4 of the Mandate which held the Mandatory Power responsible 'for seeing that no part of the Mandated Territory of Syria and Lebanon is ceded or leased or in any way placed under the control of a foreign power'. The French did, however, later secure for Syria 'a window on the Tigris' in the extreme north-east.

Lebanon was enlarged by 'all the Muslim areas it could safely dominate'[1] and made a separate state, the Greater Lebanon, three times the size of the pre-war *sanjaq* (district). Syria lost to Greater Lebanon the mainly Muslim districts of Beirut, Tripoli, Sidon, and Tyre, the fertile plains of the Biqa Valley, inhabited by Muslims and Orthodox Christians, and the Shi'a Muslim districts south of Mount Hermon. Most people in these areas did not want to be part of the Maronite-dominated Lebanon. The annexations created conflicts which still haunt the Lebanon and its relations with the Arab world.

Dismemberment of geographic Syria affected its inhabitants in a most intimate way. Barriers arose where hitherto movement to and fro had been unimpeded and almost constant. Families were separ-

ated – the merchant in Damascus or Aleppo from his brothers or
cousins in Jerusalem, Beirut, Tripoli, or Jaffa. The profound disillusion and bitterness engendered by dismemberment still shape Syrian
political development and guaranteed enduring political instability
in the entire area between Turkey and Egypt. Political instability on
the sensitive northern frontier of the Arab world affected all Arab
politics, of which Syria became the cockpit.

France partitioned what was left of Syria along religious lines,
shuffling and reshuffling its territorial organizations. The Nusayriyah
mountain and coastal area centred on Latakia was rechristened the
Alawi Territory (later the Government of Latakia or State of the
Alawis) and made 'independent' – independent, that is, of the rest of
Syria. The Jebel Druze, which militarily dominates Damascus and
central Syria, also became 'independent'. Assuming direct rule of the
nomadic Euphrates area, the French encouraged the settlement there
of Christian, Assyrian, and Kurdish minorities and the development
of separatist sentiment. The rest of Syria was divided into the two
autonomous governments of Aleppo and Damascus, perhaps in the
hope of exploiting the traditional rivalry between the two cities, but
this division could not be maintained. Aleppo and Damascus were
united in 1924 to form the State of Syria. This state, with its two
great communications and trade centres, was cut off from the sea.
The district of Alexandretta was placed under a special, virtually
independent, administration, the first step leading to its cession to
Turkey in 1939.

These divisions gave the League of Nations Permanent Mandates
Commission (PMC) 'the impression of a country which had been
parcelled out'.[2] And the frequent changes in territorial organization
and administration, 'matters so calculated to encourage controversies
inspired by races, clans, and religions', in the commission's view,
'maintained instability and unrest'.[3]

French handling of the Armenian refugee problem provoked
Syrian fears that the Armenians were cast for the same role in Syria
that the Zionists were playing in Palestine.[4] Unemployed Armenian
refugees became a burden to the Syrian states, while the employed
offered fierce competition to indigenous artisans and merchants. The
French used Armenians and Circassians as informers and auxiliary
troops in repressive actions against the population, recruited officers
and men for the local forces (after 1932 the Special Forces of the
Levant) disproportionately from the Druze, Alawi, and other
minority communities, and favoured the minorities in public appointments even at the highest levels. Christians were left in full control of
their *Waqfs* (religious endowments), while in violation of Article 6 of
the Mandate Muslim *Waqfs* were placed under a Christian authority,

the representative of the High Commissioner, and a system of centralized control. The Damascus-Medina railroad, which had been financed entirely by Muslim contributions, was turned over to a French concessionary company.

France's long-range plans for permanent domination required, behind the fiction of the Mandate, a colonial and military regime. Throughout the Mandate its military expenditures totalled almost ten times its civilian expenditures.[5] All administration and legislation emanated from the High Commissioner, whose unlimited powers resembled those of a colonial Governor-General. The first three High Commissioners were generals trained in France's African colonies. The High Commissioner appointed the governors of the states; except in the State of Syria, these were usually Frenchmen. His delegates and deputy delegates in each state or autonomous district had authority over the governors and appointed all higher local officials and heads of the principal services. An army of French advisers was attached to all these state and district officials to take all decisions, even the most trifling, for which local officials were then held responsible. Under the High Commissioner, separate all-French services – finance, justice, public works, etc. – supplemented parallel state services. With some exceptions French officials and administrators were of mediocre calibre, ignorant of local conditions, seldom spoke Arabic, and were often corrupt. Abuses committed by the Special Services (intelligence), exercising both military and civil authority, troubled the PMC[6] and drew severe criticism even in the French parliament.

Multiplication of state administrations and duplication of services were costly and all but paralyzed public services. Yet the High Commissioner's tightly centralized rule left no room for local autonomy. Wholesale suppression of civil liberties led the PMC to note 'the somewhat singular fact: the powers of the general were those of the chief of an army occupying a foreign country'.[7] Arbitrary arrest, imprisonment, deportation, suspension of newspapers, restriction of freedom of association were the norm. Martial law was lifted only in January 1925 and was periodically reimposed thereafter.

The French attempted to impose French culture somewhat as they had done in Algeria. They scrapped the educational expansion programme started by the Arab government, closed down indigenous schools, and allowed them to reopen only if they adopted a French-approved curriculum which made French-language study compulsory. Children were compelled to learn the history and geography of France, not Syria, and the classics of French, not Arabic, culture, and to celebrate French, not Syrian, holidays. French became an official language on an equal footing with Arabic.

French policies aggravated a serious economic crisis. The break-up of the Ottoman Empire cost Syria's traditional industry the greater part of its markets–millions of consumers now cut off by tariff barriers. The Mandate-inspired Open Door, in enforcing non-reciprocity in economic matters between Syria and League of Nations members, partially continued the Capitulations. Syria was deprived of protection against dumping and other competitive practices by League members, but its exports to these countries faced prohibitive tariffs. Through the Open Door cheap imports of modern goods swamped the home market, further shrinking demand for traditional products. Syria's imports for local consumption rose to five times its exports of purely Syrian goods. The growing balance of payments deficit reduced its gold reserves by 70 per cent between 1919 and 1928, and its debts to European institutions increased.

Industrial production declined. The number of textile-workers in Aleppo fell by half between 1913 and 1926, and the number of looms by two-thirds.[8] Urban unemployment grew rapidly and by the end of the 1920s involved one-quarter of industrial workers.[9] The presence of thousands of Armenian refugees prepared to work for very low wages contributed to reducing the general standard of wages in the country by 50 per cent.[10] At the same time prices of consumer goods soared: the price of flour doubled within a twelve-month period.

In the opinion of the PMC,[11] issue of a new Syrian currency tied to the franc produced unfortunate effects on the economy and risked impeding preparations for independence. Syrian currency, following the franc, experienced violent fluctuations and depreciation which caused Syrians substantial losses. The French-owned *Banque de Syrie et du Liban* (BSL) became the bank of issue and the official bank of the Levant states. Its policy of keeping a high ratio of its deposits in the Bank of France and investing most of its reserves in French securities suffocated the Syrian economy. The PMC found some basis for Syrian complaints that the French by various devices were taking gold out of Syria. The French frequently levied collective fines in gold on towns and villages, payment of which caused great hardships. A fine imposed following repression of an Alawi rebellion in 1921, for example, compelled peasants to sell their sheep and part of their land and, if they had neither, to sell or hire out their daughters on a long-term basis to rich people. The practice of 'selling girls' in the Alawi mountains–through brokers in the Latakia market place–dates from this time.

The Mandate imposed on the Mandatory Power the duty of economically developing the country. Use of the same currency, unified customs regulations, and freedom of movement for capital and labour throughout the different Levant states and administrative districts tied them together economically under the centralized Mandatory organization. The French, however, showed little concern for economic development of the Syrian states other than as – in the words of High Commissioner Henri De Jouvenel[12] – 'countries complementary to France' where French industry would find wool, silk, and vast expanses 'destined to become the cotton farm of France'. State budgets were burdened by the high salaries and allowances paid to French civilian and military officials. Unproductive expenditures in the budgets of the Syrian states accounted for two-thirds of total expenditures in 1926.[13] Surpluses of the state budgets, insofar as they were not purely paper, resulted from regressive taxation, which inhibited economic development, and from extraordinarily low expenditures on health (3 per cent of the total in 1926) and education (5·1 per cent). On a *per capita* basis, expenditure on education was much lower than in Palestine and on health much lower than in both Palestine and Iraq.

The Mandatory Power favoured French imports and promoted the interests of French companies, which controlled the railroads, ports, wharves, bonded warehouses, storage depots, tramways, flour-mills, most public utilities, the chief spinning-mills, and construction work on roads, ports, and lighthouses. Although foreign investment was negligible compared to such investment in Egypt and Iraq, these French monopolies blocked the normal development of the country and closed the door in the face of Syrian entrepreneurs whose energy and entrepreneurial skill had been proved in Egypt and in the Americas. Many businessmen emigrated at this time to Palestine and Egypt where trade and other restrictions were less onerous.

THE 1925–27 REVOLUTION

These were the main underlying causes of the 1925–27 revolution. In the first years of the Mandate, the nationalist movement suffered eclipse; its leaders, in hiding or exile in Egypt and Transjordan, did, however, continue to work and collect money for the nationalist cause. Within Syria numerous local uprisings occurred every year, and strikes and demonstrations on more than one occasion expressed popular concern over developments in Palestine as well as Syria. Following a French decision in 1925 to authorize political parties, some nationalist groupings gathered under the leadership of Dr Abdel Rahman Shahbandar and the Christian lawyer Faris Al Khuri, both of whom had been ministers in Faisal's Arab government, to form the People's Party (*Hizb Al-Sha'b*). Functionaries of the Damascus municipal government were prominent in its ranks.

Damascus now became the centre of the national movement.
No Syrian could find a national identity in truncated and partitioned Syria. The national movement insisted on the reunification of
geographic Syria, seeing its struggle for emancipation as one and
indivisible with similar struggles elsewhere in geographic Syria, above
all Palestine. Arab unity then meant primarily Syrian unity. At the
same time, by their very existence the artificial frontiers acquired a
certain reality while truncated Syria gradually developed a personality of its own. Moreover, from a practical point of view, nationalists
were compelled to concentrate on removing internal barriers within
French-mandated Syria, and to fight France for national rights,
while their brothers in Palestine confronted the British. The Western
Powers had succeeded in dividing the national movement of the
Fertile Crescent and confining each of the resulting parts in separate
compartments. The People's Party programme reflected the interests
of the urban bourgeoisie in calling not only for unity and national
sovereignty, but also for a number of modernizing reforms. These
included a demand for protection of national industry and for compulsory primary education in view of a 90 per cent illiteracy rate.

In July 1925 the urban élite of the People's Party joined with
Druze feudalists and peasants to transform the Druze revolt, led by
Sultan Pasha Atrash, into a national revolution. In the Jebel Druze,
Dr Shahbandar established a Provisional Syrian Government under
the flag of the Arab government and with Sultan Atrash as President.
The Provisional Government appealed to all Syrians to fight for 'the
complete independence of Arabic Syria' and the application of the
principles of the French Revolution. Peasants and villagers, artisans,
workers, and the jobless in the towns responded to this appeal.
Guerrilla warfare spread over much of the country, especially in the
south and centre, and into the Druze areas of southern Lebanon.
Arabs in Lebanon, Palestine, and Transjordan assisted the rebellion,
and its leaders sometimes operated from these countries, which were
still a part of Syria so far as popular sentiment was concerned.
Although only a small part of the population actively participated in
the fighting, the French needed two years to crush the rebellion.
During the conflict the French twice bombarded Damascus, causing
many casualties and destroying some of this ancient city's historic
buildings and monuments.

Druze leadership of the 1925–27 revolution in making the national
movement less a Sunni Muslim affair at the popular level contributed
to its secularization. In contrast to the local character of earlier
uprisings, the rebellion assumed a truly national character. Although
defeated, its achievements were not negligible. Through it, a
majority of the people acquired a consciousness of nationalist issues

and a sense of national dignity. Politicization of the cities of Syria made the city populace a factor to be reckoned with in national affairs. The revolution, moreover, compelled the French to realize they could not hold Syria by force alone and must at long last comply with the Mandate's requirement for a constitutional statute.

NEGOTIATIONS

Transferred to the negotiating table the struggle for independence centred around the terms first of the constitutional statute and then of the treaty that was to replace the Mandate. In this period, two national assemblies were chosen–in 1928 and 1932–in managed two-stage elections which gave the majority to French-favoured candidates. Yet the national movement dominated both assemblies, both of which were suspended before completing their terms because differences between the French and the nationalists over the degree of French control were irreconcilable. With People's Party leaders in exile, this stage of the struggle called forth a new nationalist coalition known as the National Bloc, founded by former activists of Faisal's Arab government.

The urban élite of professionals, intellectuals, notables (whose wealth was often based on landownership), and merchants supplied the National Bloc's leadership as it had that of the earlier national movement. The National Bloc's adherents came from the ranks of rural and town notables, traders in the *suqs*, and *petit bourgeois* elements. The bloc functioned on traditional clan lines, the personality and personal influence of clan chieftains and notables (rather than objective political goals) being the decisive factor. Orders went out from the notables at the top through the intermediation of lesser local notables and landlords to the people below. The bloc was directed in north Syria by Ibrahim Hananu of Aleppo, long active in rebellions against the Mandate, and in the south and centre by Hashim Al-Atasi, premier of Faisal's government in its last phase.

The first clash between the national movement and the High Commissioner came over the constitution. The High Commissioner, Henri Ponsot, rejected the draft constitution unanimously approved by the 1928 Assembly because it did not acknowledge the existence of the Mandate and insisted on the political unity of geographic Syria. He then dissolved the assembly and imposed a constitution in which the offending clauses were nullified. (The 1930 Constitution remained in force, although at times suspended, until 1950. It provided for a unicameral parliament, a Muslim President elected by, but not responsible to, parliament, and a ministry named by the President but responsible to parliament. Representation in parliament was on both a geographical and confessional basis to safeguard the rights of minorities.)

The second clash concerned the treaty to replace the Mandate. Treaty negotiations began after the 1932 elections, but the National Bloc ministers resigned when negotiations became deadlocked. A treaty subsequently concluded between the High Commissioner, Comte Damien de Martel, and the 'moderates' was abandoned in face of nationwide protest. The High Commissioner then suspended the Chamber and took the treaty out of its cognizance.

The growing impetus of the national movement became apparent when the respected nationalist leader, Ibrahim Hananu, died in November 1935. On the customary memorial day forty days later, the National Bloc proclaimed a National Pact, repeating the standard nationalist demands. A week later, nationalist demonstrations and police provocations touched off a fifty-day general strike which

> manifested itself in ways that were without parallel in the annals of the towns of the interior of Syria and above all in Damascus . . . [where] a spectator could watch a movement which started from the capital imposing itself with a certain regard for discipline and organization upon the country as a whole.[14]

The strike paralyzed business, schools, *suqs*, public services, and the courts. In it, the educated element of the rising generation played an important part. Military repression involving loss of life, hundreds of arrests, curfews, and martial law was harsh but ineffective. By the end of February 1936, the High Commissioner was compelled to begin negotiations with nationalist leaders. These were successfully concluded when the Popular Front came to power in France. On 9 September, a draft treaty, closely modelled on the 1930 Anglo-Iraq Treaty, was initialled by both sides. It provided for Syria's 'independence' and membership of the League of Nations, but accorded France extensive military, economic, and political rights in Syria.

THE PERIOD OF THE NATIONAL GOVERNMENT 1936-39

A National Bloc government took office following parliamentary elections in November 1936; Hashim Al-Atasi became President. When parliament ratified the treaty, the French began to transfer some administrative functions to the government. The National Government's three-year rule, however, proved for a number of reasons to be a profound disappointment. Its tenure of office coincided with a period of great economic distress for the majority. The élite represented in the government was not remarkable either for its social conscience or its ability to differentiate between its own material interests and the public good. Rising political impatience and new emerging political forces challenging its monopoly of power provoked the élite to try to tighten its grip. The 1936–39 Palestine rebellion revived the struggle for Syria with negative effects on its political life. France's gradual repudiation of the treaty, the government's less than militant response, and its impotence in the face of France's cession of Alexandretta to Turkey undermined its authority.

Modernization and the Crisis of the Traditional Economy

The French built roads and improved communications. While autos slowly began to replace pack animals, linking the different parts of the country, speeding transport, facilitating settlement of the beduin, and spreading acquaintance with modern technology, they remained few in number, far fewer than in the Lebanon. Modern postal, telegraph, telephone, and other services appeared. Power-stations, constructed in the main by French and Belgian companies, provided lighting for the main cities and a modicum of energy for the modern factories built in the early 1930s. Customs exemptions on machinery and fuel, a gradual rise in tariffs on imported textiles, a shortage of foreign exchange for imports during the world depression, and the return of emigrants with savings to invest combined to spur the development of modern industry. But the engineers and technicians employed were invariably foreign. By 1932, 148 small modern factories existed, producing silk and cotton, hosiery, knitted goods, matches, cigarettes, flour, and cement. But the growth of modern industry then slackened. In the early 1930s, IPC constructed a pipe-line across Syria (Kirkuk-Tripoli) giving temporary employment to some 5,000 Syrian workers.

The French established on an average seventeen new primary schools a year throughout the Mandate, and the number of pupils enrolled roughly tripled. But in 1943–44, the last year of French control of the school system, less than a quarter of the children between the ages of six and twelve attended schools; with a population of almost 3 million, Syria had only thirteen public secondary schools serving less than 5,000 pupils; at least 80 per cent of the population remained illiterate. The large role played by private schools gave education a sectarian, ethnic, and foreign basis rather than a national one. Although the small educated élite grew very slowly, members of the younger generation had difficulty in finding a place in a still backward society and often became rootless. Modernization benefited the urban well-to-do, and stimulated the growth of a small middle class, but it barely scratched the surface of Syrian society.

Agriculture

The French encouraged the growth of private latifundia, facilitating the private appropriation of land, especially by those who
collaborated with the Mandate. Land survey and compulsory registration of land titles–the only significant land reform carried out by
the Mandatory Power–confirmed the holdings of the big property-
owners since the French did not question the validity of old titles,
many of which were fraudulently acquired. Large areas, formerly the
personal property of Sultan Abdul Hamid, were registered as state
property (state domain in the Western sense), but regulations
adopted in the mid-1920s to distribute this land to smallholders were
not carried out. The French allowed this land to be sold or leased to
big landlords and influential persons at ridiculously low prices. They
also encouraged the sale of *Waqf* land to owners of latifundia and
concession companies. Ownership of state lands occupied by tribes
in the Jazira and Euphrates areas was granted to tribal chieftains,
who thus became great private landowners.

This policy of expanding big private ownership, which strengthened the big landlord class on which French rule rested, was followed
in face of the French admission[15] that

> Almost all the peasants, who are very poor, work on the land
> under a hire system which . . . is accompanied by usury. Small
> landlords are few in a country where latifundia cover the greater
> part of the land . . . Apart from a few exceptional villages, there
> is in the Syrian countryside no economically independent popu-
> lation.

Consequently, by the end of the 1930s, big absentee landlords owned
a very substantial part of the cultivable land. In the Druze and
Alawi mountain areas and the Hawran, where small and middle
properties prevailed, smallholders suffering from population pressure on the land, were often as badly off as sharecroppers on big
estates.

As applied to smallholders, land registration did tend to eliminate
one of the evils of the *musha'a* system which was common throughout
Syria. Under this system the land is held by the village and periodically reallocated (every two or three years) for individual family
cultivation. In practice, *musha'a* cultivation meant fragmentation of
the land in long narrow strips and its impoverishment for lack of any
incentive to improve it. In *musha'a* villages land registration usually
confirmed individual ownership and so gave some incentive to
improve cultivation, but at the same time it consolidated minute

fragmentation. In any case, land registration, scheduled to be completed in 1933, was less than half finished in 1942.

The French did little to extend irrigation. Although a French institute studied the irrigation potentials of the Orontes, Euphrates, and Yarmuk rivers, the only project undertaken was to raise the level of the ancient Homs dam to irrigate 15,000 hectares. Almost no modern agricultural machinery was introduced; in 1942 there were not more than thirty tractors in use in all Syria. The agricultural system remained archaic.

State Agricultural Banks, by French admission,[16] granted loans to big landlords who, instead of investing in the land, simply re-lent the money to the *fellahin* at much higher interest rates. Small and landless peasants had to turn to moneylenders, merchants, and landlords. All charged exorbitant rates, which in periods of bad harvests could reach 150 per cent.[17] Indebtedness grew, and many small peasants lost their lands. With the growing power of the big landlords, the evils of the tenancy system worsened. Tenancy contracts were verbal and terminable at will by the landlords. Hence there was no investment in the land, no improvement in agricultural methods, no tools other than those used in antiquity. Production was curtailed, peasants were reduced to serfdom, and landlords profited from exploiting not the land but the *fellahin*. At the same time, penetration of capitalist methods – cash rentals for fixed periods, use of chemical fertilizers, modern transport – undermined the position of traditional cultivators and increased unemployment in the countryside. By the mid-1930s, wages of agricultural labourers had fallen to an estimated one-third to one-half their already low level in 1929.[18]

The National Government paid no heed to the desperate plight of the rural majority. No law was enacted to better the social and economic conditions of the peasants; no attempt was made to regulate the relations between landlords and share tenants. Peasants paid a disproportionate share of taxes, but received no measurable benefit from government services. Health services did not reach into rural areas. Trachoma, tuberculosis, malaria, and undernourishment remained endemic in the villages, and few villages boasted a school. Of an Alawi village, Richard Pearse, who served as a special officer with the British army in Syria during the Second World War, wrote:[19]

... the wretched inhabitants were in a deplorable state of misery, dejection and abandon: they were past hope, resigned, their spirit utterly broken. One expects to find this sort of thing in the jungle, in China, but for a small country that had been under European mandate for 22 years the conditions every where were unbelievably bad ... Not a single week had passed since I had been in the country without my seeing an Arab suffering unnecessarily from fever, disease, torture, hunger or poverty.

Industry

In the latter half of the 1930s, industrial employment in Syrian cities was lower than it had been in Ottoman times. In 1913, traditional industry in Syria and Lebanon gave employment to 309,525 workers. In 1937, traditional and modern industry together employed only 203,927 workers.[20] Some artisan manufacturers were able to adapt to mechanical and capitalist production. Modern industry, however, was unable to make up for the decay of traditional industry: of the 203,927 workers employed in industry in 1937, only 33,149 were in modern industry and, of these, half were drivers or transport workers. The contraction of industrial activity is the more striking in view of natural population increase and the large influx of refugees from neighbouring lands.

The standard of living of the working classes, already extremely low by Western standards, had in fact fallen below that of 1913. In 1937, real wages were barely half what they had been before the First World War.[21] Working conditions remained medieval. The work week varied from 54 hours (in modern industry only) to 90 hours, with an 80-hour week prevailing in many trades. Factories seldom employed more than 10 to 15 workers; more than 40 per cent of workers were employed in home workshops. Despite prodding from the Permanent Mandates Commission, whose members sharply criticized the Mandatory Power's 'slack policy as regards labour conditions', France refused to establish a Labour Inspectorate or to enact legislation regulating working conditions aside from an admittedly unenforced decree concerning employment of children.

Beginning of the Labour Movement

Under these conditions, workers did not remain quiescent despite their fatalism and the traditionally paternalistic employer-worker relationship (often one of kinship as well). As early as 1926, a textile-worker, Subhi Khatib, established the first trade union. Printers and other workers then also started to organize. In the early 1930s, strike action spread, especially in Aleppo, where, on more than one occasion, thousands of workers struck against wage cuts and Japanese dumping which gravely threatened Syrian industry.

A 1935 decree provided for professional associations uniting all persons in the same trade and putting employers and employees on the same footing within the association. The decree also introduced many restrictions on workers. These restrictions, coupled with the disastrous consequences of the devaluation of the franc in 1936, goaded workers into their first class-battles for trade union rights. Defying the new law, they began to organize trade unions and, since employers were outnumbered in the professional associations and soon began to abandon them, meetings of the associations became–in the words of the French representative to the Permanent Mandates Commission[22]–'hardly different from those of trade unions in [Popular Front] France'.

In May 1936, trade unions held a conference at the tailoring workers' centre in Damascus and formulated their demands. They asked for a ban on child labour, wage increases to meet the rise in prices, an eight-hour day, laws guaranteeing trade union rights, and formation of arbitration commissions to settle work disputes. The authorities rejected these demands. A joint meeting of government, workers, and employers failed.

After many efforts, another general conference representing workers from all over the country convened in March 1938 and formed the Federation of Trade Unions of Syria. Its main demands were for 'pure' trade unions (that is, trade unions of workers alone), wage increases, a minimum wage, paid holidays, and the eight-hour day. Local businessmen vigorously opposing any such changes 'in the traditions and customs of the country' urged the government to act 'with great prudence'.[23] And prudent its actions certainly were. In 1939, the government recognized the right to form trade unions in forty-seven specified professions, but other labour demands were unheeded. The trade unions remained very small and weak.

Political Stirrings

Growing economic and political frustration combined with the impact of ideas emanating from rising fascist and socialist movements in Europe gave birth to new forms of political organization and action. Nazi-style para-military organizations marched and clashed in the streets of towns and cities. Doctrinal political parties, modelled for the most part on the totalitarian parties of Europe, also appeared. These parties elaborated their own nationalist ideologies and more or less consciously aimed at modernization within an indigenous national context. The new political activists, in the main Western-educated sons of the well-to-do and *petit bourgeois* elements, directed their appeals to the growing middle classes and, with few exceptions, had little concern for, or impact on, the peasant and worker majority.

One of the earliest parties of the new type was the Syrian National Party (SNP), later the Syrian Social Nationalist Party (SSNP),

founded in the early 1930s by a Lebanese Orthodox Christian, Antun
Sa'ada. Sa'ada insisted on the reality of a Syrian nation in a homeland defined as embracing all geographic Syria extended to the Suez
Canal in the south. He developed a comprehensive ideology of
Syrian nationalism coupled with a rigorous secularism which
demanded separation of Church and state and 'removal of sectarian
barriers between communities'. Yet his party found its support almost
exclusively among non-Muslim minorities. It was anti-Arab nationalist, anti-communist, and anti-feudal. In its secularism and drive to
create a modern nation-state, however, Sa'ada's party influenced
later nationalist doctrines.

The National Action League was founded in the early 1930s by
Zaki Al-Arsuzi, an Alawi from Alexandretta, and Sabri Al-Asali, a
young lawyer (and future premier), among others. The League, a
pan-Arabist movement, was influenced by Nazism and racialist
doctrines. Its aim was to 'resurrect' the glories of Arab civilization
and restore Arab racial purity. It was violently anti-communist.
Asali's decision to join the National Bloc in 1936 in order to secure a
seat in parliament weakened the movement. However, before it disappeared in 1940, the League energetically fought the French
cession of Alexandretta to Turkey.

The National Action League was later said[24] to have been the
precursor and Arsuzi, rather than Michel Aflak, the spiritual father
of the Arab Ba'th (Resurrection) Party which was founded in the
early 1940s. Aflak as a very young man was one of Arsuzi's disciples,
but his ideas later evolved. In 1932, Aflak and Salah Bitar, the future
founders of the Ba'th, returned to Syria from the Sorbonne, where
Aflak had been greatly attracted by the ideas of the French idealist
philosopher Henri Bergson. They then began to elaborate a pan-
Arab ideology. Creation of the Ba'th Party was very much influenced
by the loss of Alexandretta to Turkey.

Syrian students from Egypt, where the Muslim Brotherhood made
its appearance in 1928, began organizing Brotherhood branches
under various names in a number of Syrian cities during the 1930s.
These groups called each other *Shabab Muhammad* (Young Men of
Muhammad). They advocated reform in line with the laws and
spirit of Islam and agitated against imperialism. Some members
later became prominent in the governments and parliaments of
independent Syria.

At the other end of the political spectrum stood the Communist
Party of Syria and Lebanon, which was formally constituted in 1929.
Although ideologically committed to internationalism, the Syrian
Communist Party was greatly influenced by the rise of the Popular
Fronts in Europe and from the mid-1930s applied this concept to

Syria. The plurality of Syria's social formations made this concept a realistic one; to it the Communist Party was later to owe much of its success. It was active in the national struggle, although its strategy differed from that of most other nationalist forces during the period when the French Communist Party participated in the French government. French authorities in Syria held the communists responsible for organizing labour and articulating workers' demands. From 1936 to 1939, the party, led by Khalid Bagdash, a Kurd, was legal in Syria and Lebanon and became a political force of some consequence.

The 1936–39 Palestine Rebellion

Britain's policy in Palestine—its failure to fulfil the promise of self-government made to the Arabs, to heed Arab demands for limitation of immigration and for an end to the alienation of Arab land—coupled with the huge rise in Jewish immigration after 1933 and the gradual arming of the Jews in Palestine incited an ever more desperate Palestinian resentment in the mid-1930s. In the rebellion which began in April 1936 and was to last until autumn 1939, Palestinian Arabs fought for the establishment of a democratic government in Palestine (in accordance with the League of Nations Covenant and Article 2 of the Mandate), cessation of Jewish immigration, and prohibition of transfer of Arab lands to Jews.

This rebellion, the most important challenge to British colonial rule of the inter-war period, deeply preoccupied Syrians, for whom it was an organic part of their own liberation struggle. Syrian volunteers fought and worked in Palestine. A Central Committee of Struggle (*Al-Lajnat Al-Jihad Al-Markasiyya*), manned by Palestinians and Syrians, established headquarters in Damascus and Lebanon to collect money, equipment, and arms for the Palestinian guerrillas and to care for the wounded. A stream of messengers, volunteers, and supplies moved between Syria, Lebanon, Transjordan, and Palestine. These goings and comings, evading frontier and customs controls, symbolically restored for the people the unity of *Sham* (natural Syria). In an effort to halt this movement, the British hired Jewish labourers to build a barbed-wire fence along Palestine's northern and north-east frontiers.

The Palestine rebellion became the focus of a common Arab struggle for liberation and gave a new meaning to the ideas of Arab nationalism. But the fate of the rebellion strengthened the then dominant reactionary current of Arab nationalism. This was the British-sponsored Arab nationalist movement, led by the Hashemis, the family of the Sharif of Mecca, whose sons, Abdullah and Faisal, Britain had installed as rulers of Transjordan and Iraq respectively.

In the 1930s the Saudi and Egyptian dynasties also raised the Arab nationalist banner. Under these auspices, Arab nationalism subverted the anti-imperialist, anti-British struggle and served to cloak the rival dynastic ambitions of Arab rulers, which centred on Syria and Palestine.

Arab dynasts tried to halt the Palestine rebellion, which they feared as a threat to their own rule, and urged their patron, Britain, to make concessions to the Arabs. The concessions contained in the 1939 British White Paper bolstered their positions.[25] They were further strengthened by the fact that the rebellion's defeat removed the Palestine people from the scene as an organized political force. This greatly facilitated the later Zionist conquest of Palestine and also permitted conservative Arab rulers to take command of the Palestine struggle and so sacrifice it to their own rival ambitions. They also intervened more actively in Syria. Abdullah intrigued with Dr Shahbandar's opposition United Front. Ibn Saud, King of Saudi Arabia, recruited support in the National Bloc and established close relations with one of its leaders (and a future Syrian President), Shukri Quwatly. Intervention by rival Arab rulers in the name of pan-Arabism in the political life of Syria and Palestine led to growing confusion and divisiveness.

End of the National Government

The National Government had hardly been installed when the French began to retreat from the 1936 treaty. They exacted new compromises from the government, including a renewal of the concession of the *Banque de Syrie et du Liban* and a countrywide oil concession for the partially French-owned IPC. These government compromises roused popular opposition and split the National Bloc. In the Jebel Druze, Latakia, and the Jazira, French Special Service officers encouraged separatist movements and so sabotaged the government's attempt to establish its authority in these areas as provided in the treaty. France's step-by-step submission to Turkish demands for Alexandretta (its population was only 39 per cent Turkish) underlined the helplessness of the National Government and inflamed public opinion.

When, in 1939, the French parliament refused to ratify the 1936 treaty and ceded Alexandretta to Turkey, public opinion threatened to explode, and a nationwide revolt became a possibility. A prolonged government crisis, punctuated by violent riots, street demonstrations, French military intervention, and mass arrests, ended when the High Commissioner, Gabriel Puaux, suspended the constitution, dissolved parliament, appointed a 'non-political' Council of Directors to govern by decree under his direction, restored the Jebel Druze and Alawi provinces to autonomy, and took over administration of the Jazira.

TOWARDS INDEPENDENCE

The Second World War undermined French and British colonial positions and made imperative a more liberal Allied policy towards colonial and semi-colonial peoples. The fall of France and contradictions between French, British, and American interests proved decisive in Syria's accession to independence.

In the first years of the war, however, many nationalists in Syria and other Arab countries put their hopes in Axis victory. This was especially so in 1941 as Nazi armies advanced eastward through North Africa and the Balkans and Britain's ejection from the Arab East no longer appeared remote. In Iraq Germanophile generals and politicians, led by Rashid Ali Kaylani, were determined to keep their country neutral in the war.[26] Britain feared Nazi collusion with these opponents of its policies. Early in May this conflict erupted in fighting between British and Iraqi forces. Rashid Ali's 'revolt' inspired tremendous enthusiasm among young Syrian nationalists. A small group of Syrian volunteers, including a young lawyer from Hama, Akram Hourani, and a future Chief-of-Staff of the Syrian Army, Afif Bizri, hurried to Iraq to join the battle. Some of the future leaders of the Ba'th Party were active in the movement to aid the rebellion. With the aid of Abdullah's Arab Legion, the British by the end of May crushed the rebellion which, in the event, received very little German help. A week after this victory, Britain joined with the Free French to invade Syria on the pretext that its Vichy authorities had allowed German planes taking supplies to Rashid Ali to refuel there. Within a month, Anglo-Free French forces occupied all Syria.

On the eve of the invasion, General Catroux, then de Gaulle's representative in Cairo, in his name, promised Syria and Lebanon unconditional independence and the right to unite if they wished. The British guaranteed this promise. Soon after the invasion, de Gaulle announced that treaties guaranteeing French military, economic, and cultural hegemony would have to be signed before independence could be granted. In the meantime, the Mandate would remain in force and General Catroux with the title of *Délégué-Général* would assume the functions of the High Commissioner.

The British appointed a mission to Syria and Lebanon, and incorporated the two republics into the sterling bloc and into the economic unit governed by the Anglo-American Middle East Supply Centre. Although they had conceded to France the 'dominant privileged position' in the Levant, the British faced the problem of keeping order in the vast Arab areas under their occupation and so sought to conciliate nationalist sentiment (at least in areas of French interest). The British, therefore, prodded the French to grant Syria and Lebanon independence.

Under British pressure, the Free French in 1943 restored the suspended constitutions of Syria and Lebanon. General elections, held in Syria in July at British insistence, gave an overwhelming majority to the National Bloc, which formed a nationalist government and made Shukri Quwatly President of the Republic. A nationalist government took office in Lebanon in September. Saudi Arabia, Egypt, and Iraq recognized Syria and Lebanon. These states, including Syria, implicitly recognized the Syrian districts annexed to Lebanon by France in 1920 as part of Lebanon. Moreover, Syria's hopes of preserving its age-old economic unity with Lebanon were soon to fade. But it ignored Lebanon's bid to establish diplomatic relations since Syrians could not regard Lebanon as a foreign country.

The two governments now announced their intention to terminate the Mandates, and Lebanon revised its constitution to omit all reference to France. The French replied by arresting the Lebanese President, premier, and most ministers. A general strike and vast protest demonstrations in Lebanon, coupled with Anglo-American pressures, compelled France to yield. Syria then revised its constitution on similar lines, and France agreed to the Syrian and Lebanese demands for withdrawal of French controls. Syria and Lebanon began taking over the Common Interests and other administrations. During 1944 the USSR and United States recognized Syria and Lebanon. In February 1945 Syria declared war on Germany and so won an invitation to the United Nations founding conference. In March the pact of the Arab League was signed.

A Syrian move to end teaching of the French language in the primary schools provoked France to renew its demands for a treaty guaranteeing French-language teaching in the schools, and the independence of French schools, as well as French economic interests and military bases. The French announced they would not hand over the Special Forces and evacuate their own troops until such a treaty had been ratified. Coincident with these threats, French reinforcements arrived in Beirut. These developments provoked nationwide demonstrations, armed clashes between French army units and hastily assembled Syrian civilians and police, and a three-day artillery and air bombardment of Damascus.

British intervention compelled French troops to return to their barracks. Backed by the Arab League, Syria and Lebanon together declared their refusal to give any power a special position and their insistence on total French evacuation. The French then handed over the Special Forces, but French troops remained. Endless discussions about evacuation produced no action. Syria and Lebanon therefore complained to the Security Council where they won Soviet and American support. Under U.N. prompting, France completed its withdrawal from Syria on 17 April 1946 and from Lebanon in December. The two countries were at last independent.

[1] W. E. Hocking: *The Spirit of World Politics with Special Studies of the Near East*, New York, 1932, p. 288.

[2] League of Nations, PMC, 8th Session, 1926, p. 74.

[3] ibid., p. 207.

[4] Pierre La Mazière: *Partant pour la Syrie*, Paris, 1926, p. 201.

[5] See FRANCE Ministère des affaires étrangères: *Rapport à la Societé des Nations sur la situation de la Syrie et du Liban 1924–1938* (hereafter *Rapport*).

[6] PMC, 8th Session, pp. 84–6.

[7] ibid., p. 66.

[8] Norman Burns: *The Tariff of Syria*, Beirut, 1933, p. 63.

[9] *Rapport* 1930, p. 93.

[10] According to the ILO representative on the PMC, PMC, 8th Session, p. 27.

[11] ibid., p. 205.

[12] Statement made 22 August 1926, cited in Robert de Beauplan: *Ou va la Syrie?*, Paris, 1929, p. 133.

[13] Kurt Grunwald: 'The Government Finances of the Mandated Territories in the Near East', *Bulletin of the Palestine Economic Society*, Vol. VI, No. 1, May 1932, 33–4.

[14] R. Montagne: 'Le Traité Franco-Syrien', *Politique Étrangère*, Octobre 1936, p. 38.

[15] The French delegate to the PMC, PMC, 13th Session, p. 159.

[16] PMC, 35th Session, 1938, p. 96.

[17] S. B. Himadeh, ed., *Economic Organization of Syria*, Beirut, 1936, p. 325.

[18] ibid., pp. 98–9.

[19] Richard Pearse: *Three Years in the Levant*, London, 1949, pp. 149–50.

[20] *Rapport* 1937, pp. 218–19.

[21] ibid., p. 25; PMC, 35th Session, 1938, p. 105.

[22] *Rapport* 1937, p. 37.

[23] *Rapport* 1937, p. 28.

[24] This claim was made by some Alawi neo-Ba'thists after the neo-Ba'th's seizure of power in February 1966.

[25] John Marlowe: *Arab Nationalism and British Imperialism*, London, 1961, p. 39.

[26] In July 1940, Rashid Ali, then premier, had offered to join in the war beside Britain if Palestine was immediately established as an independent state. Churchill refused.

Chapter 5

Precarious Independence

INDEPENDENT SYRIA seemed to its citizens to be an island of liberty in an imperialist-controlled ocean, an island in constant danger of submergence under the weight of Great Power pressures and the intrigues of neighbouring client states. Throughout the area the United States challenged a war-weakened Britain for oil supremacy, markets, and political-military influence. A tremendous increase in Middle East oil production enhanced Syria's importance as an oil transit state. The Americans now wanted a trans-Syrian pipeline to carry their Saudi Arabian oil to the Mediterranean. The USSR for the first time had a diplomatic mission in Damascus, where it enjoyed local goodwill owing to the Soviet support given to Syrian independence. France fought a rearguard action to retain a hold in its former Mandates.

An extraordinary diffusion of socialist ideas throughout the Arab East in the latter years of the war and the stimulus given to Arab anti-imperialist movements by popular liberation struggles in Asia and Europe appeared to the Western Powers to jeopardize their stake in the area. So, although fiercely competing among themselves, they tried to work together against the double threat of Arab radicalization and Soviet penetration. The inter-Arab conflict for Arab leadership, which meant the conflict for control of Syria, also intensified now that Syria was independent. This conflict lent itself to exploitation by the Great Powers, especially by the United States, whose influence was decisive in Saudi Arabia and growing in Egypt, and by Britain, which still occupied militarily Iraq, Transjordan, Egypt, and Palestine.

CONFLICT OVER SYRIA

In line with its policy of encouraging dynastic Arab nationalism and in the hope of erecting a barrier to Soviet and American penetration, Britain during the war prodded its Arab protégés to organize some form of Arab unity. Wartime Arab unity talks soon developed into a contest between the Hashemi and the Saudi-Egyptian blocs for Arab leadership. Abdullah, the British-imposed Hashemi ruler of Transjordan, indefatigably promoted his 'Greater Syria' plan to bring Syria and eventually Palestine and Lebanon under his rule. Iraq's Nuri Said advocated a 'Fertile Crescent' unity uniting Greater Syria and Iraq. These Hashemi projects were doomed by King Farouk's ambitions to assume Arab leadership, Saudi hostility, and divided opinions in London over whether Baghdad or Cairo should lead. In the end, Egypt's proposal for an Arab League, an association of sovereign states in which only unanimous decisions would be binding, prevailed. Through the Arab League (founded in March 1945), which became an instrument of Egyptian policy, Egypt hoped to contain Hashemi designs on Syria.

Confronted by the Zionist drive for a Jewish state in Palestine, the Arab League undertook to maintain the 'Arab status' of Palestine. In September 1946, it proposed a plan for an independent unitary Palestine state, in which Palestinian citizenship would be open to all with ten years' residence in the country. Jewish citizens would have equal rights, and Jewish cultural and religious rights would be protected. But President Truman, soon after, publicly endorsed the Jewish Agency's August 1946 proposals for a Jewish state encompassing about 75 per cent of Palestine. This action in effect rejected the League's overture and, with other American pressures, led Britain to submit the Palestine question to the United Nations. The unwillingness of most Arab League members to jeopardize their relations with the United States and Britain, and the fact that Abdullah favoured partition (because he wanted to annex the portion of Palestine left to the Arabs), rendered ineffective any joint Arab action to halt the drive for partition.

The struggle over Palestine sharpened Abdullah's ambitions to take over Syria; Syria was time and again shaken by his Greater Syria intrigues. Most Syrians were hostile to Abdullah's mission. They considered Syria the mother country and tribal Transjordan a hopelessly backward client state of Britain. Abdullah bribed Syrian politicians, threatened the Syrian government, and intrigued with leaders of the minorities. These minorities—the Alawis, Druzes, Kurds, and nomadic tribes—were located on Syria's borders with Turkey, Transjordan, and Iraq. A network of alliances concluded among these states in 1946 and 1947 underlined for Syria, still indignant over the loss of Alexandretta, the threat of Hashemi agitation.

Abdullah's agents, however, fished in troubled waters. In Latakia province Alawi leaders, some in contact with Abdullah, threatened secession. The threat seemed the more real because a self-proclaimed god, Sulayman Murshid, formerly used by the French to encourage Alawi separatism, now again rallied Alawi peasants looking to a messianic leader for deliverance from their misery. In the Jebel

Druze, where the powerful pro-Hashemi Atrash clan resisted surrender of Druze autonomy, clan conflicts all but destroyed the government's administration. Some traditional mercenaries of the Hashemis among the nomadic tribes of the Jazira became restless.

The government's efforts to secure its authority in the potentially secessionist provinces were not wholly successful. Murshid's capture and execution left deep bitterness among Alawis who had genuine grievances. Government intervention in the clan conflicts in the Jebel Druze did not succeed in cutting down Atrash power; relations between Damascus and the Druzes remained tense. The government's closure of the Jazira to foreign travellers suggested continuing tensions although economic development in the region worked for assimilation.

A SOCIETY IN MOTION

The renewed struggle for Syria made its independence precarious, but other wartime developments created conditions which contributed to the country's consolidation. Wartime inflation, which raised prices eight times over the pre-war level without any comparable increase in wages and salaries, eroded the living standards of the majority, while war and black-market profiteering enriched speculators, traders, middlemen, and contractors. Unemployment, economic dislocation, and widespread social discontent followed on the dismissal at war's end of 30,000 workers employed with Allied occupation forces and cessation of Allied expenditures. Yet a strict ban on imports during the war, Allied demand for Syrian products, and Allied expenditures set Syria's economy in motion. Economic expansion was to continue throughout the first post-war decade, despite temporary setbacks.

Agricultural growth started during the war when a twelvefold rise in wheat prices enabled landlords and merchants to accumulate fortunes and peasants to pay off debts. Demand for food production led many people to migrate to new areas to cultivate state land. The Middle East Supply Centre made available great quantities of agricultural machinery. Speculators, merchant capitalists, and landlords acquired the tractors and combines and bought or leased from tribal shaikhs for a pittance huge tracts of land in the Jazira, uncultivated for centuries and hence very fertile. Capitalist farming and the introduction of mechanization rapidly brought these lands into production and made Syria the first country in the Middle East to employ agricultural mechanization on a significant scale.

The advance in agricultural production after the war outstripped the estimated annual increase in population. Lack of railroads between the new agricultural regions and the rest of the country compelled private entrepreneurs to develop the necessary motor transport. A sharp rise in cotton prices during the Korean War boom coupled with the introduction of American cotton seed sparked a threefold increase in cotton acreage. The need of cotton and other summer crops for irrigation stimulated private investment in pumps along the Euphrates and Khabur rivers. The irrigated area increased by almost a third by 1952. The great agricultural boom was in part a speculative operation whose long-term effects were far from uniformly beneficial. Ignorant use of machinery, the drive for quick profits, and persistence of the monocultural system of exploitation exhausted the soil. Yields fell despite the increase in the irrigated area. Cereals expanded into pasturelands at the expense of livestock. Livestock feeding in forested areas, in turn, contributed to erosion. But the immediate impact of the boom—greater production and higher export earnings, rising agricultural income and greater demand—stimulated the entire economy. And the development of eastern Syria, where the population increased by 32 to 49 per cent between 1949 and 1953 and where by the mid-1950s most of Syria's export crops were produced, contributed to the integration of the country.

Accumulated war profits and pent-up demand fuelled the expansion of modern industry. Since Syria was then bound in a customs union with Lebanon which followed a *laissez-faire* trade policy, a rising flow of foreign imports, especially textiles, soon stifled industrial growth. In 1950, under strong pressure from Syrian industrialists, the government withdrew Syria from the customs union, imposed protective tariffs and import embargoes. Modern industry then resumed its advance, though not without difficulties. Syrian industrialists had to provide their own power resources at heavy cost. The modest dimensions of domestic demand made the new industries dependent on markets in other Arab countries. These industries were restricted to already established fields—textiles, food and tobacco, building construction. By Western standards, Syria's new industry was very small: the production of one large European spinning-mill could easily exceed that of all Syria's spinning-mills combined. Moreover, industrialization in the sense of a growing diversification of production did not develop. But modern industrial enterprises were built almost entirely by indigenous capital and now took corporate form.

Artisan and small-scale manufacture, so long in decline, also grew, though at a slower rate than modern industry. Artisan manufacturers supplied local and traditional needs in a country where most people remained confined within traditional circuits of life and where many products still lacked a national market; this was due to the inadequacy and high cost of transport, and to the internal tolls still levied on goods moving from one locality to another. The ingenuity and adaptability of small manufacturers stimulated the renewed growth of such industry. In Aleppo, when fully automatic looms were introduced in modern factories after the war, artisans and workers displaced by modern machines bought the old semi-automatic looms, and, working on commission from merchants, soon accounted for a large part of rayon textile production. Small manufacturers also developed with neighbouring countries a thriving contraband trade, made possible by Syria's lack of natural frontiers and long borders. Artisan-manufactured textiles in great quantities found their way unofficially to Iraq, Jordan, and Turkey. Each year in October, tribes from Saudi Arabia and Jordan come to Syria to buy every imaginable product – thread, cloth, utensils, tools, saddles. Their purchases give employment to thousands of manual and artisan workers, and payment is made in the spring in the desert. The significant contribution to national income made by this unofficial trade does not appear in official statistics. In 1956, manual and small-scale manufacture, although slowly losing ground to modern industry, still accounted for 70 per cent of the national income accruing in the industrial sector.[1]

Economic Development and Arab Policy

Syria's economic development directly affected its Arab policy. The dependence of its national industry, both modern and artisan, on Arab markets, especially in Iraq and Saudi Arabia, gave these states a means of applying powerful pressures on the Damascus government. Such pressures became a feature of all the political crises of the turbulent post-war period. But Syria also had an effective eastern weapon. After the creation of Israel, all goods arriving in Mediterranean ports for the interior Arab countries (Jordan, Saudi Arabia, Iraq, Kuwait, and the Gulf principalities) had to pass through Syria. This commerce, plied by motor trucks, developed substantially with the rising wealth of the oil states and principalities. Syria's roads, often following ancient caravan trails, became (with the trans-Syrian oil pipelines) its Suez Canal. Transit trade brought Syria income from taxes and levies on both trucks and goods. (The motor transport business itself was shared by Syrian and Lebanese firms.) The fact that Syria had only to close its borders to bring transit trade to a halt was its trump card. Commercially, Syria could influence its neighbours and near neighbours; industrially it was the other way round.

Social Evolution

The expanding economy affected the evolution of social classes. Some feudalists were now adopting capitalist methods or investing their land rents in industry. Big merchants became agricultural and industrial entrepreneurs. Tribal chieftains, feudalists, and merchants often bought shares in industrial corporations. A number of middle-class merchants and businessmen established modern industries. A modern capitalist class gradually developed within the traditional ruling class of wealthy landowners and traders. Under protection of heavy tariffs, the rising capitalists made enormous profits on which they paid almost no taxes. They had few links to foreign capital for, until the rupture of the customs union with Lebanon, import and export trade was carried on in Beirut largely by Lebanese merchants who monopolized the agencies handling foreign goods. For the most part the new bourgeoisie, numbering no more than two or three thousand, shared the narrow traditional outlook of the old ruling class; yet its life style began to change. With the departure of the French, the urban rich moved away from the old quarters of the cities, where their homes, replete with oriental luxuries inside, were from the outside indistinguishable from the homes of the poor. In these quarters rich and poor dressed alike, and the wealthy resorted to subterfuges to hide their wealth (like baking their bread in market ovens rather than at home and going by different routes to the *suqs* so neighbours would not know how much they consumed). They now lived in villas, vacated by the French, in expensive new quarters of the city where there were no poor next door from whom wealth had to be concealed. The new bourgeoisie bought cars, hired chauffeurs, acquired (by Syrian standards at least) a taste for conspicuous consumption, and so helped create class tensions.

Post-war development accented the middle-class character of Syrian society. Small merchants and shopkeepers, artisans, and small manufacturers still carried on the bulk of commercial and industrial activity, while the educated urban middle and lower-middle class grew rapidly. The number of civil servants had by 1947 increased more than three times over the 1939 level; their salaries now consumed more than half the state budget. A great expansion of education after 1944, coupled with urbanization, modernization, and the extension of state services, offered many new employment opportunities to middle-class young people.

Not much of post-war prosperity trickled down to workers and poor peasants. Wartime inflation following on the drastic fall in real wages in the late 1930s had severely reduced the standards of Syrian workers. With the inflow of foreign imports that began in 1946 wage cuts became common, especially in the textile industry, and provoked many strikes. Working conditions in the new factories were often as primitive as in the old but without the latter's family ties and paternalism. Post-war growth of the construction industry offered some new employment, but a growing number of workers suffered unemployment and underemployment, and child labour was still widely used. In the countryside peasants owning neither land, houses, livestock, nor furniture lived much like serfs. They were subject to the *corvée*, compelled to render feudal services, pay feudal dues, make gifts to landlords, cultivate a part of the landlord's land for nothing, and send their wives to work in the landlord's kitchen. Schools and other government services sometimes could not be opened in the villages because of landlord opposition. By one means or another a handful of entrepreneurs gained control of the new agricultural lands developed during and after the war. Big landownership increased substantially between 1947 and 1952. So did the number of peasants evicted from the land.

NEW POLITICAL CURRENTS

A 'revolution of expectations' excited by the changes wrought by the war and by United Nations propaganda stimulated a growing social consciousness, especially among middle-class young people. Independence imposed a popular imperative to overcome backwardness. The movement of emancipation really began with the spread of general education and the arrival of the radio and later the transistor, which had an enormous impact. Slowly the common man began to understand that God was not the mover of all things, to lose his fatalism and submission to religious shaikhs, and to become aware of his own rights and dignity.

The labour movement counted only about 6,000 members just after the war. But the Communist Party, which after the expulsion of the Vichy French enjoyed freedom of action in Syria, became active in trade union organization and encouraged labour militancy. Now aware of the rights enjoyed by Western workers and of the gains won by the anti-fascist labour movements in Italy and France after the war, Syrian workers defined their own demands. In May 1946, the General Trade Union Federation convened its second conference, which prepared a draft labour law modelled on legislation recently adopted in Italy. This was submitted to parliament with a demand for its immediate adoption. Since the draft law did not apply to agricultural workers, the landlord-tribal majority in parliament did not greatly object. Frequent strikes and growing labour agitation had convinced the more enlightened among the bourgeoisie that labour legislation was necessary to calm social unrest as well as to bring labour under a measure of government control and give workers a positive role in industry. Parliament adopted the law with some amendments on 11 June 1946. Law 279 gave Syrian workers – on paper at least – most of the benefits Western workers had won in a century of trade union struggle. It encouraged trade union organization and established a government voice in labour matters. Most important, the new code recognized the right to strike. Although hedged with procedural conditions, this right – denied in most Arab countries – came to be accepted as normal in Syria. The Syrian labour code remained the most advanced and democratic in the Arab world until, in 1959, it was scrapped by the Nasser regime. In the first three years after its adoption, trade union membership more than tripled. The labour struggle was now directed to securing enforcement of the law, which tended to be observed only in the few large modern factories where workers were organized. Fighting against unemployment, workers also demanded a ban on employment of women, children, and workers recruited in the villages.

Akram Hourani and the Arab Socialist Party

Landless peasants in Hama Governate, a rich agricultural region then ruled and largely owned by four feudal families, found a champion in a young Hama politician, Akram Hourani, son of a self-educated tradesman. After participating in 1932 in an abortive attempt to assassinate the then President of Syria, Hourani joined Antun Sa'ada's Syrian National Party in 1936. A year later he quit the SNP and soon became active in the *Hizb Al-Shabab* (Youngmen Party) of Hama. This local movement represented a phenomenon then appearing also in other cities. This was a kind of generation reaction as nationalist youth began to question the methods of action and the authority of the National Bloc. In 1943, Hourani ran for parliament as the candidate of this local party and won on the Hama city vote.

In Hama landlord rule was more oppressive and the conditions of sharecroppers worse than in any other part of Syria. Hourani's reaction to the overwhelming influence of the landlords was originally a populist one but much more political than that of the *Hizb Al-Shabab*. Once in parliament, his activities became directly related to the real problem of his region, the plight of the destitute sharecroppers. And these very poor peasants created his political prestige.

In 1943, Hourani began a campaign to replace the two-stage indirect election procedure, which facilitated landlord control of the peasant vote, by direct elections, a fight won in time for the 1947 elections. One of his earliest initiatives—in 1944—was to call for drainage of the Ghab marshes near Hama to provide land for landless peasants, a proposal laughed out of court at the time. Early in his parliamentary career Hourani demanded that parliament authorize a study of the country's economic resources and development potential. His proposal led to an invitation to the British consulting firm Sir Alexander Gibb & Partners to make such a study. The survey, completed in 1946, became the blueprint for the country's economic development, although no use was made of it at the time.

Hourani developed as the only politician of consequence knowledgeable about, and concerned with, rural problems. For peasants he sought the political rights to which all citizens were entitled. He fought to outlaw the *corvée*, feudal services and dues. For he believed that liberation of the peasant and elimination of feudalism was a first and necessary condition to any kind of social progress in Syria. His base broadened to include not only the poorest peasants but also some of the better-off. In 1945, he organized his Arab Socialist Party which worked in the Hama region to help peasants and stimulate peasant militancy. Both peasant and city voters sent him back to parliament in 1947.

Towards the end of the 1940s the peasants' struggle began to spread from Hama to other regions; by 1950 it covered most of Syria. The Arab Socialist Party (ASP) was officially founded in January 1950, becoming a national party with branches in different parts of the country. Its base, however, remained Hama and north-central Syria. The ASP's programme called for elimination of feudalism, distribution of state land to the landless, suppression of confessionalism, emancipation of women, free elementary and secondary-school education, and introduction of technical and professional schools. The ASP promised to fight for a foreign policy independent of all foreign influence and a republican, constitutional, and parliamentary regime. It adopted the slogans of socialism and Arab unity. However, Hourani did not attempt to create a pan-Arab party. For he believed that pan-Arab unity could not be brought about until the Arab world had been liberated from imperialism and each Arab country had achieved internal unity. He became the leader of Syrian opposition to Hashemi unity schemes.

In addition to its following among the peasantry and socially conscious educated young people, the ASP won influence among young army officers. Hourani's contacts with the army began with his participation in Rashid Ali's 1941 rebellion in Iraq. After the war, Hourani opposed the National Bloc's contention that the Special Forces, the Syrian military units that had served the French during the Mandate, should be dissolved. He believed the Syrian officers were patriots. In 1944 and 1945 he took the lead in persuading these officers to give their allegiance to the Syrian government. With some of the officers of the Special Forces, including his childhood friends Adib and Salah Shishakli, he fought in the May 1945 rebellion against the French. His group succeeded in capturing and holding the Hama citadel.

Once the French had gone, the government opened the Homs Military Academy to all Syrians without class distinction and without fees, lowered requirements, and paid each student a monthly stipend. In regions which offered no economic opportunities, the gradual generalization of primary and secondary-school education that took place after independence could not but push young men into a military career. The liberal professions opened chances of promotion and economic privileges to the sons of the city bourgeoisie. In the countryside the progeny of modest and middle peasants had no means of social promotion other than the army. Thus the social base of the army became progressively more rural, and the army, a mirror of the particularisms of a Syria in which each region still had its own way of life. Hourani's concern for the peasantry, his social ideas and political courage, found him a ready audience among young cadets and officers. He also helped his young supporters to enter the Military Academy. Yet neither during this period nor later did the ASP admit officers to party membership. Officers paid no dues, had no organization, took no part in decision-making, and could be loyal partisans only. Party members entering the army had to give up their party membership.

The Ba'th Party

Akram Hourani's first contact with what was later to become the Arab Ba'th (Resurrection) Party took place in a prison cell in Deir Ezzor where he and other Syrian participants in the Rashid Ali rebellion were imprisoned following its collapse. From a fellow-prisoner, Jamal Atasi, he learned of the 'Supporters of Rashid Ali' movement in which the two Damascus school-teachers Michel Aflak, an Orthodox Christian, and Salah Bitar, a Sunni Muslim, were active. Hourani became friendly with them after he entered parliament in 1943. In 1947 they proposed merging the Ba'th and the ASP and offered him the presidency of the united party. Hourani at that time refused.

The Ba'th Party, originally organized in Syria in 1943, was officially founded in 1947 by Aflak, Bitar, and Jallal Sayyid, an intellectual from a landowning family of Deir Ezzor. A pan-Arab party, which considers Arab states to be 'regions' of the Arab nation, the Ba'th tried to establish branches in each. Aflak was the chief author of its ideology.

The basic idea in Ba'th doctrine is that the Arab nation is a permanent entity in history. The Arab nation is considered, philosophically speaking, not as a social and economic historic formation, but as a transcendent fact inspiring different forms, one of its highest contributions taking the form of Islam. It was not Islam that modelled the peoples of Arabia, the Fertile Crescent, and North Africa, equipping them with Islamic values, especially the Arabic language and Arabic culture, but the Arab nation that created Islam. This conception of the Arab nation implicitly advantages the Arab contribution to history. On the other hand, Arab decadence can be overcome through a purifying and spiritual action, not religious but moral. Here the influence on the party founders of the French idealist and puritan philosopher, Bergson, is apparent.

Arabism is defined as the feeling and consciousness of being Arab. The Arab peoples are conceived as a multitude of individuals. This conception is translated at the ideological level and in political slogans by the negation or absence of class conflict. The allusions made by Aflak to social justice are only one component in a general process of the internal liberation of the Arab individual. This internal liberation is considered to be the real way to restore to the Arabs their place in world politics and civilization.

The Arab nation encompasses the entire area between the Taurus and the Sahara and the Atlantic and the Arab (Persian) Gulf. This nation was artificially divided by the imperialist powers. To its political reunification the Ba'th subordinated all other goals. The party adopted the slogan 'Arab socialism' (partly as a means to counter the appeal of communism), but the application of Arab socialism was to await the achievement of Arab unity. Arab unity was also the precondition for the solution of all Arab problems. This assumption derived from the Ba'th's belief that a global Arab frame was essential for the nationalist struggle.

The overriding priority given to Arab unity led the Ba'th in its early years to support Hashemi projects for uniting Syria with Jordan or Iraq, then British client states, under the Hashemi crown. The Ba'th then marched under the slogan: 'One Flag, One Army, One King, One Arab World!' (It was therefore sometimes accused, especially by the French, of having British connections.) Akram Hourani and others condemned this way of thinking; in time the Ba'th abandoned it. But certain elements within the party proved incapable of assimilating this experience and could never refuse a unity project, however anti-democratic or however suspect its origin.

Jallal Sayyid left the party in the mid-1950s when this trend had been effectively isolated for the time being as a result of the Ba'th's 1953 merger with the ASP.

The Ba'th proposed to make the Arab nation a modern and secular state. Women were to have all rights of citizenship. Islam was secularized, transformed into a part of the Arab cultural heritage, and given a special place in Arab nationalism by the fact of its having been 'created out of the heart of Arabism'. All religious, communal, tribal, racial, and regional factions were to be melted 'in the crucible of a single nation'. But the Ba'th's approach to other ethnic nationalisms, notably the Kurdish, proved in practice ambiguous, if not chauvinistic. When the Ba'th and the ASP finally did merge, the Ba'th refused to admit into the new party Kurdish peasants who had been ASP members. This ambiguity was apparent also in Aflak's rejection of 'racial nationalism' and his simultaneous belief that the corruption of Arab racial purity was responsible for the national and moral decline of the Arabs.

Although the Ba'th promised a democratic state of a parliamentary constitutional type, its doctrine was frankly élitist. As in other folk nationalisms, individual rights and freedoms were subordinated to the 'higher interest' of the Arab nation, with the party cast in the role of the self-appointed 'vanguard' personifying 'the will of the Arab nation'.

The Ba'th gave priority to Arab unity but no consideration to how this unity was to be achieved. The problems created by the multiple diversities of the Arab world, the different systems of government prevailing in the Arab states, the widely varying levels of civilization achieved by their peoples, their often limited particularist horizons were all ignored. The overriding priority given to a unity so removed from the concrete context made the pursuit of unity rather like the pursuit of a myth. This was apparent despite the undeniable sense of a common identity uniting the Arabs across their many diversities and the wide appeal the unity goal came to have among literate Syrians permanently discontented over the political artificiality of their truncated state.

The Ba'th's order of priorities also introduced an external and potentially divisive pole of attraction. In 1955, Aflak recalled[2] that the national leaders of the inter-war and war periods

> never used nationalist expressions but patriotic ones, intending that all Muslims and Christians, Arabs and non-Arab minorities, should gather under patriotism to face the foreign occupant. This continued until ten years ago when our movement in the last resort obliged them to adopt the slogans of Arabism.

In 1943, at a conference in Damascus arranged between the Ba'th and various Muslim organizations, Aflak first applied the term *shu'ubiyyah* to the communists. *Shu'ubiyyah*, meaning 'belonging to the peoples', was the name taken in the early Islamic period by a movement which championed the equality of non-Arabs and Arabs within the empire. The term – by which the Ba'th means anti-Arab – became an effective weapon against not only communists but also 'regional' (Egyptian, Syrian, Iraqi, etc.) patriotism and all 'regionalists', that is all who rejected the Ba'th order of priorities. The association of Ba'th leaders with Hourani, and the eventual merger of their party with his, modified some of these approaches. The Ba'th then worked at times with the communists and other forces that did not subscribe to the pan-Arab mystique. Yet the quest for all-embracing and immediate Arab unity tended paradoxically but inevitably to generate dissension within each Arab state (and later also at times among them) and so to weaken the anti-imperialist front.

The Ba'th's claim to personify the will of the Arab nation, moreover, conflicted with the similar pretensions of other pan-Arab movements, for example, the Arab Nationalist Youth founded by George Habash at the American University of Beirut after the Palestine war. Although there was a measure of co-operation between the two movements in the early days, they always distrusted each other and later – after the Arab Nationalist Youth had transformed itself into the Arab National Movement loyal to President Nasser – became bitter enemies.

In April 1947 the Ba'th held its first pan-Arab conference and drew up its constitution. The founding elements of the party came either from Sunni and Orthodox Christian *petit bourgeois* social strata of the cities (mainly Damascus) or from families of countryside notables, especially Druzes (Atrash family) and Alawis of the Latakia plain. The party's social base remained the *petit bourgeoisie* of the cities and in the countryside middle landlords with local social prestige. However, the Ba'th did not develop importantly in the cities. Most of the Sunni *petit bourgeoisie*, even in Damascus, was influenced by the Muslim Brotherhood and later also by President Nasser. The Ba'th, however, won a following among students and military cadets – future intellectuals and army officers.

A Benighted Old Guard

The veteran nationalists who inherited rule from the French seized on the social privileges and status of the departed masters as well. The National Bloc used its monopoly of political power to feather its own nest and ensure its continuance at the helm. Flagrant venality came to prevail in public life. President Shukri Quwatly became its symbol: 'His rule was comparable to the rule of the Turkish *vali* who made no accounting to any one for his actions'.[3] The government, indifferent to the economic and social problems facing the people, embarked on a campaign of intimidation, purges, and arrests in an attempt to silence its critics and destroy all political opposition. Exacting emergency powers from parliament, it tried to muzzle the press and control political parties. As the 1947 parliamentary elections approached, public disgust and frustration gave impetus to the demand for direct elections and an end to confessional representation. The Ba'th, the communists, and others joined with the Houranists in a popular campaign which compelled the government to change the law to provide one-stage direct elections. The effort to eliminate confessional representation, a highly sensitive issue, failed.

The National Bloc during this period began to fragment. On the eve of the elections, its successor, the National Party, was founded by Quwatly, Sabry Al-Asali, and others, mainly from Damascus. An anti-Quwatly faction in Aleppo and Homs, reflecting partly a generation reaction, contested the elections and later became the People's Party. Its leaders were Nazim Al-Qudsi, Rushdi Kikhiya, 'owner of 100,000 olive trees', and the politically influential Atasi family, great landowners of Homs. The People's Party, mirroring northern Syria's commercial orientation toward Iraq, favoured a Syria-Iraq association which would abolish customs and frontier barriers but leave Syria its republican institutions. The National Party in the main represented Damascus sectional interests and leaned towards the Saudi-Egyptian bloc. But it had a wing in Aleppo based on the Christian population and also a pro-Iraq tendency, with which Sabry Al-Asali was for a time associated. There was little difference between the two parties. Professing to be anti-feudalist, both were slightly more oriented towards the rising commercial and industrial bourgeoisie than towards feudalists, but both relied on a big landlord clientele to deliver the rural vote. Both parties were perpetually torn by personal and clan feuds. In the 1947 elections, the anti-Quwatly Aleppo-based faction scored a striking victory by winning 20 seats to the National Party's 24.

Reflecting the still primitive political development of the country, the largest number of candidates and the largest group elected were 'independents'. They were for the most part heads of influential families and of ethnic and religious communities, and represented, as did the People's and National parties, the privileged élite. Independents in general pursued parochial interests. An outstanding exception was a widely travelled and Western-educated Damascene businessman, Khalid Al-Azm, who acquired a national and inter-national perspective. Parliament's adoption of progressive labour legislation in 1946 owed much to his efforts. (He was then Minister of Economy.)

The Muslim Brotherhood, becoming a political force in this period, elected a sympathizer, Dr Mar'uf Dawalibi, in Aleppo and other candidates in Damascus. Aside from the re-election of Akram Hourani, the younger and more radical elements failed. The Syrian Communist Party ran three candidates and one, its leader, Khalid Bagdash, narrowly missed election. A candidate put forward by Aleppo trade unions was defeated. So was the Ba'th's candidate, Michel Aflak.

The July 1947 election proved little beyond the continuing clan character of Syrian politics. The new government, a coalition of the National Party and a wing of the Aleppo faction, differed little, if at all, from the old. Although the Palestine question was now nearing a climax, the government's major preoccupation was to ram through parliament, probably by fraud, an amendment to the constitution to permit re-election of President Quwatly to a second term.

THE PALESTINE DEFEAT

On 27 November 1947 the U.N. General Assembly, subjected to extraordinary American pressures, adopted the Palestine Partition Resolution. The resolution gave the Jewish state more than half of Palestine, although Jews then owned only 7 per cent of the land. It provided for creation of a Jewish state whose population would include 509,780 Arabs and 499,020 Jews, and of an Arab state with a population of 725,000 Arabs and 10,000 Jews.[4] The U.N. decision provoked a violent storm of protest throughout Syria and other Arab countries. The great popular outcry compelled the Arab League to encourage recruitment of volunteers to assist the Palestine Arabs. In January 1948, Syrian volunteers—Akram Hourani and Adib Shishakli —were among the first—began to enter Palestine where they became part of a small liberation army of Arabs and Palestinians. The Zionists, on the other hand, did not want a 'Jewish State' that was half-Arab. On 1 April, a Zionist military operation began to expel Palestinian Arabs from areas assigned the Jewish state; some areas allotted the Arab state were also seized and cleared. On 9 April, 250 Arab villagers of Deir Yassin were massacred, and terrorized Pales-tinians began to flee. Many in pitiable condition arrived in Syria where their number ultimately reached 85,000. Popular demands for Arab governments to act could no longer be ignored. On 16 April the Arab League decided to send Arab armies into Palestine as soon as the Mandate ended, to try to halt the ousting of Palestinians and prevent the loss of all Palestine.[5] One Syrian brigade of 1,876 men fought in Palestine.[6] Although inexperienced, badly equipped, and short of ammunition, it made a better showing than other Arab expeditionary forces, which altogether totalled less than 15,000 men.[7] The Syrian brigade, the only Arab contingent not defeated in the 1948 war, captured and held three small areas in Palestine stretching from Lake Huleh to Lake Tiberias.

With this exception, Arab armies did not in general occupy the areas of Palestine assigned the Jewish state. Transjordan's Arab Legion was under orders not to enter the Jewish state area. Of the Egyptian columns that entered Palestine, one advanced along the coast through the Arab state area towards Tel Aviv; the other moved through Beersheba (Arab state area) to the southern suburbs of Jerusalem (international zone). Iraqi units operated in the Arab state area west of Jerusalem and small Lebanese contingents in Galilee (Arab state area). (Of thirteen military operations carried out by Zionist military forces prior to 15 May 1948, eight were outside the area assigned the Jewish state.[8]) Initial Arab 'successes' consisted mainly in the occupation of areas assigned the Arab state. During a month-long U.N.-enforced truce, 11 June to 8 July, both sides defied a ban on introduction of new military equipment and manpower, but Israel did so far more successfully than the Arabs. An arms airlift from Czechoslovakia and the arrival of a growing number of volunteers from Western countries gave Israeli forces decisive superiority. The many Palestinian refugees fleeing before the Israelis into areas occupied by Arab armies further undermined Arab military efforts. Conflicts between Abdullah and Egypt–over Abdullah's determination to annex the area assigned the Arab state–contributed to the defeat of Arab armies which, in any case, had no common military strategy. In the ten-day period of fighting between the first truce and the second, Israeli forces seized sizeable chunks of Arab territory on almost all fronts. After the second truce went into effect on 25 July, Israeli violations of the truce and of a number of Security Council resolutions gave it its largest territorial gains.

Israel's truce violations, the anti-Arab stand of both the Western Powers and the Soviet bloc in the United Nations, and the sorry performance of Arab armies humiliated and outraged the Arab peoples. In Syria, government leaders were implicated in the theft of funds collected for Palestine. Revelation of this swindle enhanced public anger and anguish. Popular demands for resumption of the war became insistent. On 29 November 1948, anniversary of the Partition Resolution, a student strike touched off a furious national uprising. This spontaneous insurrection approaching revolutionary proportions compelled the government to resign. Two weeks passed before the army under its chief-of-staff, Colonel Husni Za'im, could restore order. Khalid Al-Azm then formed a new government. His efforts to stabilize the currency by a financial settlement with France and an agreement with Aramco for resumption of work on its trans-Syrian pipeline (halted by Syria because of American support for Zionism) met overwhelming popular and parliamentary opposition.

ERA OF MILITARY COUPS

Seething popular discontent, quarrels between generals and politicians over responsibility for the Palestine disaster, charges and counter-charges of corruption created a state of near anarchy. On 29 March 1949, Colonel Za'im seized power, ousted and exiled President Quwatly, dissolved parliament, and established military rule. This first overturn in the Arab world after the Palestine war was engineered by the American embassy in Damascus. Revelations of the directing United States role made in 1969 by Miles Copeland, a member of the 1949 embassy team, confirmed long-held Syrian suspicions.[9]

To Washington, striving to develop a policy to block communism and challenge British supremacy in the Arab East, Arab armies (originally organized as internal police forces) appeared the most likely stabilizing influence in an area threatened by mass upheavals; they also seemed the most viable alternative to the old ruling oligarchy whose days were clearly numbered. John Marlowe has pointed out[10] that the armies in Syria, Egypt, and Iraq were 'reformist rather than revolutionary' and that when they took power they did so 'not to create a revolution but to avert one'. This approach suited the needs of American policy, which was also directed to shoring up the existing order; this required, on the one hand, the elimination of the most flagrant evils and compromised leaders and, on the other, the imposition of more effective controls over the people to halt the inroads of 'subversion'.

The first fruit of the new American policy was the Za'im *coup*. After a brief flirtation with Iraq, Za'im cemented close relations with Egypt and Saudi Arabia. But he was shortly overthrown by Colonel Sami Hinnawi in an Iraq-engineered *coup* in August, presumably supported by Britain. Hinnawi attempted to pull Syria into the Hashemi camp. In December, when union with Iraq seemed imminent, Hinnawi was ousted by Colonel Adib Shishakli who returned Syria to the Saudi-Egyptian orbit. And a measure of American influence was restored.

The three leaders of the 1949 *coups* were holdovers from the French

Special Forces. The army at the time numbered less than ten thousand men, but each of the putschists increased its effectives. To complement their influence among rival officers, Iraq, Jordan, and Saudi Arabia also backed rival political clans; dinars and rials flowed into the pockets of certain politicians and publishers to corrupt political life.

Za'im's Regime

The 1949 *coups* in Syria gave expression to profound frustrations and social tensions which had been sharpened by the Palestine war and its exposure of the bankruptcy of the existing order. Za'im secured the participation in his *coup* of nationalist officers–including Colonel Adib Shishakli and other associates of Akram Hourani–by promising social reforms and 'a fight to the end' against Zionism. Once in power, Za'im, who had promised the Americans 'to do something constructive about Israel',[11] abandoned Syria's demand for a cease-fire line down the middle of Tiberias and the Jordan[12] and agreed to give up the small areas held in Palestine. Under the Armistice Agreement[13] (concluded in July), these areas with adjacent Israeli-occupied land became a demilitarized zone in which neither side was to exercise sovereignty.

Za'im's *coup* was popularly acclaimed as a 'blessed revolt' against the old order. To the Ba'th it heralded the dawn of a 'new age'. Ba'th leader Michel Aflak sought to become Za'im's mentor. Za'im's commitment to reform–'I come to liberate the peasants'–won him Hourani's support. Hourani became legal adviser to the Defence Ministry. And Za'im did carry out a number of reforms which offended the traditionalists. He extended suffrage to literate women and in his proposed constitution abolished confessional representation. A modern civil code, modelled on Egyptian legislation, restricted the authority of the *Shari'a* (Muslim religious law) and the power of the religious hierarchy. Za'im removed an obstacle to land reform in abolishing family *Waqfs* (land endowed to future pious purposes when the founders' descendants have died out), and he proposed to limit large landholdings and distribute state land to the landless. He even set up a committee to plan this distribution. After his 'election' as President on 25 June, however, he named a great landowner of Hama, Muhsin Barazi, to head the government. This choice emptied his land reform programme of content and alienated the Houranists and other social reformers.

Za'im's pro-American and pro-Turkish policies offended the people. Syrians were indignant over the American role in the Palestine disaster and still resentful over Turkey's annexation of

Alexandretta. Za'im ratified the agreement to allow construction of
Aramco's pipeline, endorsed the United States project for a Middle
East military pact, and proclaimed his solidarity with Turkey. Moreover, his stifling of political activity had a much more immediate
impact than his reforms. Not even a reduction in the price of wheat
and bread, made possible by a good harvest, could eradicate growing
popular irritation. Fiercely anti-communist at home as well as
abroad, Za'im had immediately outlawed the Communist Party.
Soon he dissolved other political parties, restricted political activity,
and suppressed newspapers. A rigged referendum approved direct
election of the President, and Za'im was 'elected' to this office. His
partiality toward Kurdish and Circassian units in the army and
growing delusions of grandeur ruffled army and popular sensibilities.
Za'im granted SSNP leader Antun Sa'ada political asylum following
an abortive SSNP *coup* in the Lebanon, only to hand him over soon
after to Lebanese authorities who promptly executed him. Although
the SSNP had little following in Syria, this action did not endear
Za'im to the people. On 14 August, a group of officers, including
some of the same Druze and SSNP officers who had brought him to
power, overthrew Za'im and killed him.

Hinnawi's Interregnum

Colonel Sami Hinnawi, leader of the August *coup*, asked the
venerable Hashim Al-Atasi to form a government, withdrew the army
from politics, and legalized all political parties except the communist
and the rightist Socialist Co-operative Party. Akram Hourani became
Minister of Agriculture and Michel Aflak Minister of Education in a
Cabinet dominated by the People's Party. Elections for a Constituent
Assembly to draft a new constitution were held on 15 November with
eighteen-year-olds and women voting for the first time; they gave the
People's Party dominance in the assembly. Although the National
Party boycotted the elections, 13 Nationalists were elected. The
SSNP, the Ba'th, and the Muslim Brotherhood each won one seat.
Trade union candidates in Aleppo, Damascus, and Homs were
defeated. Aflak, a defeated candidate, left the government, charging
fraud. The assembly elected Atasi temporary President of the
Republic (and later President) and began to draft a constitution.

Serving in his first ministerial post, Hourani dug out of the files,
where it had long been gathering dust, the Alexander Gibb study of
Syria's development potential. He had it translated into Arabic and
began to campaign for action on certain projects, including the
drainage of the Ghab and construction of a dam on the Euphrates.

The question of unity with Iraq, however, overshadowed all

others. In the assembly the unity question focused on a conflict over the wording of the oath to be taken by the President and the deputies. Opponents of unity with Iraq, led by Hourani and Mustafa Siba'i of the Muslim Brotherhood, insisted that the oath should pledge jurors to work not only for Arab unity but also for maintaining the republican regime. The assembly's rejection of this amendment appeared to be a vote for unity with Iraq. Strong opposition to Syria-Iraq unity existed in the army, some of whose higher officers had planned a *coup* to prevent it but hesitated to act. Two junior officers—Amine Abu Assad and Husain Hiddi—now gave Hourani a memorandum signed by many of their colleagues. This memorandum declared their intention to make a *coup* to abolish the assembly, which they claimed was about to vote for unity with Iraq, and asked Hourani to become President. Hourani replied that unity, if made, would be made by Hinnawi, not the assembly, and that he would not tolerate abolition of parliamentary life; he declined to become President under such circumstances.[14] On 19 December, Hourani's longtime friend, Colonel Adib Shishakli, overthrew General Hinnawi. In his first communiqué Shishakli defined his movement as a 'correction' inside the army, made necessary by Hinnawi's decision to unite with Iraq, and announced that parliamentary life would continue.

Indirect Army Rule

During the following two years the army remained in the background, interfering relatively little in politics. Shishakli exercised control by playing on the contradictions within the bourgeoisie and its political parties. Sharpening social struggles, especially in the countryside, and feverish popular resistance to Western pressures to draw Syria into military pacts gave political life vitality and scope. Dissensions raged between the government and the assembly, the politicians and the officers, and among the politicians themselves, yet important steps were taken along the road to modernization.

The task of drafting the constitution occasioned many bitter quarrels. The question of secularism provoked a prolonged and passionate controversy. The assembly finally rejected the clause in the original draft making Islam the state religion to declare Islamic law the main source of legislation and, as in the 1930 Constitution, required the President of the Republic to be a Muslim. The constitution declared Syria to be part of the Arab nation and looked forward to the day when 'our Arab nation should be united in one state'. Most significantly, it reflected social aspirations at stake in current social strife. A 28-article bill of rights guaranteed not only the usual freedoms of speech, press, assembly, and association, but also economic and social rights–to a job, free education, and social insurance.

Property was classified as both public and private and the state given the responsibility of ensuring that it fulfilled its 'social function'. State ownership was established over all sub-soil wealth and all other sources of natural wealth. The constitution called for special legislation to ensure the most productive use of the land, reversion of neglected land to the state, distribution of state land to the landless as well as creation of co-operatives and model farms, limitation of landholdings, and progressive settlement of the beduin. Hourani's demand that the state's right to limit landholding be retroactive failed by only two votes. The peasants' movement won a notable victory in a clause requiring enactment of a law on agricultural relations. Compulsory labour was prohibited. Legislation was to guarantee workers' rights. The constitution provided for a permanent Economic Council to propose 'economic plans and programmes to develop the potentialities of the country'.

All these provisions amounted to a statement of principles whose practical application was left to subsequent legislation. In many cases the necessary laws did not materialize, but social laws had been laid down. Many later national movements also found in Syria's 1950 Constitution the social content of their programmes. The constitution's commitment to these principles, however delayed their fulfilment might be, revealed a new climate of opinion created by radical political currents and continuing social strife.

The assembly–transformed over much opposition into a parliament following adoption of the constitution on 5 September 1950–began to establish some of the conditions essential for Syria's independent economic development. External trade was liberated from foreign control by ending the customs union with Lebanon, by requiring representatives of foreign agencies and companies operating in Syria to be of Syrian nationality, and by other measures. Failure of foreign-owned public utilities to keep pace with growing power needs induced parliament to nationalize electricity, and these companies were taken over one by one. Foreign-owned railroads, water services, the French-owned tobacco monopoly, and all other foreign-owned enterprises were also nationalized. With the setting-up of the Ghab Administration, the work of draining and reclaiming the Ghab marshes, the most important development project of the first two post-war decades, was at last begun. Construction started on the port of Latakia with the help of a 6-million-dollar Saudi loan. Money was also appropriated for irrigation works on the Khabur and Euphrates rivers. Average annual government expenditures on development rose sharply.

In 1950 and 1951 the peasants' movement reached its height. Peasant unrest erupted in all parts of the country. Peasants refused to render feudal services and dues and effectively abolished these practices in most areas. In the Ghab, when reclamation work started, peasants fought landlords who arrived to lay claim to the land. Landlords expelled peasants from their villages, killed their livestock, and harassed them in every possible way. But other villages gave ousted peasants refuge; peasants remained united and stood together against the landlords. In mid-September 1951, thousands of delegates from all over Syria thronged to a peasants' congress in Aleppo convened by Hourani's ASP. Here they raised the slogan 'land to the peasants', demanded real agrarian reform and a law to regulate relations between landlords and peasants. The congress gave the peasant struggle a political character. The first grass-roots congress of its kind ever held in the Arab world, it provoked landlord fears and worried both the Saudis and the Americans, who backed Shishakli because of his anti-Hashemi policy.

Even more disturbing, especially to the Americans, was the accelerating momentum of the anti-Western upsurge in Syria. Anglo-American pressures on the Arabs to make peace with Israel infuriated all classes. In February 1950, Premier Khalid Al-Azm announced Syria's decision to do without American aid. Later he rejected Point IV Aid. The Muslim Brotherhood, reorganized in November 1949 as the Islamic Socialist Front, became the first to speak out boldly for an Arab *rapprochement* with the USSR to counter Anglo-American pressures. Hourani, then Minister of Defence, seconded this call. Economy Minister Mar'uf Dawalibi warned in April 1950 that the Arabs would rather 'become a Soviet republic' than submit. He soon opened trade talks with the USSR because 'we have need of markets for our products which we are ready to exchange for machinery and the necessary raw materials for our industry'. These initiatives were widely acclaimed by a public scornful of Western aid, tied as it was to settlement of the Palestine refugees in Arab countries despite U.N. resolutions calling for their return to Palestine.

The ASP and the Ba'th (which under Hourani's pressure had begun to retreat from its advocacy of Hashemi unity projects) took the lead in a campaign demanding Syria's neutrality in the Cold War. Even pro-Western politicians insisted on satisfaction on the Palestine question as a condition for alignment with the West. The outbreak of the Korean War and Egypt's refusal in the Security Council to support the U.S./U.N. intervention (because the U.N. had failed to act against aggression in Palestine) strengthened popular pressures for neutralism. Syrian newspapers rejoiced in U.S. defeats. At the U.N., growing Syrian and Egyptian abstention on

Cold War resolutions contributed to the formation of the Afro-Asian bloc. The remarkable success of the communist-inspired Partisans of Peace testified to broad popular support for rejection of any alignment with the West. The Peace Partisans claimed some 60,000 signatures to their anti-war, and anti-atom bomb, petitions in 1950 and 185,000 in 1951. Signers included intellectuals, cultural personalities, politicians, the Speaker of Parliament, nearly all deputies, several ministers and former ministers, and a number of religious leaders. A succession of Anglo-American military and political personalities who made the grand tour of the Middle East in these years to solicit support for a Middle East defence pact provoked in Syria great protest demonstrations which gave radical parties experience in organization.

Shishakli's Dictatorship

Throughout this period Shishakli engaged in a running fight with the People's Party, which dominated parliament and still manoeuvred to bring about unity with Iraq. The dynamism of Hourani's Arab Socialist Party and its success in rallying the peasantry alarmed the People's Party and other conservative forces. Some of these elements blamed Shishakli for not using the gendarmerie more effectively against the peasants. The People's Party challenged army authority by insisting that the Interior Ministry, and not the army, should control the gendarmerie and that a civilian should be Minister of Defence. In autumn 1951, American pressures aimed at bringing Syria into a Middle East pact created further dissensions within the government and contributed to a government crisis. When People's Party leader Mar'uf Dawalibi, an anti-militarist, attempted to form a new government, he ignored demands made by Shishakli. Shishakli feared his indirect control was threatened. On 19 November, he made his second *coup*.

He dissolved parliament, ousted President Atasi and the politicians, conferred all legislative and executive power on his spokesman, Colonel Fawzi Selu, and soon outlawed the political parties (including the Ba'th and the ASP which had supported him). He also suppressed newspapers, prohibited students, teachers, workers, and civil servants from engaging in political activity, abolished the Supreme Court, and tightened police controls.

The developing industrial bourgeoisie constituted the social base of Shishakli's regime and often determined its orientations. The Khumasiyya Company (Company of Five), formed in 1949 by a merger of the five largest industrial concerns, had an important voice in the regime's higher councils. Ma'mun Kuzbari, the company's chief attorney and the son-in-law of one of its directors, became one of Shishakli's protégés and the Speaker of his 1953 parliament. The fact that the rising Damascus industrialists were more interested in the Saudi than in the Iraqi market reinforced Shishakli's adherence to the Saudi-Egyptian camp. Industrialist influence was responsible for Shishakli's invitation to the German 'financial wizard' Hjalmar Schacht to examine the Syrian economy and for financial and monetary reforms that followed. A Central Bank was established. Syria was put on the road to complete independence in monetary matters. Shishakli enacted many measures to assist national industry to overcome the difficulties it was then experiencing. Industry was granted tax and customs exemptions and government loans. Internal tolls were abolished. The Chambers of Commerce and Industry were reorganized. The Damascus Fair was instituted. The competence of the government's economic and financial administration increased with the employment of young technicians and professional men.

For Shishakli the land question was secondary, but the dimensions taken by the ASP-led peasants' movement provoked him to act. In an attempt to blunt this movement's growing force, he issued in January 1952 his 'programme for workers and peasants'. By Decree 96 of 30 January 1952 he proposed to end illegal occupation of unregistered state land and to limit landholdings. Fraudulently acquired land would be distributed to the needy. Since the location of unregistered state land was not known and no legal procedures existed to establish ownership of these lands, the decree could not be carried out. Later decrees abrogated Decree 96, redefined the state domain, and substantially raised the limit on landownership; however, these decrees also remained inapplicable because the area of state domain was not known. To workers Shishakli preached class harmony and promised state assistance for labour funds while he established stricter government control over the trade unions.

When his programme proved ineffective in calming peasant unrest, Shishakli directed a pitiless repression against the peasants. The gendarmerie and army forces evicted peasants from their villages and expelled them from their home districts. Thousands of peasants were imprisoned and many were tortured.

Shishakli hoped to create a modern and internally united state by eliminating foreign influence and removing the separate status of religious and racial minorities and the tribes. He abolished the privileges of tribal chiefs, brought foreign and private schools under a measure of government control, and tried to assimilate the minorities, sometimes by questionable measures. Thus he made many enemies, especially among the Druzes who were, in any event, pro-Hashemi.

Shishakli created his own monolithic political party, the Arab

Liberation Movement (ALM), but it failed to rally mass support. His repression of the peasantry and abolition of parliamentary life made an implacable enemy of his lifelong companion, Akram Hourani, who commanded the loyalties of not a few army officers. The ASP and the Ba'th waged an underground campaign inside and outside the army for the dissolution of the ALM and restoration of political liberties. In December 1952 Shishakli arrested some ASP, Ba'th, and Communist Party members, including Hourani, Aflak, and Bitar, as well as some officers on charges of plotting a *coup*. Hourani and the two Ba'th leaders escaped to the Lebanon.

Attempting to give his regime a constitutional foundation, Shishakli submitted his constitution to a managed 'popular referendum' and on the same day, 10 July 1953, was 'elected' President by direct suffrage. The 1953 Constitution created a presidential system. The ban on political parties – the communists excepted – was lifted before the 9 October parliamentary elections, but only the ALM, the SSNP, and the Socialist Co-operative Party participated. The ALM won 72 seats out of 82, the SSNP one, and independents the rest.

The fact that most political parties boycotted the election heralded the gathering political storm. Already in June 1953, more than a hundred political and professional leaders had called on Shishakli to put an end to 'individual absolute rule' and restore public liberties. Less than a month later, representatives of the National, People's, Ba'th, Arab Socialist, and Communist parties and independent politicians met in Homs as a National Congress to conclude a National Pact to overthrow the regime. This unprecedented alliance of Syria's customarily fragmented political forces boded ill for Shishakli. Yet he declared a general amnesty for political prisoners, allowed Hourani, Aflak, and Bitar to return to Syria, and put no hindrance on the public activities of the parties which were secretly organizing his overthrow.

Army officers were drawn into the movement mainly by Hourani. Some political leaders, including Sabry Al-Asali, received money from the Iraq government to further the conspiracy, while Iraq simultaneously revived its agitation for Fertile Crescent unity. A Druze uprising was to have been the signal for the revolt, but the arrest of Sultan Pasha Atrash's son Mansour, a Ba'th Party member, for distributing leaflets brought the army prematurely into the Jebel Druze. Its brutal attacks on the population stoked the fires of Druze hostility to Shishakli. Student strikes and demonstrations started in Aleppo and spread throughout the country. Shishakli imposed martial law and arrested leading political personalities; he then attempted to come to terms with the imprisoned politicians, but was unsuccessful. On 25 February 1954, an army mutiny began in

Aleppo under the leadership of Captain Mustafa Hamdoun, one of Hourani's partisans. All garrisons except that of Damascus joined the rebellion. That same evening, Shishakli resigned and left Syria under a safe conduct.

[1] Adel Akel: 'Analysis of Syrian National Income Estimates 1953–1960', *EFSPA*, 1961, No. 43.

[2] *Fi Sabil Al-Ba'th Al-Arabi*, Beirut, 1959, p. 164.

[3] *Memoirs of Muhammad Kurd 'Ali, A Selection*, trans. by Khalil Totah, Washington D.C., 1954, pp. 214–17.

[4] Report of Sub-Committee 2, UN Doc. A/AC. 14/32 & Add. 1, para. 59.

[5] UNTSO Chief of Staff Lt-Gen. E. L. M. Burns commented: 'It would seem that Arabs outside Palestine should have as much right to come to the assistance of Arabs in Palestine as Jews outside Palestine come to the assistance of Jews within'. *Between Arab and Israeli*, London, 1962, p. 127.

[6] Official files of the Syrian Ministry of Defence, cited by Walid Khalidi: *From Haven to Conquest*, Beirut, 1970, p. 867.

[7] ibid.

[8] These military operations have been described in authoritative Hebrew sources published in Israel, notably *Ha Sepher Ha Palmach* (The Book of the Palmach), Vols. 1 and 2, and *Qurvot (Battles) 1948*. See Walid Khalidi: 'Plan Dalet', *Middle East Forum*, Vol. 37, No. 9, November 1961.

[9] Miles Copeland: *The Game of Nations*, London, 1969, pp. 37–44: 'A "political action team" under Major (Stephen) Meade systematically developed a friendship with Za'im, then chief of staff of the Syrian Army, suggested to him the idea of a coup d'état, advised him how to go about it, and guided him through the intricate preparations in laying the groundwork for it . . .'

[10] Marlowe, op. cit., p. 56.

[11] Copeland, op. cit., p. 42.

[12] According to Khalid Al-Azm, premier of the government overthrown by Za'im, U.N. Mediator Ralph Bunche had promised to support this Syrian demand which accorded with normal international practice: if inland waterways serve as international boundaries, the frontier usually runs down the middle. See Khalid Al-Azm's posthumously published memoirs in *Al Nahar* (Beirut), 21 June 1972.

[13] During the first half of 1949, General Armistice Agreements were concluded between Israel, on the one hand, and Egypt, Lebanon, Transjordan, and Syria on the other. According to these agreements, the armistice demarcation line was 'not to be construed in any sense as a political or territorial boundary' and was 'delineated without prejudice to the rights, claims and positions of either Party . . . as regards the ultimate settlement of the Palestine question'. The provisions of the armistice were 'dictated exclusively by military and not by political considerations'; 'no military or political advantage should be gained under the truce . . .' The basic purpose of the armistice demarcation line was 'to delineate the line beyond which the armed forces of the respective Parties shall not move . . .' 'No aggressive action by the armed forces–land, sea or air–of either Party shall be undertaken, planned or threatened . . .' Execution of the agreements was to be supervised by Mixed Armistice Commissions whose Chairman in each case was to be the U.N. Chief-of-Staff of the Truce Supervision Organization or a senior of that organization designated by him.

[14] Akram Hourani to the author, 2 June 1971.

Chapter 6

Road to Union

SHISHAKLI'S OVERTHROW DIFFERED from earlier military *coups* in that–in Michel Aflak's words–'the people began and the officers followed'. The popular watchword became: 'No more dictatorships!' Almost universal revulsion against military autocracy compelled the army to return to its barracks. But politicized officers did not renounce their sense of mission. They were now divided into rightist and leftist currents. The rightist group consisted of a pro-Iraqi bloc, strengthened by the reinstatement of officers dismissed by Shishakli, and a handful of SSNP militants. The radicals were mainly partisans of Hourani's Arab Socialist Party now merged with the Ba'th.

In 1953, the two parties–drawn together by their common fight against Shishakli–had united to form the Arab Ba'th Socialist Party. Although the terms of the merger required a new name and a new constitution, the merger was made so hastily that no time was found to modify the Ba'th's constitution, and the new party was commonly called simply the Ba'th. In the decade of its existence, each of the two wings retained its identity. The Aflak-Bitar 'resurrectionists' became identified as the right wing; Hourani's socialists, as the left.

Even at the beginning, harmony was not achieved. Party unity was many times threatened from top to bottom owing to basic political and intellectual differences. Yet the merged party changed the history of Syria. The ASP gave the new Ba'th a dynamism and a mass base lacking in the old as well as a significant following in the army. Like the ASP, the new party, although it ardently proselytized in the army, did not accept military men as fully-fledged dues-paying members. Hourani opened the doors of the Military Academy to many young Ba'th militants, but a party member entering the army was required to give up his party membership. These regulations, while preserving party independence from the military, did not prevent the Ba'th's officer partisans from wielding considerable influence in the party.

The new Ba'th refused to participate in the conservative coalition government (People's and National parties and independents) established once the 1950 Constitution had been restored and the 1950 parliament recalled. Neither government nor parliament, both dominated by the People's Party, represented the balance of forces in the country. Speaking for the Ba'th, Hourani warned parliament that, if social reform were delayed, the Ba'th would regroup workers and peasants 'to break the yoke of feudalism and capitalism'. Premier Sabry Al-Asali's hints that Syria might join a recently concluded Turkish-Pakistan military pact—apparently a *quid pro quo* for Iraq's help in ousting Shishakli—provoked such protest that he was compelled to promise not to commit the country to any external alignment before national elections.

SEPTEMBER 1954 ELECTIONS

Although the politically conscious public hoped for significant change from the coming parliamentary elections, political confusion prevailed. The political parties, so recently united against Shishakli, fell out with each other and were splintered by personal feuds. Former President Quwatly's return from Egypt, where he had spent most of his years in exile since Za'im's *coup*, roused passionate protest from the many for whom he remained a symbol of old regime bankruptcy. Already looking ahead to the 1955 presidential election, Quwatly tried but failed to form a conservative coalition. The two conservative parties entered the elections separately. Shishakli's Arab Liberation Movement, reactivated by Ma'mun Kuzbari, contested the elections. The Muslim Brotherhood did not enter candidates, but some brothers resigned to run as individuals. Khalid Al-Azm, forming a group of independents later called the Democratic Bloc, campaigned on a platform calling for modernization of agriculture and industry, a developed social programme, and rejection of collaboration with all powers sustaining Israel. The Ba'th spurned communist overtures to form a common front. But the Communist Party and neutralist partisans of Azm made common cause in Damascus.

A non-political caretaker government conducted the elections. Under popular pressures, it provided a secret ballot and enclosed polling booth, and transferred all provincial officials involved in the voting process to new posts on the eve of the elections in order to prevent the customary deals between local notables and election officials. But the electoral lists, which had not been revised for many years, were not brought up to date, and many eligible voters were unable to vote. Although only 40 per cent of eligible voters went to the polls, the election with some justification has been called 'the first free election in the Arab world'.

The results revealed a significant change in the balance of political forces. Representation of the People's and National parties substantially declined, while radical and modernizing groups came to the fore. The Ba'th won 16 seats as a consequence of the clean sweep made by Hourani's complete lists in Hama and nearby Ma'arat Al-Numan against the traditional victors, the big landlords. Al-Azm's neutralist bloc numbered 38 in the new parliament. Many other victorious independents ran on neutralist platforms. One communist candidate was elected and four others might have been, had not the government intervened against them.[1] The Communist Party and Ba'th polled roughly the same number of votes. Communist Party General Secretary Khalid Bagdash became the second communist deputy to be elected in the Arab world. (The first was Abdel Kader Isma'il, elected to the Iraqi parliament in 1937.) Ten former Shishakli partisans and an SSNP candidate were also victorious.

The voting put Syria on the road to democratic development and had a profound impact throughout the Arab world. On the paramount issue, Syrians voted overwhelmingly against military co-operation with the West. This clear popular mandate from one of the two Arab countries where the people's voice could be heard–coming just a month after Egypt and Iraq had agreed at Sursink to co-operate militarily with the West through the Arab Collective Security Pact (ACSP)[2]–played a decisive role in the Arab and Great Power conflict, of which Syria was the focus, and in the subsequent Arab breakaway from Western control. It influenced the Cairo regime's evolution towards neutralism and Baghdad's eventual resort to armed conspiracy to gain its ends in Syria.

Displacement of the old guard had begun, but the new forces were not united, and no party was strong enough to impose its control. The old guard still held the command posts, as Azm's inability to form a government representing the modernizing forces demonstrated. The seventy-seven-year-old Christian nationalist Faris Al-Khuri formed a conservative coalition government dominated by the People's Party.

THE BAGHDAD PACT

The Anglo-Egyptian Agreement for British withdrawal from Egypt, concluded a month after the Syrian elections, provoked a storm of criticism in Syria and the Arab world, because its provision for the return of British forces in the event of an attack on the Arab states or Turkey was seen as a link to NATO. Reversing the neutrality policy of the former Egyptian regime, Gamal Abdel Nasser sought Western military aid for the Egyptian-led Arab Collective Security Pact. He later revealed[3] that the United States had consented to let Egypt take the lead in building a regional pact that would be supported by the West but not directly allied either to the West or Turkey. This formula for Arab military co-operation with the West was unacceptable to Britain and Iraq. With the Anglo-Iraq treaty soon to expire, Britain needed a means to retain its bases in Iraq (already threatened by popular insurrections in 1948 and 1952) and to halt American encroachment on its Middle East positions; Iraq was unwilling to concede to Egypt the Arab leadership it wanted for itself. The Baghdad Pact was already in gestation.

In Syria, which rejected *any* military link with the West, both Left and Right then opposed the Nasser regime. Syrians had not forgotten Cairo's violent attacks on the political front which had overthrown Cairo's friend, Shishakli. In the Nasser-Naguib conflict, democrats sided with Naguib against Nasser's 'military dictatorship'. The Muslim Brotherhood, under attack in Egypt for its opposition to the Anglo-Egyptian Agreement, had moved its headquarters to Syria, where it conducted a virulent campaign against the Cairo regime. Syria's refusal to bow to Egyptian demands to expel Egyptian Brotherhood leaders who had taken refuge there caused a continuing crisis in Syrian-Egyptian relations. Violent demonstrations in Syrian cities protested Egypt's execution of Brotherhood leaders who had tried to assassinate Nasser.

Faris Khuri's government, committed to shun all external alignments, was the only Arab government to oppose the decision taken by Arab League foreign ministers in December 1954 to collaborate with the West through the Arab Collective Security Pact. The Arab decision became meaningless when Iraq, backed by Britain, seized the initiative to conclude a pact with Turkey. The Iraq-Turkey pact – nucleus of what soon became the Baghdad Pact – took both Washington and Cairo by surprise. The United States refused to join the pact or give it economic aid. The sudden conclusion of the pact angered Egypt and Saudi Arabia, the avowed enemy of the Hashemis. Aware of the divergence between American and British policies, Nasser focused his anti-Baghdad Pact campaign against Iraq and Britain. Washington responded by maintaining cordial relations with Cairo. American disassociation from the Baghdad Pact was underscored by the fact that Saudi money, derived from American oil royalties, financed Cairo's anti-Baghdad Pact campaign. Saudi gold poured into Syria, Lebanon, and Jordan to persuade newsmen, politicians, and officers to oppose the Baghdad Pact and align these countries with Egypt. These Saudi activities and the 'curious alliance' between Saudi agents and the Left became the subject of more than one editorial comment in the Syrian and Lebanese press. Britain and Iraq, holding the United States responsible for the Saudi campaign, tried – unsuccessfully – to persuade Washington to use its influence in Riad to call it off and countered the Saudi subsidies with their own.[4]

Popular pressures generated by the Saudi-Egyptian campaign made untenable the Khuri government's attempts to avoid offending either camp. Violent Egyptian accusations that Syria was playing the Iraqi game brought about the fall of the Khuri government. A government more representative of the September election results took office on 13 February when the anti-pact forces (Ba'th, communists, and Azm bloc) found allies in the anti-Iraq wing of the National Party. Asali became premier; Azm, Foreign Minister and acting Defence Minister; and a Ba'thist was named Minister of Health. Azm and, from behind the scenes, Hourani became the moving powers in the new government.

Egypt and Saudi Arabia besieged the government to join their alternative to the Baghdad Pact: a military, economic, and political treaty tying the anti-pact states into an Arab Federation. The heart of this proposal was a Joint Military Command which would bring the Syrian army, and hence Syrian foreign policy, under Egypt's control. To win Syria to this plan, Nasser sent Brigadier Mahmoud Riad to Damascus as his new ambassador. On 26 February, Egypt's Salah Salim arrived to negotiate Syria's adherence to the treaty. But the Syrian government hesitated before the risks involved. The People's Party and the SSNP were accusing it of leading the country to communism and hinting at Iraqi intervention. Turkey joined Iraq in warnings and threats, while clashes occurred on the Turkish-Syrian border. Israel's attack on Gaza on 28 February persuaded Azm and Asali to agree to the Egyptian demands, but the government, still fearing to alienate dangerous neighbours, continued to hesitate.

Mounting pressures from both sides had the effect of turning Syria towards the USSR. Since Shishakli's overthrow, Syrian-Soviet relations had developed steadily. Owing to Soviet bloc participation, the Damascus Fair in September 1954 was so successful that it was made an annual event. Syria's trade with the USSR, eastern Europe, and China quickly developed. In December 1954, the army acquired military equipment from East Germany. In March 1955, Azm, then in Cairo, asked the Soviet ambassador for military aid. Turkish and Iraqi troop concentrations on Syria's borders at this time prompted Soviet Foreign Minister Molotov to assure Syria of Soviet support. In June, at the U.N. Conference in San Francisco, he told Azm his government had agreed to Syria's arms request.

Cairo's reaction to the developing Syrian-Soviet *rapprochement* suggested that the Nasser regime did not favour an independent Syrian foreign policy. But at the Bandung Conference, in which an important delegation led by Azm participated, Syria's neutralism was strengthened and its growing self-identity with Afro-Asia was confirmed. In July, Syrian parliamentary delegations visited the USSR to consolidate relations and seek economic aid.

THE STRUGGLE WITHIN

Conflicts over the Baghdad Pact had internal repercussions. On 22 April, Deputy Chief-of-Staff Colonel Adnan Malki, the most influential neutralist leader in the army, was assassinated by a sergeant, an SSNP agent. Since the SSNP was fanatically pro-West, the assassination was assumed to be a Baghdad Pact plot to overthrow the government. But a bitter feud within the army between Malki and a small SSNP faction led by an Alawi officer, Ghassan Jadid, also played a part. Jadid, who was accused of organizing Malki's murder, had recently been dismissed from the army by Malki on the grounds that he was in contact with the Americans.

In the wake of Malki's assassination, the government tried and convicted more than a hundred SSNP members (some *in absentia*), outlawed the SSNP, and imprisoned all the SSNP members it could find. Sweeping purges ousted SSNP sympathizers from the army and the administration, opening the way for the Ba'th and its followers. Communist co-operation with the Ba'th in the anti-SSNP and anti-Baghdad Pact campaign laid the basis for a future common front. The prestige won by Abdel Hamid Sarraj, newly appointed head of the army's Second Bureau (Intelligence), by his conduct of the investigation became the springboard for his rise in the army in alliance with the Ba'th.

The Malki affair roused nationalist fury to a fever pitch. Ba'th and communist influence, riding the anti-Western tide, developed rapidly. The Ba'th and the Communist Party shared control of the streets in a part of the world where the monopoly of power held by the traditional ruling class made street demonstrations a normal and necessary part of the political process. Akram Hourani and Khalid Bagdash were acknowledged to be among the country's most able politicians. Demands for social reform went hand in hand with the Left's anti-pact campaign. Left publications multiplied. Writers and artists lent their talents to the nationalist cause. Syria's political freedoms and ferment attracted refugees and exiles from dictatorships in other Arab countries. In this period Syria became the political and cultural mecca of the Arab world.

Social Aspirations

Workers, who had suffered much under the Shishakli regime, began almost immediately after Shishakli's fall to strike against widespread undercutting of the minimum wage and dismissals for joining trade unions. Some employers, notably Damascus textile firms, replied with lockouts and threats to emigrate. Parliament therefore amended the labour law to allow the government to compel owners to reopen factories and workers to return to work. Damascus textile firms then yielded.

After the September 1954 elections, the trade union movement became much more active. A sweeping programme submitted to the new government called for help for the unemployed, social insurance, laws to protect agricultural workers, creation of a Ministry of Labour and Social Affairs, and adoption of an economic development programme. The Asali government incorporated some of these demands in its Ministerial Declaration of February 1955. A wave of strikes at this time revealed a growing militancy in the trade unions, where both the Ba'th and the communists were extending their influence. The trade union movement also threw itself into the anti-Baghdad Pact campaign and began to work towards co-operation with other Arab trade unions.

A developing economic crisis underlined the Left's social demands and put pressure on the government to fulfil its promises. On social questions, however, the government was split. Nor could a parliamentary majority be found to enact social legislation. Parliament rejected a draft law submitted by Akram Hourani to protect sharecroppers and agricultural workers, but passed overwhelmingly a law devised to protect big landlords in ownership of the state domain. Parliament also denied women the right to vote in coming municipal elections.

The Left's economic demands found wider support. Pressure from the Communist Party and the Ba'th put new vigour into the government's three-year-old demand for higher royalties from IPC. IPC soon conceded a tenfold increase in these transit fees and the principle of 50–50 profit sharing. The agreement provided for the annual sale to Syria of 600,000 tons of crude oil and so posed the need to build an oil refinery. Completion of a World Bank survey of the potential for economic development induced parliament to set up economic development institutions and to adopt a seven-year programme for the expenditure of £S659 million ($184 million) on development.

Presidential Election

Traditional forces remained in control of parliament. Left demands were radical only in the traditionalist context. But Syria's lively political life – and the fact that communists participated in it –

alarmed the traditionalist Iraqi monarchy, and worried the West, especially the United States. Egypt and Saudi Arabia, eager for Syrian ratification of their proposed alliance, objected to Syria's independent foreign policy *vis-à-vis* the USSR. The Syrian presidential election, to be held in parliament in August 1955, assumed crucial importance in the struggle for Syria. The contenders were Khalid Al-Azm, backed by the Ba'th, the Democratic Bloc, and the communists, and former President Quwatly, the candidate of the National Party.

Western observers usually dismiss Azm as an unprincipled opportunist governed only by an ambition to become President and willing to play the Soviet-communist game to achieve this end. Many Syrians, however, respected Azm as the only real statesman Syria possessed. Originally an advocate of Syria's collaboration with the West, Azm was convinced by the West's consistent support for Israel against the Arabs of Syria's need for a counterweight against Western pressures. When Soviet policy shifted towards the Arabs in the early 1950s, he found that counterweight in the USSR. He believed that, if Syria gave an advantage to either side in the Cold War, the Middle East would become a theatre of war, and so he insisted on a neutralist policy. A staunch capitalist, Azm considered that Syria's economic and social development could be achieved only by a combination of private and public enterprise, since private capitalists lacked the resources to undertake necessary social overhead projects. Syria, he said, borrowing what Mao Tse-tung had said of China, 'suffers from an excess of imperialism but not at all from an excess of national capital. On the contrary, it is too feeble'. Azm, the architect of Syria's industrialization, worked tirelessly to encourage state-directed economic development. He was prepared to co-operate with any group, including the Communist Party, so long as it pursued national goals.

The United States opposed Azm, pioneer of Syria's neutrality and good relations with the USSR. So did Egypt and Saudi Arabia. The Saudi-Egyptian candidate was Saudi Arabia's longtime protégé, Quwatly, who had spent his years of exile in Egypt and there formed close relations with the ruling officers. Quwatly's victory was achieved by the lavish expenditure of Saudi funds and a last-minute switch of the People's Party to his support. Saudi interference was so blatant that many deputies complained. One vote was cast for the Saudi ambassador in what Damascus newspapers called 'a funloving gesture to epitomize Saudi efforts to influence the election'. Azm and the Ba'th minister promptly resigned. A new conservative government took office.

Egyptian Ascendancy and Soviet Arms

Quwatly's election proved to be a major step towards Syria's adherence to Egypt's pact. Another was Nasser's purchase of Czech arms. For, in breaking the Western arms monopoly, Nasser became overnight the national hero of the Arabs. (The Syria–USSR arms agreement had not been revealed.) The Syrian government could not now resist the great popular demand to join the Egyptian pact. The Cabinet signed and parliament ratified the military accord with Egypt. A similar Saudi-Egyptian accord was concluded a week later. As a reward for Syria's adherence to the pact, Saudi Arabia promised to buy more Syrian industrial goods, postponed repayment of its 1950 loan, and offered another of $10 million. Syria then rejected a $25-million World Bank loan, long under negotiation, because the bank required the use of contractors and advisers from its member countries.

A large-scale Israeli attack on Syrian posts near Lake Tiberias in December 1955 pushed Syria closer to the USSR. UNTSO commander Elmo Hutchison called this three-pronged attack by land and sea

> a premeditated raid of intimidation, motivated by Israel's desire to test the strength of the Egyptian-Syrian Mutual Defence Pact, to disrupt unity further, to bait the Arab states into some overt act of aggression that would afford Israel the opportunity to overrun additional territory without censor and add to their growing list of hostages.[5]

Although France had earlier promised weapons for Syria's French-equipped army, it now refused Syria's plea for arms because of Syrian criticism of French actions in Algeria. So Syria took up the Soviet arms offer. A month later it signed a contract to buy arms from Czechoslovakia. Voluntary contributions poured into army funds. Many young people enrolled for military training. A popular insurrection in Jordan against Britain's attempt to bring Jordan into the Baghdad Pact greatly excited Syrians. Along with Saudi Arabia and Egypt, Syria offered to replace King Husain's British subsidy, but the king refused. Rising tensions led Syria to reconsider its defence expenditures. A large proportion of the increased oil revenues and the new Saudi loan were diverted to the military. Most taxes were raised by 10 to 20 per cent.

The Ba'th, the Communist Party, and a wing of the National Party began to work together after the presidential election. In November they formed a National Front electoral alliance against the People's Party in a Homs by-election. The National Front candidate, a non-party trade unionist, won by some 3,000 votes.

Nasser's arms deal set in motion a powerful pro-Egyptian current, with the Ba'th in the lead agitating for union with Egypt. Egyptian ambassador Mahmoud Riad, now one of the most influential figures in Syria, encouraged this campaign. The potent appeal of the Arab unity slogan among Syrians resided in their belief that only unity could bring about the liberation of Palestine. In March 1956, Syrian and Jordanian trade unions succeeded in holding a congress, in which Egyptian and Libyan trade unions also participated, to found the International Confederation of Arab Trade Unions (ICATU). This achievement gave further impetus to the unity trend. The Syrian government provided the facilities and financing for this congress. The veteran Syrian trade unionist Subhi Khatib became the confederation's first President. ICATU's constitution pledged Arab workers to work for Arab unity and Arab liberation from imperialism.

By early 1956, the unrepresentative character of the government had become apparent. Popular opinion was exercised about the French war in Algeria. When, in June, the government lifted a ban on wheat shipments to France, students revolted, and the government fell. Sabry Al Asali's new National Union Government, formed on 15 June, brought together the more or less mutually hostile National and People's parties, Azm's Democratic Bloc, the right-wing Constitutional Bloc, and the Ba'th. The Ba'th, which won the key ministries of foreign affairs and economy, made its participation conditional on the opening of such talks with Egypt. Parliament duly approved creation of a committee to begin unity talks with Egypt. The Ba'th at this time sought the support of rightist officers to make Abdel Hamid Sarraj chief-of-staff, but Tawfik Nizam Al-Din, a conservative, secured the post. One of the government's first acts was to welcome Soviet Foreign Minister Shepilov, who paid a brief visit to Damascus; another was to recognize China.

The Iraq Conspiracy and Suez

In the Syrian-Egyptian pact, in Egypt's growing ascendancy in Syria, and in the rising influence of the Ba'th and Communist Party, Iraq's Nuri Said saw a plot 'to strangle Iraq through the communists in Syria'. He, therefore, asked Britain and the United States for a 'free hand' to get rid of 'the communists' in Syria and a 'guarantee' that the United States and Britain would 'restrain' Israel during these efforts.[6] An Iraqi conspiracy to overthrow the government in Syria and eliminate the Ba'th and the Communist Party began at this time. It soon involved a broad spectrum of right-wing politicians

–members of the People's Party, the Constitutional Bloc, and a few in the National Party–and exiled Syrian officers and SSNP leaders in Beirut, including Ghassan Jadid. Former dictator Adib Shishakli, who was originally involved, withdrew when he decided the plot could not succeed. With the connivance of the United States and Britain, preparations went forward throughout 1956.

Nasser's nationalization of the Suez Canal Company on 26 July evoked a great popular mobilization in defence of Egypt. Hourani warned that, if Egypt were attacked, Syria would cut off Western oil. People of all ages rushed to join a Popular Resistance Force created under the wing of the army. In response to an ICATU appeal, Syria and other Arab countries observed a general strike against the London Conference on 16 August. Relations with the Soviet bloc expanded with the conclusion of new trade and cultural accords and the visits of many delegations from these countries. The Cabinet considered but could not agree on a Czech offer to build the projected oil refinery.

Meeting in September, Nasser, Quwatly, and King Saud of Saudi Arabia agreed once more to offer Jordan, then suffering punishing Israeli raids, financial assistance and a chance to join the Joint Command. Nationalist forces in Jordan won a sweeping victory in parliamentary elections held in October. The new National Government swiftly aligned Jordan's policies with those of Egypt and Syria, putting the Jordanian army under the Joint Command. When Israel attacked Egypt, the Syrian and Jordanian armies prepared to invade Israel in a move designed to cut it in two. Egyptian Commander-in-Chief Abdel Hakim Amr, who feared a tripartite invasion of Syria if it participated in the fighting, vetoed this proposed action. Under Amr's orders, a Syrian division entered Jordan at this time to bolster it against possible Israeli attack. Syria broke relations with Britain and France, and also rejected French and British offers to build an oil refinery and a new international airport. Workers and officers acting unofficially blew up the IPC pipeline, thus contributing to the defeat of the 'tripartite aggression'. Quwatly flew to Moscow on a previously arranged visit. Syrians enthusiastically welcomed the assurances he received of Soviet moral support. On the other hand, they had no appreciation of the American role in the Suez crisis. For the Iraq conspiracy, in which the United States was involved, was discovered at this time. Syrians considered this conspiracy and the Suez aggression to be part of one imperialist plot.

Throughout the summer and fall of 1956, Syrian Army Intelligence, under the direction of Sarraj, had gradually unravelled the tangled threads of the Iraq conspiracy. When Iraqi arms were smuggled into the Jebel Druze on the eve of the invasion of Egypt, the government began rounding up the conspirators. On 22 December, a bill of indictment was brought against forty-seven persons, including Adib and Salah Shishakli, Ghassan Jadid, Adnan Al-Atasi (son of two-term former President Hashim Al-Atasi), Druze leader Hassan Al-Atrash, and certain leaders of the People's Party, the Constitutional Bloc, and the right wing of the National Party. Colonel Afif Bizri presided over the military court that tried and convicted the accused, many of whom had already escaped. The trial broke the power of the People's Party, weakening traditional conservative forces in Syria.

Soon after discovery of this conspiracy, Hourani and Azm took the lead in organizing a parliamentary National Front with the aim of rallying all deputies who would subscribe to its programme. The Front's Charter called for a firm anti-imperialist stand, including 'action to liberate Arab states under the imperialist yoke and especially to aid the Iraqi people in their fight against imperialism', and for 'austerity' to enable the country to cope with the dangers it faced. It proposed a programme to overcome backwardness, including tax reform and legislation to protect workers and peasants. The Front pledged itself to combat 'atheism' and anti-Arab national movements. The People's Party, the largest in parliament, refused to subscribe to the National Front Charter. Some 65 deputies (out of 142) ultimately endorsed the Charter. This democratically constituted coalition–joined by officers friendly to one or other of its member parties[7]–formed the basis of the National Front that was to guide Syria's destiny in the year ahead.

Asali then reshuffled his government to eliminate the People's Party and the Constitutional Bloc (because of the involvement of some of their leaders in the Iraq conspiracy). He brought in Azm (out of politics for the previous sixteen months because of two heart attacks) as Defence Minister. The new government, representing the National Front, Ma'mun Kuzbari's Arab Liberation Movement, and certain independents, became the first Arab government to denounce the Eisenhower Doctrine proclaimed in Washington at the turn of the year.

THE EISENHOWER DOCTRINE

The Eisenhower Doctrine announcing the American intention to fill the 'vacuum' in the Middle East offered aid and protection to any state in the area threatened by 'international communism'. On 10 January 1957, the Syrian government issued a statement in which it denied the existence of either a 'vacuum' or a 'communist menace', rejected external interference, and insisted that the main threat to the Arabs came from imperialism and Zionism, 'the aggressors of

Suez'. A vast Western press campaign at this time pictured Syria as already falling under communist Soviet domination. Kennet Love, then correspondent of the *New York Times*, later wrote of the origins of this campaign:[8]

> The US Embassy in Syria connived at false reports issued in Washington and London through diplomatic and press channels to the effect that Russian arms were pouring into the Syrian port of Latakia, that 'not more than 123 Migs' had arrived in Syria, and that Lieutenant Colonel Abdel Hameed Serraj, head of Syrian Intelligence, had taken over control in a Communist-inspired coup. I travelled all over Syria without hindrance in November and December and found there were indeed 'not more than 123 Migs'. There were none. And no Russian arms had arrived for months. And there had been no coup, although some correspondents in Beirut, just a two-hour drive from Damascus, were dispatching without attribution false reports fed to them by embassy visitors from Damascus and a roving CIA man who worked in the guise of a US Treasury agent.

Behind the screen of such propaganda – maintained in similar vein throughout 1957 – the Eisenhower Doctrine aimed at isolating and subverting Syria's National Front regime.

Kings Saud and Husain and Presidents Nasser and Quwatly formally condemned the doctrine at a Cairo conference in mid-January. But on his return to Jordan King Husain, whose National Government was then preparing to establish diplomatic relations with the USSR and China, warned of the 'communist menace' in a move designed to fulfil the conditions for Eisenhower Doctrine aid. King Saud travelled to Washington to become an advocate of American policy.

The choice of the antedeluvian Saudi monarch as the anchor of the Eisenhower Doctrine made sense from the American point of view. Since America's longstanding opposition to Hashemi expansionism removed Saudi fears of Hashemi unity projects, Washington could hope for a reconciliation of Saud and Husain under its aegis. Saud's intimate ties with both Egypt and Syria could also be valuable. Shishakli's former Chief-of-Staff, Fawzi Selu, then a resident at the Saudi court, acted as confidential messenger between Saud and Quwatly throughout 1957. And Quwatly, who visited Egypt regularly for medical treatment, used these occasions to consult with President Nasser. Apart from his then immense personal prestige, Nasser had a base in the Syrian army and he enjoyed the support of the Ba'th Party. Egypt and Saudi Arabia were thus intimately involved in, and able to influence, Syrian affairs.

Saud's intervention in Syria began at a four-nation conference held in Cairo in late February to hear his report on his American trip. But his demand for a joint condemnation of 'subversive activities' in the Middle East—in furtherance of the American campaign against Syria—was refused when Azm denied the existence of any such activities capable of endangering the area's stability. Saud then sent a note to Quwatly charging Syrian officers with responsibility for opening the door to Soviet penetration in the Arab East. The timing of this note may have been dictated by the fact that the Syrian government's decision to accept a Czech bid to build its oil refinery was soon coming up for ratification in parliament. Saud's note prompted Quwatly and Chief-of-Staff Nizam Al-Din to order the transfer of some 120 nationalist officers to remote or minor posts. But the officers refused to move and Azm refused to countersign the transfers. The crisis was eventually resolved when the Joint Command (Nasser and Field Marshal Amr) persuaded the chief-of-staff to rescind the transfers.

The next step in the application of the Eisenhower Doctrine came in Jordan, where King Husain, with Saudi and American help, succeeded in ousting the National Government and qualifying for American aid. The Syrian division stationed in Jordan since the Suez war made no move to assist the National Government during this crisis, but the Saudi troops which entered Jordan at this time began subjecting this division to daily provocations. Syria's Colonel Afif Bizri, accompanied by a high Jordanian officer sympathetic to the ousted National Government, went to Cairo to consult with Nasser and Amr about the Syrian division. Believing that Syria would be the next target of the Eisenhower Doctrine, they tried to persuade Nasser that the best defence would be to take the offensive; they claimed that nationalist units in the Jordanian army, with the help of the Syrian division, could restore the situation in Jordan. Nasser, not wanting to give the United States a pretext for intervention in Syria, ordered the division withdrawn.

A Saudi effort during talks in Baghdad in mid-May to ease tensions between Egypt and Iraq soon resulted in the replacement of Nuri Said as premier by Ali Jawdat Al-Ayyubi, a less dedicated anti-Egyptian. When King Saud sent his pro-Egyptian Deputy Foreign Minister, Yusuf Yasin, a Syrian, to inform Quwatly of the Baghdad talk results, Quwatly arranged a meeting between Yasin and officers of the High Command–Bizri, Amine Nafouri, and Abdel Hamid Sarraj. Yasin tried to persuade these officers to align Syria with Saudi Arabia behind American policy and to steer clear of union with either Iraq or Egypt until it could unite with both. The officers encouraged Yasin to talk. After hearing him out, they ordered him to leave the country.

Western concern about the 'communist menace' in Syria then intensified. Committed to Syria's defence, President Nasser sought to acquire a decisive hold. Policies that were to lead to the union of the two countries now began to develop. Within Syria, Egyptian representatives tried to moderate the Syrian tone, isolate the communists, and consolidate Egyptian influence. To his many friends on the Left, Egyptian Ambassador Riad emphasized Nasser's progressive aims while warning of the need to contain the communists. His Counsellor, Fathi Ridwan, whose friends and contacts were on the Right, reassured conservative politicians and businessmen that Nasser would safeguard their interests and put the communists in their place as he had done in Egypt. A new Egyptian military attaché, Abdel Mohsin Abu Nour, arrived in Syria to take in hand the Egyptian intelligence network in the Syrian army, while his assistant, Ahmed Zaki, concentrated on working with Ba'th officers. Anwar Sadat's Islamic Congress cultivated the *ulama* (Muslim learned men) and other religious leaders. President Quwatly, who had been convinced by the army's rebuff to King Saud that the army would never tolerate a pro-West alignment, now looked to Egypt for help in containing the National Front's growing influence.

POPULAR ADVANCE

During this period Turkey and Iraq again massed troops on Syria's frontiers and halted trade with Syria. The United States dumped wheat in Syria's customary markets, especially Greece and Italy (where Syrian hard wheat is used for making *pasta* and macaroni), and refused to sell Syria spare parts needed for its civil air transport. The National Front, however, stood firm. It presented candidates in four parliamentary by-elections held to fill seats left vacant by the verdicts in the Iraq conspiracy. National Front victories in all these elections in May revealed the Front as the most effective political force in the country. In Aleppo alone, fourteen new trade unions were organized in the first half of 1957. Communists and Ba'thists were elected to the boards of all three trade union federations, the communists winning 7 out of 12 seats on the board of the General Federation. Many without party affiliation, especially among the young, were drawn into political activity. The National Front programme inspiring this lively political life was nationalist and democratic in content: it aimed at maintaining Syria's independence, modernizing and developing the country, and giving fair shares to the underprivileged. This effort, of course, did threaten landlord and traditional interests, and so was considered 'communistic'. These interests, still predominant in parliament, were able once again to defeat a draft law on agricultural relations submitted by the Ba'th. However, a one-article substitute resolution prohibiting eviction of peasants from their houses was adopted by 36 votes to 2, the rest of the 142 deputies having withdrawn to avoid the vote.

Early in June conservatives in parliament struck back. People's Party leader and wealthy landlord Rushdi Kikhia, insisting he had been insulted by communist deputy Bagdash, resigned from parliament; 40 or more People's Party deputies threatened to follow suit. The Western press hailed these moves as a protest against 'communist domination of Syria'. Some National Front leaders believed the resignations should be accepted: new elections would produce a more democratic parliament. But the People's Party, itself becoming aware of this probability, had second thoughts. Resignation threats were quietly withdrawn. Deputies who had started to boycott parliament returned. The intervention of the Egyptian ambassador persuaded all National Front leaders to join with other deputies in rejecting Kikhia's resignation.

SOVIET AID AGREEMENT

Divergences between the policies of Cairo and Damascus appeared sharply in summer 1957. Cairo hoped to normalize relations with Washington in order to secure release of its frozen assets and World Bank help in settling the problems left over from Suez. Damascus, mobilizing to withstand unabated American pressures, was militantly anti-American. Defence Minister Azm provoked a Syrian-Saudi crisis in June when he denounced Kings Saud and Husain as 'American tools' and warned Saud to stop interfering in Syrian affairs. In retaliation, Saud froze all Syrian holdings in Saudi Arabia and threatened to break relations. A two-pronged Egyptian mediation—in Damascus to persuade the government to disassociate itself from Azm's remarks and in Riad where Field Marshal Amr secured from Saud a renewed pledge of neutrality in return for a promise to do something about communism in Syria—averted a break in Saudi-Syrian relations.

Late in July, Azm went to Moscow to negotiate an economic aid agreement for which he had prepared the way. This first major Soviet aid agreement in the Arab world provided technical aid and substantial Soviet credits on reasonable terms. They were to be used for construction of dams and power stations, irrigation projects, oil and mineral prospection, fertilizer factories, and a railroad linking the Jazira to the port of Latakia. The agreement excited popular enthusiasm because it would permit realization of long-dreamed-of state building projects. Yet conclusion of the treaty opened a fissure in the National Front between the Ba'th, backed by the Egyptians, on the one hand, and the Azm partisans and the communists, on the other. For the United States' massive propaganda campaign about the 'communist threat' in Syria was beginning to have its effect both in Syria and Egypt. President Nasser's misgivings over the Soviet aid agreement and 'communist influence' in Syria were made known to the Americans.[9] The Ba'th ministers had participated in the government's decision to seek Soviet aid, but the Ba'th, never pro-Soviet, feared – or professed to fear – the communization of Syria and began a whispering campaign against both Azm and the communists. From the Ba'th's point of view the National Front had served its purpose. The Ba'th whispering campaign foreshadowed its break-up.

AMERICAN CRISIS DIPLOMACY

A week after the Soviet aid agreement was announced, the Syrian government disclosed an American plot to overthrow the regime and expelled three American diplomats. Of the Syrian charges, Patrick Seale wrote:[10]

... it is hard to dismiss them as fabrications. Convinced that Syria was 'going communist', the United States had been exploring ways of reversing the trend. Its officials had had clandestine contacts with members of the Syrian armed forces with a view to organizing the overthrow of the Government. This, at least, is what emerges from the evidence ... Half a dozen officers approached by American officials immediately reported back to the authorities so the plan was doomed from the start.

Army Chief-of-Staff Nizam Al-Din, backed by President Quwatly, resisted the demands of Bizri, Amine Nafouri, and Sarraj for dismissal of certain officers suspected of involvement in the American conspiracy. When the three officers, with the tacit support of Azm and Asali, refused to take no for an answer, Nizam Al-Din resigned. Afif Bizri, a popular non-partisan officer who had held aloof from factionalism in the army, became chief-of-staff and a general. Although friendly to the communists, Bizri was not a communist and he as often as not ignored communist advice. But the Western press interpreted his appointment as a 'communist *coup d'état*' in Syria. British Labour Member of Parliament Richard Crossman commented: 'The Communist coup in Syria is an invention of American propaganda designed to conceal a humiliating diplomatic defeat'.[11] This invention became the pretext to concentrate 50,000 Turkish troops on Syria's frontiers,[12] station the American Sixth Fleet off its shores, airlift American arms to its neighbours 'to protect them against possible Syrian attack', and dispatch an American emissary, Loy Henderson, to nearby countries to determine what 'aid' the United States could give in what it professed to see as a desperate emergency. These pressures and Turkish provocations on the frontier (the Turkish army was eight times larger than the Syrian) sent Bizri and Sarraj to Cairo to find out what help the Joint Command could offer should Syria be attacked by Turkey or Israel. At Bizri's request, Nasser agreed to send artillery and anti-aircraft personnel to Syria, and did so in October. The USSR meanwhile warned Turkey that action against Syria could not remain 'localized'; a visit of two Soviet destroyers to Latakia lifted Syrian spirits.

American crisis diplomacy proved somewhat embarrassing to Arab governments allegedly threatened by Syria. They were unable to respond to Syria's polite inquiries to specify the threat and faced a hostile public opinion at home. The manufactured crisis, however, unnerved the Syrians and prepared the way for a mediation effort by King Saud to close the breach between the United States and Syria on American terms. This involved splitting the National Front and so ending its dominance in Syria. The king's mission was both encouraged and assisted by the strains that had already appeared within the Front in the wake of the Soviet aid agreement. He first secured from the allegedly threatened Arab states promises to support Syria against aggression; he then visited Damascus, where he suggested to President Quwatly that misunderstandings between the United States and Syria could be dissipated if Syria would halt the purge then under way of right-wing elements in the army and security forces, welcome all efforts to achieve an inter-Arab *rapprochement*, and make a genuine effort to normalize relations with the United States. During Saud's Damascus visit, Secretary Dulles in Washington announced his readiness to meet with Syrian Foreign Minister Bitar, then at the United Nations. The outlines of an understanding gradually emerged. Washington was prepared to moderate the rigidities of the Eisenhower Doctrine in return for a modification in the content of Syrian neutralism and a Syrian effort to improve relations with the West.

In Syria, most National Front leaders continued to rally the people to stand firm against all pressures. They organized and armed popular resistance forces all over the country. In Damascus, however, efforts were already under way in line with King Saud's mediation to form a new coalition around the Ba'th, to isolate communist and pro-Soviet elements, and apply a more 'truly neutral' foreign policy. The new coalition was devised to break up the National Front. The last common action of the Front was the election of Hourani as Speaker of Parliament by a narrow margin. Soon after, Hourani refused to make a common front with the Communist Party in municipal elections scheduled for 15 November, in which the National Front had been expected to make large gains. This decision –made on the grounds that such a front would be harmful to Syria in view of Western propaganda about the 'communist threat'–in effect buried the National Front. The Ba'th now began rallying all anti-communist forces.

Saudi mediation efforts also played a role at the United Nations in preventing action on the complaint Syria submitted about the Turkish troop concentrations. Although the Damascus government refused Saud's mediation offer, U.N. debate on this complaint was twice adjourned to permit behind-the-scenes mediation. As a result, the Syrian case was quietly shelved, and by the end of November Turkish troops were withdrawn. During this affair, Bitar met privately on 7 November with the American delegate to the United Nations, Henry Cabot Lodge, and Assistant Secretary of State William Roundtree. Soon after this meeting, the American ambassador, withdrawn from Damascus when the American conspiracy was discovered, returned to his post. American Socialist Party leader Norman Thomas accompanied Bitar back to Damascus and under Ba'th auspices gave lectures in which he expressed American sympathy for anti-communist Arab socialist movements. Although the National Front's Political Committee had earlier unanimously decided to insist that municipal elections be held as scheduled, the Ba'th now joined with the People's Party and other right-wing groups in withdrawing its candidates. The elections were therefore indefinitely postponed.

An Egyptian parliamentary delegation visited Damascus in November to join with the Syrian parliament in asking the two governments to conclude a 'federal union' as soon as possible. In characterizing the projected union as 'federal' the resolution followed the Syrian conception, but Cairo's propaganda said that coming negotiations would realize 'total unity'. Cairo's call for 'total unity' was taken up by Salah Bitar, but Hourani and other Ba'th leaders continued to advocate 'federal union'. Early in December, Azm, already Minister of Defence and Finance, became deputy premier as well. The Ba'th professed to see in this appointment the threat of a communist seizure of power. It appeared to fear that Azm, who was then trying to organize his own political party, would become, with communist backing, a formidable rival in the 1958 parliamentary elections. His appointment, in any case, became the pretext for the Ba'th to lead a stampede into union with Egypt.

The Ba'th turned to the army to accomplish what could not be achieved through normal processes of government. Ba'th leader Salah Bitar encouraged Ba'th partisans in the army to take matters into their own hands. The officers were the more susceptible to Ba'th urgings because they had been much affected by the crisis atmosphere of the past year and by American pressures, of which the army itself had been a primary target. The break-up of the National Front had left the nationalist officers without a common programme and so had enhanced factionalism.

On 12 January, a fourteen-man military delegation led by Chief-of-Staff Bizri left secretly for Cairo to ask Nasser for immediate union of the two armies as the first step to the union of the two countries. This action was taken without reference to the civilian government and constituted in all but name a *coup d'état*. In an ultimatum delivered after arriving in Cairo, the delegation informed the Damascus government of its action. Foreign Minister Bitar, sent to Cairo by the Cabinet to determine Nasser's views on unity, had no authority to negotiate a union but promptly joined the officers in doing so.

To the officers and Bitar, Nasser delivered his own ultimatum: unconditional 'total union' including liquidation of all political parties and the Syrian army's renunciation of all political activity. This was a card played at the last moment when withdrawal was virtually impossible. Azm's demand that parliament and the political parties be consulted and the question fully studied was ignored. Nasser's terms – involving eradication of Syria's identity – were accepted in great haste. On 1 February 1958, Presidents Nasser and Quwatly proclaimed the creation of the United Arab Republic (UAR) from the balcony of Abdin Palace in Cairo. On the 5th, the two parliaments ratified the decision. On the 21st a referendum in both countries confirmed the merger and 'elected' Nasser President by 99.9 per cent majorities.

Ba'th leaders agreed to total unity in defiance of party instructions to accept a federal union; they did not consult their membership or follow party rules. They confidently expected to dominate the new UAR. When asked to explain their casual surrender of Syria's independence, they replied: 'Don't worry. In a year's time we will be running the UAR'.[13] No evidence has ever been produced of the alleged communist plot the Ba'th used as a pretext for the stampede into union. The effectiveness of the National Front did not lie in the strength of any one of its components. No one of them was anywhere near strong enough to go it alone, as the Ba'th itself demonstrated in calling in Nasser. The Front drew its strength from the fact that it was a workable formula for bringing together some of Syria's diverse social formations on a programme guided by national political objectives rather than by personal, clan, or regional interests. The Front had enhanced the influence of all its participants, the Ba'th as well as the Communist Party and Azm. The communists needed the Front to maintain their position and so sought its continuance. Moscow's policy was to counter the Eisenhower Doctrine by supporting neutralists and neutralist governments. The USSR was clearly not prepared to compromise this policy or to run the risk of a confrontation with the United States for the sake either of local communists or of acquiring a client state of uncertain value.[14] The Syrian Communist Party and Moscow did not like the union, but did not want openly to oppose what appeared to be a popular goal. The communists and Azm, however, were not alone in preferring a loose federal union to 'total unity'.

Chief-of-Staff Bizri, often called a communist by Western propaganda, played an important role in securing Syrian acquiescence to Nasser's terms. His own account of the negotiations[15] partially explains this. President Nasser, he said, gave certain guarantees, including a promise that cessation of political party activity would be for an interim period only; he also promised that there would be no discrimination against elements of the National Front and no economic domination of Syria by Egypt. Bizri later explained[16] that he had believed that unity would strengthen both countries against imperialism and Israel and was 'deceived by Nasser's assurances as to the nature of the union'. He therefore 'refused to heed the advice of Bagdash and other friends' who counselled him 'against any union not made on a democratic basis'.

President Nasser always claimed that the Syrians forced him into union. But his representatives in Syria encouraged the Ba'th's unity campaign almost from its beginning. Moreover, powerful forces in Egypt, including business groups led by the Misr Bank and government economic agencies, also pressed hard for unity. Nor could Nasser have long remained unaware of the prestige the union would bring him. Without the crisis atmosphere manufactured by the year-long American campaign against Syria, the stampede into unity would not have been possible. And by this time, the union suited American purposes. Since August 1957, at least, Cairo had shared Washington's concern about 'communism' in Syria. Having failed on other fronts, Washington's policy, which throughout 1957 moved gradually towards an accommodation with Nasser, now seemed prepared to see him undertake the task of ridding Syria of the 'communist menace'. Akram Hourani later charged[17] that the United States fully supported Syria's union with Egypt in order 'to

secure elimination of the patriotic elements in Syria and settlement
of the Palestine question'.

[1] Manfred Halpern: 'The Middle East and North Africa', in Black & Thornton: *Communism and Revolution*, Princeton, N.J., 1964, p. 314.

[2] On Egypt's initiative the ACSP was established by the Arab League in 1950 to provide protection against Israel. For Cairo it was also a means to prevent Hashemi control of Syria.

[3] *New York Times*, interview, 4 April 1955.

[4] See Anthony Eden: *Full Circle*, London, 1960, pp. 334, 341–3.

[5] Elmo Hutchison: *Violent Truce*, New York, 1956, pp. 109–10.

[6] Waldemar J. Gallman: *Iraq Under General Nuri, My Recollections of Nuri As Said 1954–1958*, Baltimore, 1964, p. 161.

[7] Notably, Abdel Hamid Sarraj, Mustafa Hamdun, and Abdel Ghani Qannut (friendly with the Ba'th); Afif Bizri (friendly with the communists); and the 'independents' Amine Nafouri and Ahmed Abdel Kerim (friendly with Azm).

[8] Kennet Love: *Suez The Twice-Fought War*, New York, 1969, p. 653.

[9] P. W. Thayer, ed.: *Tensions in the Middle East*, Baltimore, 1958, pp. 42–9; and Copeland, op. cit., p. 186.

[10] Patrick Seale: *The Struggle for Syria*, London, 1965, pp. 293–4.

[11] *Le Monde*, 28 August 1957.

[12] Figure given by Dwight D. Eisenhower: *The White House Years II: Waging Peace*, London, 1966, p. 203.

[13] Michael Adams from Rome, *Manchester Guardian*, 28 September 1961.

[14] As Soviet policy towards the Iraq Revolution in July 1958 was again to demonstrate.

[15] Bizri statement to the Beirut press, 10 May 1959.

[16] Bizri to the author, 19 November 1962.

[17] Memorandum issued to the press, *Arab World*, 6 June 1962. See also Miles Copeland, op. cit., pp. 176, 186.

Chapter 7

Pursuit of a Myth

PRESIDENT NASSER'S PLEDGE at Saladin's tomb in Damascus 'to follow Saladin's example to realize total Arab unity' and appeals from UAR leaders to other Arab states to join the union electrified the Arab peoples. The UAR's magnetic attraction threatened to undermine the always fragile balance in the Lebanon as well as enfeebled Arab monarchies. To shield himself from the winds of change blowing from Damascus and Cairo, Imam Ahmed of the Yemen linked his Imamate to the UAR to form the United Arab States. A less astute King Saud became the target of a violent attack by Nasser when Sarraj uncovered an alleged Saudi conspiracy to assassinate the UAR President. Cairo's anti-Saud campaign provoked a palace revolution in Riad which compelled the king to transfer full powers to his brother, Faisal, then considered to be pro-Egyptian. The UAR seemed poised on the verge of new triumphs.

The euphoria produced by the union was nowhere greater than in Syria itself. Reality, whatever it proved to be, could only be a let-down. The extraordinary fashion in which the union had been concluded—by a handful of people in a few days' time without study or preparation of any kind—virtually assured the domination of the smaller partner by the larger. Cairo's ignorance of Syria, its assumption that Syria's problems could be solved merely by extending Egyptian laws and practices to Syria, and more than a touch of Egyptian arrogance hastened the onset of disillusion.

Reorganization of Syria's political structure to make it the Northern Region of the UAR produced the first uneasiness. The 1956 Egyptian Constitution, modified to give the President even greater power, served as the basis for the UAR Constitution. Under this constitution, the President appointed the members of the Legislative Assembly, could convoke, dismiss, or dissolve the assembly as suited his convenience, could rule by decree without restrictions, and proclaim a state of emergency without reference to the assembly. A presidential decree would define the manner in which the National Union, the sole political organization, would be formed.

The President then named the members of the UAR Central Government and of the Executive Councils or Local Governments of each region. His Central Government appointments hurt Syrian pride since Egyptians filled all important ministries and only three posts went to Syrians: Akram Hourani and Sabry Al Asali became Vice-Presidents and Salah Bitar a Minister of State. The functions attached to these offices were very vaguely defined. The Syrian Executive Council provided a façade of internal autonomy, but in reality President Nasser held absolute power in Syria as in Egypt. All decision-making of any importance was transferred to Cairo. The fact that all but two of the Syrians appointed to the Executive Council were army officers or technicians without governing experience underscored this subordination. The Ba'th, however, could take some comfort from these arrangements. It occupied two of the three Syrian posts in the Central Government, while Hourani was President of the Executive Council in which the Ba'th held the Economy, Agriculture, and Labour and Social Affairs ministries. Abdel Hamid Sarraj, then still a Ba'th sympathizer, enjoyed real authority as Minister of Interior with overall control of the Syrian security network.

Before a 13 March decree dissolving political parties, all parties except the communist 'voluntarily' liquidated themselves. Communist leaders, who left the country on the eve of parliament's ratification of the union, refused to dissolve the Communist Party 'for the good reason it was never authorized in Syria'. Ba'th leaders did not take the decree seriously except as it applied to other parties. 'We shall be officially dissolved', asserted Michel Aflak,[1] 'but we will be present in the new unified party of the National Union. Born of the union of the two countries, this movement cannot but be animated by the principles of the Ba'th'. The Ba'th discreetly managed to maintain its identity and from its dominant position in the Local Government began to eliminate its rivals from posts in the administration, the schools, and the trade unions, establishing what its non-Ba'th colleagues later called 'Ba'thist domains'.[2]

Damascus, formerly a lively capital with an often dramatic political life and, in Syrian eyes, the heart of Arabism and Islam, subsided into a dusty provincial backwater. With the Central Government handling all foreign affairs, embassies departed; Syrian diplomats got no important posts in the UAR diplomatic service. The reservations of those who had been stampeded into supporting the union–including not a few among the religious minorities, business circles, liberals, democrats, and leftists–began to appear. General Bizri's dismissal as Commander of the First (Syrian) Army late in March, because he protested against Field Marshal Amr's purge of leftist officers, contributed to nascent malaise. Dismissal and transfer of many local officials and the arrival of a succession of

Egyptian missions concerned with one or another aspect of administration in Syria enhanced the Syrian sense of inferiority.

UAR RAPPROCHEMENT WITH THE UNITED STATES

In 1958 President Nasser won from both the United States and the USSR recognition of his non-alignment policy and substantial aid agreements. The USSR offered to build the High Dam at Aswan and to assist industrial development. A radically new American aid policy soon made Egypt on a *per capita* basis the largest consumer in the world of American surplus food, and American loans, covering growing Treasury deficits, became a major resource on which the UAR budget was based. Troubles that erupted in the Lebanon in May–in which for a time the United States took one side and the UAR the other–only temporarily halted the UAR-U.S. *rapprochement*.

Tension in the Lebanon had been rising sharply since President Chamoun in early 1957 had abandoned the country's traditional neutrality to accept the Eisenhower Doctrine. This decision, coupled with his determination to seek a second term in defiance of the constitution, provoked profound opposition not only from Muslims but also from many Christians. UAR appeals to other Arab states to join the union were seized on by Chamoun, who charged that Nasser intended to annex the Lebanon. The assassination on 8 May of a prominent Lebanese newspaper editor and critic of Chamoun, Nassib Matni, touched off a rebellion known as the 'Revolt of the Pashas'. Britain, Iraq, and Turkey hastened to Chamoun's aid. Fearing Soviet penetration in the Middle East, the United States sent arms to Chamoun's supporters. Although U.N. observers could find no evidence of the 'massive intervention' of which Chamoun accused the UAR, Abdel Hamid Sarraj, Syrian Interior Minister, did send arms and 'volunteers' from Syria to aid the opposition.

Cairo and Washington, however, were already considering a compromise–selection of Lebanese army chief General Chehab to succeed Chamoun–when the Iraq revolution put an end to the Baghdad Pact plan to rescue Chamoun and brought American and British troops to the Lebanon and Jordan respectively. With American behind-the-scenes management, Chehab became President of the Lebanon on 31 July 1958. President Nasser gracefully accepted a 'no victor, no vanquished' formula in the Lebanon as part of a new orientation in his Arab policy inspired by the Iraq revolution.

The Iraq Revolution

On 14 July, Iraqi army officers led by Brigadier Abdel Kerim

Qasim seized power in Baghdad, putting an end to the anachronistic Hashemi-Nuri Said regime. The initiative and participation of left and democratic opposition parties, organized in a National Front, transformed this military *coup* into something close to a popular revolution. All members of the royal family, including the young King Faisal II, were put to death. So was the hated Nuri Said, whose corpse was dragged through the Baghdad streets by an angry and vengeful mob.

In its early hours the Iraq revolution appeared to be pro-Nasser; the Egyptians expected the new regime's prompt adherence to the UAR. On learning of the American and British troop landings in Lebanon and Jordan, Nasser flew to Moscow, where he secured Soviet Premier Khrushchev's promise to exert all international pressures short of war or the risk of war on behalf of the new Iraq regime. An Emergency Session of the U.N. General Assembly settled the crisis created by the Anglo-American intervention when U.N. Secretary-General Dag Hammarskjold brought Western and Arab views together. The West gave strong backing to an Arab-sponsored resolution calling on the Arabs to settle their own affairs and on the U.N. Secretary-General to facilitate withdrawal of the Anglo-American forces. The resolution also adopted a suggestion made by President Eisenhower for creation of an Arab development agency, to which the President had already promised American aid.

By this time, however, the Iraqi government's intention to steer clear of absorption in the UAR and the popular character of the revolution had become clear. The revolution thus posed a formidable challenge to Nasser's Arab leadership and even to the existence of the UAR. For Baghdad offered Syria – no longer threatened by the Hashemis – the perspective of escaping Egyptian domination in a larger association of Arab states. In this context, the joint Arab resolution at the U.N. marked the beginning of a UAR effort to 'contain' the Iraq revolution and a shift in UAR policy towards conciliation with the Saudi monarchy and the surviving Hashemi dynasty in Jordan.[3] But Nasser's effort to build an anti-Iraq front was never wholly successful since the two monarchies, however sympathetic to his anti-communist crusade, ultimately saw in Iraq's independence *vis-à-vis* the UAR a guarantee of their own.

Aware that Syrians found appealing the liberal and democratic Arabism then expounded by Baghdad, President Nasser quickly strengthened his hold on Syria. A government reorganization made the Syrian Executive Council directly dependent on the Central Government; Akram Hourani, head of the council, was removed; six additional Syrians were named to unimportant ministries in the Central Government. Hourani, now Central Minister of Justice, had to reside in Cairo and was thus removed from the Syrian political scene. Of twenty-five Syrian newspapers, nineteen were closed down. Egyptian censors moved into every newspaper office.

Anti-Communist Crusade

Towards the end of November, the Syrian Communist Party issued a manifesto calling for 'democratization' of the union. Iraq, where the Communist Party was influential, had already started attacking Egyptian rule in Syria. Discovering a 'communist menace' in Iraq, Cairo presented itself as 'the bulwark against communism' in the Middle East and moved closer to Washington. On 22 December, Nasser's spokesman, Hassaneen Haykal, wrote in *Al-Ahram* that, although the communists 'had fought alongside the nationalists in violent struggles against imperialism, imperialist agents, and feudalists, this struggle is now finished or about to finish'. The next day at Port Said, President Nasser made a violent attack on Arab communists, and Syrian communists in particular, as enemies of Arab nationalism and Arab unity. On New Year's eve, mass arrests of communists in both regions began. These arrests started a police rule; ultimately all who in any way opposed the regime were to become victims.

The Mosul Revolt

Preparations to overthrow Abdel Kerim Qasim's government in Baghdad were soon under way. The Syrian and Iraqi Ba'th originally inspired the Mosul revolt. The Ba'th aim was to bring Iraq into the UAR so that Syria and Iraq together could stand up to Nasser and put the Ba'th on an equal footing with the UAR President. Though the conspiracy was largely a Syrian operation organized by Sarraj and the Ba'th, Nasser was persuaded to support it. Mosul became the site of the revolt largely because of its rail connections to Syria and because the Mosul plain is the home of the Shammar tribes which move freely back and forth across the Syro-Iraq frontiers. Iraqi officers maintained contacts with Sarraj's agents in Damascus and Beirut. A Syrian officer, Colonel Haydar Kuzbari, was assigned to assist the Syrian military commander of the Jazira, Colonel Amine Al-Hafez (future President of Syria), in arming and organizing the Shammar tribes. Truckloads of arms came from Syria to Ba'th and Nasserist para-military organizations in northern Iraq. Sarraj's agents established a broadcasting unit in the Syrian village of Kharabo not far from Mosul. From here the proclamation of Iraqi Colonel Shawaf, nominal leader of the revolt, was broadcast.

The Mosul revolt was crushed less by Qasim's government and the regular army than by Kurdish peasants, Arab workers of Mosul, and rank-and-file soldiers who turned their guns against rebel officers. Failure of the Ba'th-Nasserist *coup* and the revelation that most of the Iraqi people were not beguiled by Cairo's unity appeals ended the Syrian dream of becoming part of an Arab commonwealth. Instead of attaining equal status with Egypt and other Arab countries in a larger state, Syria remained subjected to its dominant partner within the UAR's restricted borders.

The belief that unity would lead to the liberation of Palestine also evaporated as the Palestine question once more became a pawn in the virulent inter-Arab conflicts that reached a new intensity after the abortive Mosul revolt. Nasser, Qasim, and Husain each claimed to speak for Palestine and each tried to use the Palestine question to his own ends. To undermine Nasser's claim to Arab leadership, Qasim proposed to create a Palestine Republic and a Palestine Legion. Claiming that a liberated Palestine belonged in the UAR, Nasser organized Palestinians in Gaza and Syria into a Palestine National Union. Husain asserted his exclusive sovereignty over Palestine. By 1960, UAR-Jordanian cold war hostilities developed to the point of assassination and sabotage. (Jordanian personalities, including Premier Majali, were murdered by Sarraj's agents. Jordanian agents committed acts of sabotage in Syria and attempted to subvert Syrian army officers.)

When Arab governments failed to take a strong stand against the Hammarskjold plan to settle the Palestine refugees outside Palestine, though annual U.N. resolutions had asserted their right to repatriation, popular suspicions were aroused. Cairo's reaction to the Hammarskjold plan was sufficiently equivocal to make credible Iraq's charges that the UAR endorsed the plan.

When Israel's work on its diversion of Jordan waters to the Negev also failed to evoke a strong response, the image of the UAR as a powerful bloc in the face of Israel was further eroded. An inter-Arab technical committee was set up to make a plan for Arab use of the Jordan waters, but President Nasser refused to take any other action against Israel, despite the urgings of Ba'th leaders. His stand was a major factor in the split between the UAR President and Hourani that came into the open at the end of 1959.

NASSER-BA'TH CONFLICT

The rift between Nasser and the Ba'th began early in the union when he rejected a Ba'th proposal that the UAR be ruled by a secret committee of three Egyptians and the three Ba'th leaders, Aflak,

Bitar, and Hourani. Nasser found irritating the Ba'th claim that it had supplied him with 'a philosophy and an ideology' and its stubborn obstruction of his endeavours to organize the Syrian National Union, the government-controlled political organization called for in the constitution. After the Mosul revolt's failure, Nasser decided to deal with the Ba'th and organize the National Union at one stroke. The National Union was to be a single party of all the people (excluding communists and opponents of Arab nationalism). Its aim would be to create 'a co-operative, democratic, socialist society free of any political, social, or economic exploitation'. A manifesto revealing growing Syrian discontent over the Egyptianization of Syria was issued by General Bizri in Beirut on 10 May 1959. This may have contributed to Nasser's decision to hold elections for the National Union without further delay. He scheduled for July elections for the National Union committees of the villages and city quarters, the first stage of a five-stage indirect election procedure for a National Union Assembly. These committees would later elect District Committees; the District Committees, in turn, would elect Governate Committees; and the Governate Committees, a General Congress. From the General Congress the President would then name the members of the National Union Assembly or Council of the Nation, half of whom would be former deputies in the Syrian and Egyptian parliaments. All candidates in these 'elections' were required to have the approval of a committee appointed by the President and, if rejected, had no right of appeal.

The wide revulsion against the Ba'th leadership in Syria caused Nasser to allow the elections in Syria a measure of freedom that similar elections in Egypt did not have, in order to let Syrians themselves put the Ba'th in its place. Mahmoud Riad, Nasser's personal adviser on Syrian affairs, met with old-line political figures and businessmen and gave these groups enough latitude to reform their ranks, organize anti-Ba'th coalitions, and even hold anti-Ba'th demonstrations. When the Ba'th realized what was happening, it withdrew its candidates in many districts and won only 250 seats out of 9,445.

Thrown into disarray, the party began to fragment. Its fourth National Congress, held in Beirut in August 1959, fiercely debated – and many condemned – the national leadership's 1958 decision to liquidate the Syrian party. Many Syrian members accepted only reluctantly the congress's ultimate affirmation of this decision. Some began on their own to try to rebuild the party in Syria wholly apart from the national leadership. Others quit the party to work independently. A major split occurred after the congress with the expulsion of an extreme pro-Nasserist faction which advocated total dissolution of the Ba'th in favour of Nasserism. A conflict pitting Aflak and Bitar against Hourani had already developed. Hourani made several attempts to persuade Nasser to change his policy and proposed that a federation replace the centralized unity. Nasser's answer was to appoint Abdel Hakim Amr his representative in Syria with supreme legislative and executive powers. Convinced that Nasser would never relinquish Egyptian domination, Hourani from this time began to boycott government meetings.

The Amr Mission

On his arrival in Damascus, Amr established a Bureau of Grievances to allow ordinary citizens to voice their complaints, and thousands did. He made concessions to landlords and businessmen, and tried to stimulate the stagnant economy. At the same time, he tightened police controls. Within two months the Ba'th ministers in the Central Government resigned. Clashes between Ba'thists and Nasserists occurred at Damascus University. Sarraj, moving away from the Ba'th as his power grew, became Amr's right-hand man and head of the National Union in Syria. Resignation from the Central Government in early 1960 of three independent Syrian progressives showed that the departure of the Ba'th had not resolved Egyptian-Syrian differences. The National Union structure, however, was completed. In July, when the General Congress of both regions met in Cairo, Nasser appointed from its ranks the members of the Council of the Nation: 400 Egyptians and 200 Syrians, of whom 46 were former deputies in the Syrian parliament. Syrian National Union members were in the main careerists drawn from various political trends. The National Union had no other function than to regiment public opinion on behalf of the regime. The Council of the Nation was not consulted about legislation or even asked to approve it.

Another government reshuffle in September 1960 again enhanced the power of Sarraj, who became President of the Syrian Executive Council and Minister of State as well as Minister of the Interior. He soon replaced Amr as Nasser's pro-consul in Damascus. His appointment constituted an admission that Syria could be controlled only by the police. The sources of Syrian discontent were many. For Egyptian rule—a combination of reforms, Egyptianization and colonization, and destruction of civil liberties—eventually alienated nearly everyone.

REFORMS

Agrarian Reform

The Agrarian Reform and Agricultural Relations Laws—enacted

in September 1958 after the imminence of land reform had been announced in Iraq – constituted the most important reforms made by the UAR regime in Syria. They were carried out in the context of a severe three-year drought which reduced cereals production to less than half the 1957 level and agricultural income to 60 per cent of that of 1957. Pastures and water-holes dried up. Sheep, goats, and cattle died of hunger or thirst. The government did little to help the poor peasants who bore the brunt of the catastrophe. Peasants complained of the corruption and incompetence of officials who delivered seeds too late for planting and fodder after animals had died of hunger. Near-famine conditions drove tens of thousands of peasants to seek food and work in the cities or in the Lebanon, but cities had little work to offer and bread was short everywhere.

In these circumstances the reforms did little to ease the lot of the peasants. The Agricultural Relations Law, prepared earlier by the Ba'th, for the first time regulated working conditions of sharecroppers and agricultural labourers, setting limits to the landlord's share of the crop according to the nature of the land, and allowing modifications according to the kind of crop and the supplies furnished by the tenant. The law required written leases, limited the landlord's right to cancellation, prohibited life contracts (the basis of serfdom), and granted agricultural workers the right to form unions. The law also emphasized the duties of workers and tenants and prohibited strikes. In general, the Ba'th-controlled Ministry of Labour and Social Affairs made a genuine attempt to enforce the law, but President Nasser would not permit the formation of agricultural workers' unions. Moreover, landlords were able to profit from certain loopholes in the law to evict tenants. In spite of the law, verbal contracts remained common.

The land reform law was modelled on the Egyptian law and hence was not suited to Syrian conditions, since Syria's agriculture is extensive and Egypt's intensive. Only two categories of land were recognized: irrigated and non-irrigated. But there are great differences in the value of land irrigated by pump and by flow, between pasture and fertile land, between land in zones of maximum rainfall and that which gets almost no rain at all. Failure to take these differences into account made for great inequities. The maximum landholding was set at 80 hectares of irrigated land and 300 of non-irrigated. But each landlord was allowed an additional 10 irrigated hectares and 40 non-irrigated for each dependent up to a total of 120 irrigated hectares and 460 non-irrigated. Syrian landowners claimed such holdings yielded about a quarter of the income produced by the maximum landholding in Egypt. A maximum of 8 hectares of irrigated land and 30 of non-irrigated was allotted to beneficiaries. In much of the non-irrigated land a plot this size is not sufficient to allow the peasant to be self-supporting.

Some 3,240 landlords or 0·6 per cent of the rural population were found to own and use roughly 35 per cent of all the cultivated land. The reform would strip them of 1·3 million hectares–about 17–18 per cent of the total cultivated area. During the three years between the enactment of the law and Syria's breakaway from the UAR, nearly two-thirds of the land subject to expropriation was provisionally expropriated. But only 63,000 hectares–less than 5 per cent of the land subject to the reform and less than one per cent of the total cultivated area–was distributed. This to fewer than 5,000 peasant families.[4]

The execution of the reform was dilatory, especially after Field Marshal Amr's assumption of supreme authority. Amr assured landlords he would end abuses. As a further gesture, the government agreed to take over payment of debts owed by landlords subject to the reform. The delay in carrying out the reform brought about a prolonged period of uncertainty during which landowners stopped investing in the land, often ceased providing agricultural credits, or even abandoned the land for fear of nationalization of capital equipment. As a result, production was reduced and the land was further impoverished.

Compulsory membership in co-operatives for beneficiaries and small owners ran up against the highly individualistic character of the Syrian peasant, who had no tradition of agricultural co-operation. The government, short of experts, resources, and technical equipment, could establish only a limited number of co-operatives. These were placed under the National Union. Many existed only on paper, since co-operatives were declared established before the land was distributed. Sometimes 'co-operation' consisted in no more than allotting the village mukhtar (headman), a National Union member, a sum of money to be used for loans to peasants in his village. Peasants complained that the money often remained in his pocket or was diverted to other purposes. Loans advanced by the government were guaranteed by the crop. Peasants said that when the harvest season arrived, the government took all the crop, even though only a part was owed, put it in store, and told them to wait 'until we sell the crop'. At the end of 1962, some villages were still waiting for payment for crops taken by the government in 1960 and 1961.

On the other hand, some model co-operatives operated efficiently and brought substantial benefits to their members. These fortunate peasants became ardent partisans of President Nasser and the union. The land reform, although only minimally applied, contributed to creating a pro-Nasserist movement among peasants of the Euphrates and Hawran plains. These Sunni peasants were also influenced in this direction by a number of army officers from these regions who became Nasserists.

The land reform proved to be an essential first step in breaking the political power of the landlords. Practically, it too often meant distribution of non-irrigated land, much of it of poor quality, to poor peasants lacking the resources to cultivate it properly. They could not look to the government for the necessary assistance, since the government also lacked the necessary skills, money, and equipment. The peasant who got the land had to pay for it in forty annual instalments at 1·5 per cent interest. Only after the entire sum was paid, that is only after forty years, would he get title deed to the land and be able to register it at the Land Office. The beneficiary therefore had little sense of ownership and security. Experience showed that the new owners could not pay the instalments due and could not find the resources to cultivate the land. Many therefore turned it back to the former owner for a modest rental and returned to share-cropping.

An intensive government programme of irrigation and land reclamation was needed to permit distribution of irrigated land to the landless. Such a programme was under way in the Ghab. The USSR had assumed responsibility for preliminary economic and technical studies for the Euphrates dam project in the 1957 Syrian-Soviet aid agreement; Moscow handed over a 12-volume report in 1960. Since Cairo-Moscow relations were then strained, Cairo sought and secured in 1961, not Soviet but West German aid to build the dam. The break-up of the UAR soon after upset this plan. The Syrians, in any case, feared that Cairo planned to settle Egyptian fellahin in Syria's north-east. Such plans had been discussed since the beginning of the union. In March 1958 the influential Misr Bank *Bulletin* insisted that agriculture must remain Syria's principal vocation and that farmers from the Southern Region must emigrate to the Northern to alleviate population pressure in Egypt and assure full land exploitation in Syria. But at the time of the rupture of the union nothing concrete had yet been done in this direction.

Development Planning

A real effort to carry out a development plan under state direction also marked an advance for Syria, since the Suez crisis had side-tracked earlier development programmes. Syrian economists originally drafted the First Comprehensive Five-Year Plan 1960–65. The Egyptian contribution was to raise planned investment by 36 per cent. This decision was taken although less than half the development projects authorized in 1959, and less than a third of those authorized in 1960, were actually executed. This level of spending proved to be beyond Syria's financial and, above all, its technical resources. (Over the full plan period the public sector invested less than half of the amounts projected.) Costs turned out to be greatly underestimated. In the first year, the public sector fulfilled only about three-fourths of planned investment while the private sector overfulfilled its goals, especially in industrial investment. Some capitalists explained the upsurge in industrial investment by their determination to frustrate 'Egyptian efforts to sabotage Syria's industrial development'. Under the plan, surveys for iron-ore and oil were undertaken. A number of industrial enterprises were established. The USSR agreed to begin construction of the Latakia-Qamishli railroad, and work progressed on several irrigation and reclamation projects in addition to the Ghab. But the public was more conscious of the inflationary pressures to which the development programme contributed than of the long-term benefits it would bring.

The 'Socialist Decrees'

President Nasser's July 1961 'socialist decrees' as applied to Syria fully nationalized banks, insurance companies, and three industrial firms, and partially nationalized twenty-four other industrial companies. They imposed a progressive income tax, placed ceilings on compensation to be paid company presidents and directors, and allotted workers a 25 per cent share in company profits and representation on company boards. The period between the issuance of these decrees and the break-up of the union was too short to permit most of the decrees to be applied. The nationalizations, which were carried out, had a somewhat different significance in Syria than did similar measures in Egypt, where they affected many capitalists of foreign origin. In Syria, about 17,000 people held shares in these firms which belonged to indigenous capitalists.

The long-term significance of the 'socialist decrees' was to establish a precedent for government social action. The short-term effects of nationalization proved negative. Production in the affected industries declined. Production costs soared. Junior army officers named as managers and directors often had no idea how to carry on. Business confidence inevitably ebbed. Disinvestment accelerated. Syrian entrepreneurs withdrew from thirty-three development projects which would have given employment to 20,000 workers. Large stocks of unsold goods accumulated.

The Ba'th, although publicly welcoming these measures, criticized them within the confines of the party as a stratagem devised both to pacify mounting popular discontent and to strengthen the bureaucracy.[5] Many Syrians shared this view. Workers employed in the nationalized and partially nationalized firms numbered at most 15,000[6] out of nearly 150,000 employed in manufacturing. Roughly 10 per cent of industrial workers[7] were affected by the provisions giving workers in joint stock companies representation on company boards and a 25 per cent share in profits. Only 10 per cent of company profits went directly to workers, the other 15 per cent being paid into social security funds. The decrees were far from being unanimously welcomed by workers. Some feared that profit-sharing, uncertain in its application, would replace the traditional bonus (13 months wages for 12 months work). Many suspected the decrees were designed to block their demands for trade union liberties, wage increases, and better working conditions. For the experience of workers under the UAR regime had not been a happy one.

THE LABOUR MOVEMENT: REFORM OR REPRESSION?

The UAR regime aimed to integrate the Syrian labour movement into the National Union and so make it, like the Egyptian trade union movement, an arm of the government. The Ba'th, controlling the Ministry of Labour and Social Affairs, set out to establish Ba'th dominance over the unions. The ministry waged systematic war against unions not under Ba'th control, interfered directly in trade union elections, and sometimes organized elections for the sole purpose of ousting the elected leadership; if necessary, candidates were disqualified arbitrarily. In the September 1958 elections for the General Federation's Executive Committee, contested by the Ba'th and an independent list, the Ba'th list won by the margin of 24 votes because the Labour Ministry barred thirty-six non-Ba'th unions from voting.

The other side of this policy was a campaign to organize the unorganized. This was especially successful among government employees. By the end of 1960 trade unions claimed nearly 62,000 members. Two labour federations in which communists had had some influence were eliminated. A single General Federation was established, although not all unions adhered to it. This federation and the Egyptian General Federation were affiliated to the pan-Arab Confederation, the ICATU.

Two weeks after the creation of the UAR, the right to strike was, in practice, cancelled. Workers also complained that guarantees against dismissal without just cause began to be ignored. The UAR Labour Code of April 1959—Law 91—drew in general upon the most advanced Egyptian and Syrian labour legislation. Yet for Syria it was in certain important respects a step backward. The new code established a much closer government control over both unions and workers than had the Syrian Labour Code. It denied the right to strike and introduced the Egyptian system of fines for a wide range of breaches of discipline defined by employers, a system hitherto virtually unknown in Syria. Minimum wages, formerly fixed by regional committees whose trade union members really represented the workers, were now fixed by the government, the committees having only a consultative status and for the most part remaining inactive. Even compensation and sick-pay benefits were not as favourable to workers as under the Syrian legislation.[8] The new law, however, was more effectively enforced than the old. The Social Insurance Code – Law 92 – introduced to complement the Labour Code, did institute obligatory insurance against work accidents and diseases, guaranteeing that compensation would actually be paid.

Restructuring the trade unions under Law 91 and integration of the labour movement into the National Union provoked great protest and resentment. Since all candidates for union office had to have National Union approval, the regime was able to staff unions with its own agents. In January 1960, representatives of more than 300 unions held a conference in Damascus to petition President Nasser for restoration of trade union rights. They demanded the right to strike, an end to unwarranted dismissals, amendment of the Labour Code, liquidation of National Union control, and a 10 per cent increase in the minimum wage, because wages had declined at least that much in 1959. Many of these union leaders were arrested. The Executive Committee of the General Federation, which had been handpicked by the Ba'th in September 1958, resigned in protest. This action reflected both the pressure of workers from below and the fact that the Ba'th's co-operation with the Nasser regime had drawn to a close.

Field Marshal Amr then installed a new union leadership and integrated the unions more closely into the National Union. Trade union leaders now occupied themselves mainly with National Union, Arab, and international affairs; they frequently travelled abroad. Workers, however, suffered from rising prices (which cut purchasing power by at least 20 per cent in the nearly four years of the UAR regime[9]) and from mounting unemployment caused by industry's inability to move its stocks, a drastic decline in foreign trade, and peasant migration from the drought-stricken countryside. Abandoned by government-appointed trade union leaders, workers still sometimes tried to enforce their demands by one- or two-hour work stoppages.

In the circumstances, the 'socialist decrees' of July 1961 could not greatly alleviate widespread and bitter labour discontent. But some workers did welcome the decrees as heralding a socialist era.

EGYPTIANIZATION AND COLONIZATION

The idea that Syria should serve as an agricultural hinterland and market for Egyptian industry pervaded Egyptian business circles and the economic authorities of the Nasser regime, although President Nasser himself disclaimed this view. Syria's traditionally liberal economy and Egypt's far more developed centralized economy were competitive rather than complementary. Economic policies imposed by Egypt had a disrupting effect in Syria, especially since Egyptian big business, one of the main promoters of the union, remained until almost its end free to exploit the weaker partner and did so.

Syria's economic system depended in significant measure on its economic relations with neighbours, for whose needs its simple manufactured production is well suited. Cairo's cold wars against Iraq, Jordan, and other Arab countries artificially restricted these relations. As a result, Syria's official exports to Iraq had by 1960 been reduced to 90 per cent below the level of 1956. In the first half of 1961, Syrian exports to Iraq, Jordan, Saudi Arabia, and Kuwait were 52 per cent below the comparable period in 1956 and its imports from these countries 74 per cent lower.[10] Yet Syria did not wholly lose its Arab vocation. A significant expansion in contraband export of manufactured goods to neighbouring countries compensated for a part of the fall in official exports. Contraband trade, however, also became a road for the flight of Syrian capital abroad and in this way worked to the detriment of the economy.

Trade with Egypt, feeble before the union, increased substantially, but took on a colonialist aspect and Syria's trade surplus with Egypt declined. Raw materials for industry made up the bulk of expanded exports to Egypt, while Egyptian exports to Syria consisted mainly of industrial products, especially textiles. A study of Egyptian-Syrian trade prospects made in early 1961 by the UAR Planning Ministry concluded that more than 80 per cent of Syria's exports to Egypt would consist of foodstuffs and raw materials, while industrial products would make up more than 75 per cent of Egypt's exports to Syria.

UAR regulations opened the Syrian market to Egyptian goods while putting obstacles in the way of Syrian penetration into the Egyptian market. Egyptian goods entered Syria tax-free and customs-free, but a 7 per cent tax and a 1·5 per cent tariff levy were imposed on Syrian goods entering Egypt. Syrian products sold in Egypt were required to pay all taxes and levies imposed on similar Egyptian-made goods, but Egypt did not pay Syrian taxes on Egyptian goods sold in Syria. Syria, moreover, was required to import certain goods – carburants, sugar, iron and steel, certain chemicals, fine yarns – only from or through Egypt. Egypt thus secured a controlled market and collected import duties, commissions, and price mark-ups on goods destined for Syria. Sometimes Egypt was unable to supply goods needed for Syrian industry. By the end of 1960, for example, it had furnished only one-fourth of the iron sheets and bars it had contracted to deliver, and at higher prices than provided in the original agreement. Such delays compelled a slow-down in Syrian construction and other projects.

Restrictions on Syria's direct trade with the Soviet bloc reduced the share of these countries in Syrian exports. A number of trade accords with other countries concluded in the name of the UAR did not allow for Syrian participation. Khalil Kallas, Syrian Minister of Economy during the first two years of the union, charged that Syria was compelled to sell its cotton to France and West Germany under an arrangement whereby the Egyptian Cotton Commission bought Syrian cotton with Egyptian currency and sold it to western Europe for hard. Syrian cotton in this way earned hard currency for the Egyptian Treasury.

Overcharges paid by Syria on goods imported from or through Egypt fed Egypt's export subsidy fund which, among other things, enabled Egypt to dump in Syria products competitive with Syrian production. Since Syria did not produce finer grades of cotton yarn in sufficient quantity to meet its own needs, it was required to buy Egyptian yarn which was priced above the world market level. With the cost of production of its textiles thus increased, Syria had to meet subsidized Egyptian competition both at home and in other Arab markets when these were not closed to it by Cairo-imposed political restrictions. As a result, many textile companies were reduced to operating at much below capacity, while the annual reports of Egyptian textile firms revealed they had disposed of large surplus stocks in Syria. But some Syrian industries not competitive with Egyptian – especially specialized industries like brocades, gold thread, certain types of curtains, and furniture covers – found a new market in Egypt and flourished. And, according to President Nasser, Syrian merchants and businessmen flocked to Cairo and Alexandria where they established many shops and enterprises.

Salaries paid to Egyptian experts, expenditures on secret police and security forces (external and internal security accounted for 58 per cent of budget expenditures in 1958), the cost of such operations as the Mosul revolt – all ate into Syria's monetary reserves. Certain Egyptian practices drained foreign exchange reserves already much diminished by reduced export earnings caused by the drought. Large quantities of Egyptian banknotes were brought from abroad to be exchanged in Damascus against hard currency. (In return, Syrians created a black market in the Egyptian pound in Egypt.) Each Egyptian visitor to Syria could bring with him £E50 to be exchanged for the freely convertible Syrian pound at a rate of £S9–10 to the Egyptian pound rather than the £S6–7 market rate. Nearly every week boatloads of Egyptians arrived in Latakia to buy medicines, perfumes, nylons, frigidaires, and other imported products for which Syria paid in hard currency and Egyptians in soft. Shortage of foreign exchange hampered industrial production, public works, and building construction since necessary materials could not be purchased abroad.

Egyptian banks, especially the then privately owned Misr Bank and the semi-private Cairo Bank, were permitted to work in Syria although Syrian banks could not work in Egypt. The Misr Bank opened eleven branches in Syria, extending its activities especially in the Jazira where it lent money to big capitalists who, in turn, lent to small farmers at high interest rates. Egyptian banks invested no capital in Syria but attempted to establish domination by using Syrian capital. A Cairo decree ordering Syrian public administrations to place their deposits in the Misr Bank put nearly £S30 million at its disposal. The bank financed a good part of the Syrian cotton crop and established a company to handle Syrian cotton exports.

Ordinary budget expenditures soared, owing in part to a big increase in the number of government functionaries. Public expenditures almost doubled between 1957 and 1961. Budget deficits accumulated. The government resorted to the Central Bank to cover not only investment but also current expenditures. In the three years 1957–60, *per capita* national income in constant prices declined by more than 22 per cent, while exports fell by more than 25 per cent and imports increased by almost 25 per cent.[11] Inflation eroded the purchasing power of the currency.

Early in 1961 Cairo imposed exchange control in Syria, abrogating all monetary laws on which Syria's monetary regime was based. This measure, devised to halt the flight of capital and steady the Syrian pound, was taken without consulting the Syrian financial authorities. It foreshadowed the unification of the Syrian and Egyptian currencies and the further economic subordination of Syria to Egypt. The flight of capital abroad was accelerated. Many capitalists left Syria to invest in other Arab countries and Africa. Arab capital also departed. Syrian economists maintained that, far from conserving foreign exchange, exchange control deprived Syria of foreign exchange which had been flowing through free market facilities and which to some extent had relieved pressures on the Central Bank.

1 The Barada in Damascus (1843). On the right the famous
   Al Tekkieh mosque built by Suleiman the Magnificent in 1555

2 Isle of Arwad, Tartus in the distance (1843)

3 Faisal leaving the Hotel Victoria in Damascus, 3 October 1918, after learning from General Allenby that the Arab administration would cover only internal Syria east of the Anti-Lebanon

5 Aleppo citizens gathering to greet Faisal, October 1918

4 Faisal's troops in Damascus, October 1918

6 General Georges Catroux, Délégué-Général of the Free French, broadcasting on 1 October 1941 a few days after the proclamation of Syrian 'independence'. On his left, wearing sash, a longtime servant of French interests, Shaikh Taj Al-Din Al-Hasani, newly appointed by Catroux President of Syria

7 Distribution of cereals to Kurds who can afford to pay in April 1943. Here they are getting receipts for their money

8 Shukri Quwatly, President of Syria 1943–49 and 1955–58, here
greets Druze leaders

9 Khalid Al-Azm   10 Akram Hourani

11 Dr Yusef Z'ayyen

12 Nur Al-Din Atassi

13 People's Army on parade in Damascus

14 The four leaders of the then projected Federation of Arab
Republics at the tomb of President Nasser, 1971. *From left to right*:
Presidents Hafez Assad (Syria) and Jafaar Numeiri (Sudan),
Colonel Mo'ammer Qadafi (Libya), and President Anwar Sadat
(Egypt)

15 Israeli transport lorries advancing through south-west Syria
during the June 1967 War

16 Syrian soldier killed defending his post in the Golan, June 1967

17 Syrians driven from the Qunaytra region by the Israelis after the 1967 War

18 One of four UNRWA emergency camps established after the June 1967 War for Palestinian refugees expelled—along with more than 100,000 Syrians—from the Qunaytra region by the Israelis

19 The Eighth of March State Farm established in 1967 in the
Damascus Ghouta

20 Demonstration in Damascus in autumn 1969 against the Lebanese government's attempts to restrict the activities of Palestinian commandos in Lebanon

21 Aleppo merchants at a café near the Citadel

22 Syrian women learn to read and write in classes conducted by the General Women's Federation

23 A courtyard near the great covered *suq* of Aleppo

24 The Citadel of Aleppo, dating back into antiquity, was recon-
structed by Nur al Din in the twelfth century

25 The famous Hamidiyaa *suq* in Damascus

28 (*Above*) Old waterwheels in Hama

26 (*Left*) A new quarter of present-day Damascus

27 The port city of Latakia

29 Palmyra: The Arch of Triumph

30 The Euphrates at Deir Ezzor

In March 1961, a State Economic Organization was created over the protests of all Syria's economic and financial authorities. Arabization of all Syrian banks gave the Economic Organization, which was partly owned by Egyptian banks, a 35 per cent interest in every Syrian bank. Since the Economic Organization was authorized to buy into any Syrian industrial or commercial firm, Syrian businessmen feared their enterprises would be both Egyptianized and, as the Misr Bank had been nationalized in 1960, also partially nationalized.

'Decentralization'

The 'socialist decrees' enacted a few months later provoked both a class and a national opposition in Syria, since many Syrians regarded them as a further step in Egyptianization. These decrees were a major factor in precipitating the break-up of the union. Another was President Nasser's decision in August to complete Syria's annexation to Egypt. He abolished the Syrian and Egyptian Local Governments to create only one UAR government for the two regions and decreed that the 'decentralization' or local government law, which had been applied in Egypt in 1960, should be imposed in Syria without further delay. This law divided Syria into a number of Governates, each directly linked to the Cairo government but without links to each other. Each Governate would have its own Governor, appointed by the UAR President, its own capital, budget, taxes, and council. The council, partly elected and partly appointed, would be controlled by the National Union and linked through a pyramid structure to the Presidency or Vice-Presidency in Cairo. Having experienced similar divide and rule tactics under the French, Syrians were not unaware that the law's real purpose was to divide Syria 'in order to provincialize it in a definitive manner'.[12]

On the eve of government unification, President Nasser removed Sarraj from Syria and from control of the Syrian intelligence machinery by naming him a Vice-President of the UAR, and he sent Field Marshal Amr back to Damascus. Sarraj resigned in protest. The power conflict between Sarraj and Amr and the resulting disarray in the intelligence services (from which many of Sarraj's men were purged) created the opportunity for Syrian officers to act. For conflict between the Syrian and Egyptian military bureaucracies had become acute.

THE ROLE OF THE ARMY

In making the union Syrian officers had reluctantly agreed to withdraw from politics, but they had not foreseen the extent to which the army would be brought under Egyptian control. Beginning in

March 1958, the Egyptians purged first the communists, then progressives, later Hauranists, then 'Aflaks', and finally any who opposed Egyptianization. Even seventy-five Palestinian officers given commissions in the Syrian army after the Palestine war as a first step towards training a Palestine army were purged; the Egyptians considered them 'Bizri's men' because Bizri had removed certain discriminations to which they had been subjected. Communists were ousted and later imprisoned. Ba'th partisans were usually posted to the diplomatic service or transferred to Egypt. The purges involved some of Syria's most qualified officers.

A number of Ba'th officers stationed in Egypt reacted to the sharpening conflict between the Ba'th and Nasser in 1959 by forming a secret organization, later known as the Military Committee, to await the moment to rectify the situation. They did not tell even the Ba'th Party leadership about their organization. Their leaders were three Alawi officers – Salah Jadid, Hafez Assad, Muhammad Umran – and a Druze, Hamad Ubayd.

In an effort to keep retired officers quiet the UAR regime raised pensions to the point that their payment became a burden on the state budget. Altogether during the union, 4,800 commissioned and non-commissioned officers were ousted or transferred; the Syrian officer corps was reduced by half. Some 2,300 Egyptian officers came to Syria, where even the lowliest received, in addition to his basic pay, a monthly salary of at least £S800 paid by the Syrian Treasury.[13]

The Egyptians abolished Syria's system of military conscription, dismantled the Syrian Air Force, and transferred the Military Academy and Air Force College to Egypt, admitting thereafter only a token sprinkling of Syrians. Young and inexperienced Egyptian junior officers were put in charge of Syrian units. Syrian officers later said that Egyptian officers 'came to us in the spirit of secret police officers', their main mission being to spy on their Syrian colleagues. They also charged that many Egyptian officers had secret radio transmitters and communicated directly with Cairo, and that some had large bank accounts in Damascus to be used for corruption. According to official charges made at the 1962 Chtoura Conference – indirectly confirmed some years later with the arrest of a number of officers in Field Marshal Amr's entourage – high Egyptian military representatives in Syria engaged in hashish smuggling through the military mail. Many Egyptian officers, as well as civilian officials, were involved in illegal commercial operations. The morale of the Syrian army suffered, as did standards of personal conduct and professional performance. Frequent political purges affected the soldiers' attitude to their officers. Discipline lapsed. Clashes occurred between Egyptian and Syrian soldiers in which a number were killed.

POLICE STATE

The junta of Syrian officers that took control of Damascus in the early morning of 28 September 1961 acted without reference to the people. However, the union was already doomed by the wide popular revulsion against the UAR's police dictatorship with its suffocation of freedom of expression and its destruction of civil liberties. No less than four secret police networks operated in Syria. The ordinary citizen walked in fear of a legion of secret agents. His mail was censored, his telephone tapped, his conversations reported, his goings and comings watched. Thousands were imprisoned for shorter or longer periods during the union. Some apparently were arrested for ransom. An undetermined number of political prisoners disappeared, some of whom were tortured to death. Secret police operations financed from the Syrian secret budget reached into every social group to establish what former President Quwatly called 'a regime of tyranny, domination, and repression' which operated by 'securing a minority, posing the majority as traitors, and putting into power fabricated organizations and individuals'.[14] Responsibility for this state of affairs was not only Egyptian. Three of the four intelligence networks were under Syrian direction; the other was attached to the President's Office in Cairo. Moreover, the Ba'th's Aflak-Bitar wing originally pushed its cadres to take posts in the intelligence services and to work with the secret police agencies.

President Nasser's popularity in Syria was eroded by the dictatorship. Yet to some degree he was sufficiently remote to escape blame for prevailing conditions, which were attributed to subordinates. For many Syrians he was still the hero of Suez and the only Arab statesman of international stature. His occasional tours of Syria drew big and apparently enthusiastic crowds. This phenomenon, however, could not conceal the fact that Syria's withdrawal from the union was for Syrians—in the words of the French writer Jean-Jacques Berreby[15] —'a true liberation like that of a fascist-occupied country'.

[1] *L'Orient* (Beirut), 25 March 1958.

[2] During the March-April 1963 Cairo Unity Talks, BBC *Summary of World Broadcasts*, 1963, Part IV, ME 1285.

[3] See Marcel Colombe: 'La Nouvelle politique arabe de la République arabe unie', *Orient*, 1959, 3me tri., No. 11.

[4] SAR Central Bureau of Statistics: *Statistical Abstract* 1968, p. 113.

[5] *Nidal Al-Ba'th*, Vol. IV, 247–8, Beirut, 1963.

[6] *EFSPA*, February 1962, No. 50, 40.

[7] Department of Labour, Ministry of Labour and Social Affairs, December 1962.

[8] Under the Syrian Code, for example, a dismissed worker received severance pay on the basis of one month's wages for each year of service. The UAR Code gave him a half-month's pay for each of the first five years and only then a full month's pay. Under the Syrian Code a worker was entitled to full pay during sick leave, while under the UAR Code he got only 70 per cent of his normal wage.

[9] Chafik Akhras: 'Force et faiblesse de la livre Syrienne', *EFSPA*, No. 56, August 1962.

[10] 'Perspectives économiques régionales', *EFSPA*, November 1961, No. 47.

[11] Adel Akel: 'Economic Stabilization in Syria', *EFSPA*, No. 47, November 1961.

[12] Marcel Colombe: 'Indépendance et tentatives de regroupement des pays arabes du moyen orient', *Revue Française de Science Politique*, Vol. X, No. 4, 1960.

[13] *Watha'iq Mou'tamar Shoutura* (Documents of the Chtoura Conference), Syrian Government Publishing House, Damascus, 1962.

[14] *Arab World*, 24 October 1961.

[15] 'L'Egypte et la Syrie après l'éclatement de la République Arabe Unie', *Politique Étrangère*, 1961, No. 5–6.

Chapter 8

The Bitter Harvest

THE AUTHORS OF THE 28 September 1961 *coup* declared they wanted Syrian autonomy within the UAR, not separation from it. But President Nasser refused to yield to this demand. Moreover, the process, once set in motion, acquired its own momentum and could not be stopped. Syrian *coup* leaders Lt-Col Abdel Kerim Nahlawi and Air Force Brigadier Mawafak Assassa negotiated at General Headquarters with Field Marshal Amr in the presence of the Commander of the First (Syrian) Army and the Syrian ministers of the UAR. Amr in principle accepted their demands which were concerned primarily with the grievances of Syrian officers but, awaiting Nasser's word, did not sign Communiqué 9 which announced the agreement.

Nasser, however, ordered the First Army to march on Damascus and, since Aleppo and Latakia had not yet rallied to the *coup*, sent a naval force to Latakia and 2,000 paratroopers to nearby Jebla to crush a rebellion he apparently believed was confined to Damascus. But no unit of the First Army obeyed his order. And, by the time Egyptian forces arrived, both Latakia and Aleppo had gone over to the insurgents. The 200 Egyptian paratroopers who actually landed promptly surrendered. Nasser then recalled his naval forces, announced he would never transform unity into a military operation, and accepted the *fait accompli*. He refused, however, to recognize Syria 'until the people have spoken in free elections' – and did not do so even after they had.

Cairo soon began to employ another kind of violence against Syria which it treated as a province in rebellion: a cold war of lies, rumours, incitements to revolt, strikes, and clashes, organized by the network of Egyptian agents left behind in the army, trade unions, and other groups. Money, agents, and arms were infiltrated from the Lebanon to feed this network and maintain constant pressure against the government. Cairo waged its cold war in the name of 'Arab socialism' and 'popular Arabism' against 'capitalists and reactionaries'. Its propaganda blamed the break-up of the UAR on a minority of 'feudalists and reactionaries' who acted 'against the will of the Syrian people' and simultaneously emphasized the 'revolutionary' character of Nasser's 'socialist doctrine'. This theme was devised to conceal the opposition of virtually all Syrians to the UAR's repressive rule and to divert attention from popular Syrian demands for restoration of democratic institutions, demands which could have an echo in Egypt itself. Cairo's cold war prevented re-examination of the priorities of pan-Arabism and compelled Syrians to exhaust their energies in self-defence instead of using them to put their own house in order.

Cairo's propaganda ignored the basic forces behind Syria's withdrawal from the UAR, but its claim that some of the officers involved had links to Jordan was well founded. Both Col Nahlawi and Lt-Col Haydar Kuzbari (a cousin of Ma'mun Kuzbari, a power in the Khumasiya Company) received help from Jordan and Saudi Arabia to facilitate the *coup*. Moreover, the elements brought to power by the *coup* were of the Right. This was hardly surprising since the UAR regime itself had strengthened the Right and had emasculated the democratic and progressive movements. Big landlords, if put on the defensive by the land reform, remained powerful. Wealthy capitalists had reinforced their position. During the union many capitalists sent their money out of the country, where they succumbed to the 'Lebanese disease', preferring speculative profits in foreign deals to investment at home. National capitalists involved in the independent economic development of the country had been undermined; in face of Cairo's cold war, they now had little confidence in Syria's future. Purges of nationalists, progressives, and leftists from the army, trade unions, schools, the civil service, press, and publishing had left the field clear for the Right and the careerists. The UAR's political organization, the National Union, brought to the fore political opportunists and even old-time collaborators with the French, while in the army Cairo had relied on old-line French-oriented officers.[1] The Muslim Brotherhood had expanded its following and influence (as its success in the December 1961 elections was to show). The trade unions remained in the control of Egyptian-picked leaders, some of whom were no more than agents of the *Mabaheth* (Egyptian Intelligence). Peasants were exhausted and heavily indebted after three years of poor harvests. Years of repression and thought-control had left their mark on the intelligentsia.

The Ba'th Party was disorganized and split. Akram Hourani's socialist wing supported Syria's withdrawal from the UAR. Hourani himself became the first Syrian politician to take a strong stand against President Nasser. From this time his faction became in effect a separate party, although the split was not formalized until May 1962. Confusion reigned in the Aflak-Bitar faction. Bitar joined with Hourani to sign a manifesto issued by eighteen politicians in support of the separation. Aflak refused to sign. When the Ba'th's National

Command attacked 'secession', Bitar repudiated his signature. Another group of Ba'thists, led by Sami Sufan, angered by Hourani's and Bitar's signature of the separation manifesto, quit the party to organize the pro-Nasser Socialist Unionist Movement. Ba'thists and former Ba'thists in the provinces, who had secretly tried to rebuild the party during the union, were in revolt against the authority of Aflak and the pan-Arab National Command. The Ba'th Military Committee in the army maintained its own independent and secretive organization. Some fifty Ba'th officers, including the Military Committee, returned from Egypt to support Syria's withdrawal from the UAR and co-operate with the ruling Nahlawi junta.[2] These officers turned against 'secession' only after Colonel Nahlawi, in a drive to clean the army of partisans of political parties, cashiered them. When they found they had gained nothing from the separation, they joined with Nasserist officers in attempts to overthrow the 'secessionist' government. Like the Ba'th provincials, the Ba'thist officers were primarily interested in Syria. If sincere about unity, they had no intention of subordinating their country once again to Egypt.

Decimated by persecution and by a large number of defections during the union, the communists were kept in jail until January 1962, and Khalid Bagdash was not allowed to return to Syria. Communists found their return to economic, political, and public life blocked. The Nasserists, although not strong in numbers, retained considerable influence due to the key positions they continued to occupy in the army, the security forces, the trade unions, and the government administration. For there was no systematic purge of Nasserist elements, although some were discharged from the army and police, and Sarraj and his collaborators were arrested. (In recognition of his anti-communist services Sarraj was later allowed to escape to Cairo.) Cairo's *Al-Akhbar* (28 March 1962) could boast six months after the September *coup*:

> In Syria today a strong machinery is working in favour of Egypt against the secessionist regime. Heading this machinery is a number of personalities who retain the sensitive and key positions they occupied during the union.

The union had weakened Syria's state structures, emasculated its political cadres, disrupted its economy, and shaken its self-confidence and morale. To overcome the wounds left by this experience required time and, above all, democratic liberties. Cairo's cold war denied the time. The new Syrian authorities were unwilling to concede the liberties.

POLITICAL CONTROLS

Within 24 hours of the beginning of the revolt, the Nahlawi junta proclaimed the end of the union and–to emphasize its dedication to Arabism–renamed Syria (formerly called the Syrian Republic) the Syrian Arab Republic. The officers then sought out the politicians to constitute a government. Their third choice,[3] Shishakli's onetime protégé Ma'mun Kuzbari, who had served as Secretary of the National Union in Damascus during the UAR regime, accepted. He formed a Cabinet of National and People's Party politicians, businessmen, and lawyers. This government, evoking no enthusiasm among the people, tried to win public confidence by promising to restore political liberties, freedom of the press and opinion, to abolish the emergency laws, and to extend the rights of workers and peasants.

The Nahlawi junta ostensibly withdrew from politics. But Nahlawi soon established a National Security Council–in which the Army Command as well as the President and five key ministers were members–to supervise the government. The junta's political and social policies closely resembled those of the UAR regime: strong police controls over the people combined with a number of social measures for the poorer classes. The junta quickly assured workers that their participation in profits and company management would be continued and peasants that the land reform would be maintained. Workers were granted half-pay for their previously unpaid Friday rest day and unpaid holidays. Peasants renting state and agrarian reform land were exempted from paying rent for the 1960–61 winter season; the Agricultural Bank declared a moratorium on debt payments. On the other hand, the junta retained the emergency laws, banned political parties, advocated the formation of a 'popular rally' (on the lines of the National Union) to support 'the principles of the Revolution', prohibited workers from engaging in political activity, denied freedom of the press and civil liberties, and refused to reinstate thousands who had been purged from their jobs by the UAR regime.

The democratic movement, although weakened and shackled, worked to restore civilian and democratic government. For a time it managed to advance step by step towards this goal–only to be defeated in the end by having to do battle on too many fronts at once.

THE DECEMBER 1961 ELECTIONS

A provisional constitution, published in mid-November, provided that an elected assembly should designate the President of the Republic for the next five years and should become a Constituent

Assembly for six months to draft a constitution. While awaiting a definitive constitution, the new Cabinet would exercise power according to the 1950 Constitution. Parliamentary elections, originally promised by the junta in four months, were rushed through in two before clear-cut political currents could develop and political groups could reconstitute themselves.

Many restrictions circumscribed the electoral campaign. Propaganda on radio and television was prohibited. Only 'sincere' criticism was permitted. Some seventy political personalities belonging to the former political parties were persuaded by the army junta to sign a Pact of National Union designed to eliminate all partisan conflict for the next four years; it called for non-alignment, decentralized Arab unity, and Arab socialism.[4] The election, held under the emergency laws and with political parties banned, proved something less than democratic. Progressives were too weak to field more than a few candidates. Yet the vote was not without significance. In face of a tremendous campaign by Cairo Radio to get Syrians to boycott it, the turnout was heavy, 50 to 60 per cent, higher than in any previous elections. Just over 97 per cent of the voters approved the new constitution, equivalent to approval of withdrawal from the UAR.

Khalid Al-Azm, a forceful advocate of full democratization and an opponent of the union from the beginning, won the highest number of votes. Salah Bitar was defeated along with all candidates of his faction of the Ba'th. Resentment over this failure and consequent exclusion from power played no small part in the decision of the Aflak-Bitar Ba'th to fight the 'secessionists' and to choose the road of conspiracy. On the other hand, Akram Hourani, the dissident Ba'th leader, swept to victory with his entire ticket and, with his allies, captured about 15 seats. The composition of the new assembly was much like that of the 1954 parliament. The People's Party, with 33 seats, constituted the single biggest grouping. The National Party won 21 seats, the Muslim Brotherhood ten, and Independents 62. The Right was clearly in the ascendant. Ma'mun Kuzbari was elected Speaker of the assembly by 114 votes to 47 for Jallal Sayyid, an index of the relative strength of the Right and its opponents. People's Party leaders Ma'ruf Dawalibi and Nazim Qudsi, both of whom had won respect by refusing to become involved in the National Union during the UAR regime, became premier and President of the Republic respectively.

ECONOMIC AND SOCIAL POLICIES

The elections touched off a spirited debate among students, businessmen, workers, politicians, and intellectuals over economic and social policy. A broad current of opinion held that private savings and the private entrepreneur still had an important role to play in Syria's undeveloped economy and that co-operation between public and private enterprise was essential to economic advance. The state should undertake social overhead projects – the Euphrates dam, oil and mineral exploitation, communications, public utilities, and basic industries – since private enterprise lacked the capital for such projects. Private enterprise should develop consumer and light industries and commerce since the state lacked the technical and administrative apparatus to handle industrial and commercial affairs as well as major development projects. Khalid Al-Azm, other important spokesmen for the business community, the Hourani socialists, and the communists all supported this view. The socialists and communists argued that strong social legislation and full freedom of trade union organization for workers and peasants were also essential.

On the other hand, landlords, the bigger capitalists, and the traditional Right maintained constant pressures to secure cancellation of the economic and social measures taken by the UAR regime. The Dawalibi government and, even more, the rightist majority in the assembly proceeded to weaken the most important of these measures. The assembly lifted ceilings on landownership so high as to reduce the amount of land subject to requisition by two-thirds and improved the terms of compensation to landlords. It denationalized all industries totally or partially nationalized in July 1961. An attempt by the government to maintain partial nationalization of the banks (which had been fully nationalized in 1961) was overridden by the assembly majority. It also insisted that foreign banks be authorized to hold a 25 per cent share in Syrian banks. This conflict caused the measure to be postponed. But the law requiring workers' representation on company boards and a 25 per cent share in profits was amended in a sense more favourable to workers. They were allotted the full 25 per cent share, whereas under the UAR regime they received only 10 per cent, the other 15 per cent going into social insurance funds; the law was made retroactive to 1 January 1961 so that shares could be paid sooner; the government paid the workers the profit share in advance so that payment would be assured.

Trade agreements restored Syria's traditional trade with its neighbours. Egypt's intensifying cold war spurred a dramatic *rapprochement* with Iraq. Iraqi military and economic delegations visited Syria. A meeting in mid-March 1962 between Iraq's Abdel Kerim Qasim and President Qudsi at Rutba on the Syrian-Iraq border suggested something close to a Syrian-Iraq alliance, the prevention of which has always been a primary objective of Egyptian policy. An Israeli attack in the demilitarized zone at this time provided an additional reason for Syria's turn to Iraq, since Egypt was then treating Syria as an enemy and, according to Damascus, refused to hand over Syrian military equipment valued at £S200 million.

Throughout this period Cairo's *Sawt Al-Arab* (Voice of the Arabs) maintained an unremitting attack on the 'secessionist' government, accusing its members of every conceivable sin: the 'secessionists' not only cancelled 'Nasser's socialism' and 'exploited and tortured workers and peasants', but also were 'paid agents of the imperialists'. These broadcasts—directly addressed to Syrian officers—incited them to revolt and had an enormous effect. The government's cancellation of the nationalizations and emasculation of the land reform played into Cairo's hands by giving credibility to its charges, however fanciful. 'We believed them all', the then Commander-in-Chief of the Army, General Abdel Kerim Zahr Al-Din, later admitted.[5] The Syrian government, moreover, made no reply to Cairo's ever more bitter attacks. For President Qudsi had ordered an end to all anti-Nasser and anti-UAR statements and propaganda. Even deputies in the assembly were muzzled.

DEMOCRATIC CAMPAIGN

However, an ever stronger demand arose for cancellation of the emergency laws, lifting of the censorship and all restrictions. Khalid Al-Azm and Akram Hourani led this campaign in the assembly, where it won strong backing, since most deputies wanted to get rid of army control. The campaign was echoed in a grass-roots drive for democratization in which Hourani's socialists took the lead. Although severely hampered by the police and the censorship, this movement gathered growing popular support. By mid-March demands for democratization had become so insistent that Premier Dawalibi was compelled to permit the assembly to debate the question. The assembly demanded he resign to make way for a National Union Government pledged to cancel the emergency laws and restore political and civil liberties. Dawalibi resigned on 25 March. Consultations on the formation of a new government were interrupted by three military *coups*—the first in Damascus, the second in Homs, and the third in Aleppo.

THE COUPS OF MARCH AND APRIL 1962

The first *coup* was made during the night of 28 March by Colonel Nahlawi and some of the officers of his original junta. Its proclaimed aim was to restore the land reform, the nationalizations, and the union. The Nahlawi officers arrested most deputies and ministers. They tried to persuade President Qudsi to dissolve the assembly and act as their front, but he refused. From that moment the Nahlawi *coup* began to go wrong. Nahlawi was unable to rally support either in the army or among the politicians. Popular demonstrations in provincial towns and outlying districts insisted upon a return to civilian government. Huge demonstrations in Aleppo demanded the release of Qudsi and other arrested politicians. These popular actions taken in defiance of a military curfew and martial law showed the people resolutely opposed to any further army intervention in political life. Unable to form a government and faced by popular revolt, the Nahlawi junta began to lose control.

During the night of 31 March, Nasserist officers led by Jasim Alwan and Ba'thist officers recently dismissed from the army, joined by others earlier dismissed by Nasser, made the second *coup* in Homs. These two groups acted together but their aims were divergent. The Ba'th officers, led by the Military Committee, acted because they wanted both to get back into the army and to prevent Nahlawi from restoring the union with Egypt. They had suffered from the union. If unity was to be restored, they were determined they would be in charge and control its terms and timing. The Nasserists acted to regain posts of prestige in the army and to restore the union under their aegis. Other non-party officers participated for opportunist reasons.

The Homs *coup* split the army. The commander-in-chief, General Zahr Al-Din, therefore convoked a conference in Homs of all army commands on 1 April. The third *coup* in Aleppo was really a continuation of the Homs *coup* by diehard Nasserists, led by Alwan, who refused to accept the decisions of the Homs conference. This group seized the Aleppo radio station and broadcast as 'the UAR Broadcasting Station in Aleppo', proclaiming: 'We are your lion cubs, O Gamal!' These officers called on the Egyptian embassy in Beirut for parachutists. On 3 April, however, they were compelled to yield.

The various groups involved in these *coups* had one goal in common – to prevent the restoration of democracy in Syria, since a democratic regime would exclude the army from power. This aim was revealed on the eve of the 28 March *coup* in reports that the military were determined to avoid the 'embarrassment' of a return to political, press, and trade union freedoms and wanted a Shishakli-type regime.

Another widely shared goal was to restore the land reform and the nationalizations. A good many of these young officers were from the countryside or from the lower-middle classes of the provincial cities. Some Ba'thist and Nasserist officers came from the Hawran. The Hawran's economic destinies were largely controlled by the big merchants and businessmen of Damascus, just as the economic destinies of the Jazira were largely dependent on the wealthy merchants and businessmen of Aleppo. Jasim Alwan, who was of beduin origin, came from Deir Ezzor, a rather poor city in constant contact with the beduin. Many of the Ba'th officers were from the underprivileged provinces of the Jebel Druze and Latakia. The social ideas of these officers were not developed. But their background gave them a genuine interest in social reform. They had little stake in the Damascus-Aleppo controlled existing order. *Sawt Al-Arab*'s daily harangues heightened their awareness of this fact.

All three *coups* were made in the name of restoring the union. Yet in discussions the Army High Command and the commander-in-chief held with 'unionist' politicians and public figures before the *coups*, only one individual (the Nasserist officer Nihad Al-Qasim) was willing to accept unconditional union. The rest, though ready enough to resort to conspiracy, wanted only a 'moderate' union.[6] The Syrian people did not take seriously the unity slogans chanted by the putschists. The prevailing view was that 'the officers do not want a return to union but want to rule themselves'. But on this question the officers were, in their own fashion, true believers.

Cairo was involved in the Homs and Aleppo *coups*; it may also have had a hand in the Damascus *coup*. Its aim was not only to bring down the 'secessionist' government and so vindicate Nasser's rule in Syria, but also to put an end to the Damascus-Baghdad *rapprochement*. Cairo itself later revealed that three of Nahlawi's officers, on a mission to Egypt in January 1962 concerned with negotiating the return of Syria's military equipment, discussed their projected *coup* with Nasser. Cairo's propaganda, in any case, prepared the way for the *coup*. Cairo's participation in the Homs and Aleppo *coups* was revealed during the Egypt-Syria-Iraq unity talks in Cairo in March and April 1963 and by Jasim Alwan himself in later testimony before a Military Tribunal.[7] General Zahr Al-Din described Cairo as 'the known financier and planner' of the *coups*, while asserting that the American embassy in Damascus and the American consulate in Aleppo financed and planned the *coups* 'behind the scenes'.[8] The then police chief of Aleppo testified[9] that the American consulate attempted to assist the Nasserist *putsch* by distributing photographs of President Nasser and tying up telephone lines to police headquarters to prevent action against the putschists.

THE HOMS DECISIONS

The Homs Conference reached a compromise settlement. The Nahlawi group, ordered to go into exile, did so. Jasim Alwan, also exiled, managed to go underground. The extremists were to be dismissed from the army. Civilian government was to be restored, but the assembly would not be recalled. The army, in effect, would retain control.

The *coups*, however, provoked a great upsurge of anti-Nasserism, which meant anti-authoritarianism, and insistence on civilian rule. Under popular pressure the army was compelled to proclaim once more its withdrawal from politics, although it continued to exercise ultimate authority in virtually every field. Qudsi, having dropped his demand for recall of the assembly to restore legality, was brought directly from Mezza prison to the Presidential Palace to resume his functions. Detained politicians were gradually released over the next six weeks. An 'independent progressive', Dr Bashir Azmeh, President of the Doctors' Association, was named to head a 'transitional government' of technicians of varying political hues. His government duly renationalized the Khumasiya Company, and restored the agrarian reform with amendments devised to do away with its inequities and to give the peasant title deed to the land when it was distributed, and not forty years later. It also enacted legislation providing for nationalization of all foreign banks and a 25 per cent government share in all Syrian banks. Although promising democratization, the government took no steps in this direction.

A NEW CONSPIRACY

These actions conformed to the policies demanded by the officers, but neither the officers nor Cairo were satisfied. *Sawt Al-Arab* was soon calling for Azmeh's overthrow; within weeks the officers again became involved in conspiracy. A many-sided struggle now began in Syria.

The split between the Hourani and Aflak-Bitar factions of the Ba'th became final. The party's fifth National Congress in May 1962 expelled Hourani. This congress tried to paper over basic differences between the party's National Command and the Syrian provincials or (as they came to be called) regionalists, who had tried to maintain a party organization on their own during the union. Regionalist demands for a reorganization of the party from its base and election of a new National Command were rejected.

After this Congress, Cairo's attacks on the Syrian Ba'th tapered off, and Ba'th leaders Aflak and Bitar began to take a line on Syrian affairs not much different from Nasser's. For, a month earlier, the Aflak-Bitar Ba'th had become involved – along with Hani Al-Hindi's Arab National Movement and various other Nasserists and unionists – in still another Egyptian conspiracy. The Egyptian embassy in

Beirut, which organized this conspiracy, maintained contacts with both the civilian and military leaders of these groups and promised to give Salah Bitar a ministerial post. Among the reasons drawing Ba'thist and Nasserist officers into this conspiracy was their desire to save themselves from trial and jail for killings and other acts committed during their recent *coups* and to return to the army. The *putsch*, however, required several months' preparation.

POPULAR ADVANCE

Akram Hourani now launched a campaign for restoration of democracy under the slogan: 'Democracy Before Union'. The grass-roots democratic movement rallied its forces and began to expand its activities. The mounting campaign for political liberties won its first important victory when press censorship was lifted early in June. The press immediately took up the popular slogan: 'No Union With Dictators'. Political party activity, although nominally illegal, became intense. Some twenty political manifestos were issued in a two-week period in June. Under popular pressures, pro-Nasser ministers left the Cabinet one by one. By the end of June the democratic anti-Nasser forces had become the ruling influence in Syrian politics.

At this time, former Premier Dawalibi, Khalid Al-Azm, and other politicians started a campaign for return to legality. In face of warnings from Azmeh that it would bring trouble from the army, 110 deputies of the dissolved assembly signed a petition demanding restoration of the assembly and democratic freedoms. They were concerned about the lack of legality in the country. According to the 1950 Constitution, parliament could not be dissolved within the first eighteen months after its election. Its dissolution was therefore illegal. The deputies proposed that the assembly be recalled to amend the constitution so that the assembly could vote confidence in a new government, to which it would grant legislative powers. Other amendments would allow the President to dissolve the assembly whenever he chose, revise the article requiring elections within sixty days of parliament's dissolution, and would give the premier greater executive power. Once these constitutional changes had been made, the President would dissolve the assembly, and a new parliament would be elected within six months.

The struggle of rank-and-file workers to rid their trade unions of *Mabaheth* agents also began to achieve some success. Hitherto, the General Federation's Executive Committee, handpicked by the Egyptians, joined by the Egyptian-chosen committees of certain unions, had called strikes and demonstrations demanding the overthrow of the 'secessionist' government and Syria's return to the UAR. With the lifting of press censorship, many unions petitioned for convocation of a General Assembly to discuss removal of the federation's Executive Committee.

At this time, trade union delegates who had attended a labour conference in Cairo informed the government that certain of their number had conspired with Abdel Hamid Sarraj and Egyptian intelligence officials to provoke troubles in Syria. When investigation proved this charge had substance, the government acted. It issued a new set of rules for trade union organization which had the effect of doing away with the pyramid structure imposed by the UAR regime and abolishing the federation's Executive Committee. The new law (50 of 1962) also established (very complicated) procedures for trade union elections and prohibited trade union political activity. The government at the same time issued regulations devised to protect workers from arbitrary dismissals. The Nasserist leadership of the federation called strikes in Aleppo and Damascus to protest against the new law and demand immediate reunion with Egypt. Cairo's *Sawt Al-Arab* incited Syrians to rise and overthrow the Azmeh government and 'restore union with Abdel Nasser'. A series of bomb explosions occurred in different parts of the country. The strikes came to an end when the government arrested the ringleaders and when other labour leaders began to explain the new law. The workers themselves decided they did not want to continue a strike for restoration of a union 'from which we suffered a great deal'.

Labour troubles, clashes, bomb explosions, Cairo's incitements to revolt, and the infiltration of money and arms from the Lebanon heralded the approach of the new Egyptian conspiracy. Field Marshal Amr predicted on 28 June that 'the situation in Syria could be rectified by the Syrian army'. In speeches celebrating the anniversary of the Egyptian revolution late in July, President Nasser spoke of Syria as 'the Northern Region of the UAR' and declared he could no longer stand idly by while 'reactionaries continue to persecute the Syrian people'. By this time, however, the Syrian authorities had the situation in hand. The government announced that an attempted Nasserist-Ba'thist *coup* on the night of 28–29 July had been frustrated. Documents, tapes of wireless conversations between the conspirators and Cairo, and confessions of the accused exposed the plot. The conspirators, meeting on 6 July, had decided to seize power on the 28th and install a civilian government including Nasserists and Ba'thists with Salah Bitar as premier. They had then asked Nasser for a public declaration of support. His speeches of 23 and 27 July fulfilled this demand. The conspirators received arms from Egyptian ships bringing water-melons to the Lebanon.

Discovery of the plot provoked the now predominantly anti-Nasser government to complain formally to the Arab League about Egypt's constant interference in Syria's internal affairs. A League conference, held at Chtaura in the Lebanon, in late August heard the complaint. The conference became a stormy affair. The Syrian delegation offered a wealth of documentation: the tape recordings, written documents of a similar nature including instructions from the Egyptian embassy in Beirut, confessions of the conspirators, and so on. (These were later published in book form, but the UAR and Lebanese governments prohibited its distribution.) The Syrian delegation invited other delegations to visit Syria to see for themselves that Egyptian charges that 'Syria was one big prison' were false. No delegation accepted. The presence in the Egyptian delegation of four Syrians, who had defected to Cairo when the UAR broke up, did not help Egypt's case. The Egyptian delegation, making no effort to answer Syria's charges, limited itself to violent attacks on the Syrian government as 'unrepresentative of the people'. These attacks themselves substantiated the Syrian complaint. The Egyptian delegation, highly embarrassed, then walked out, threatening that Egypt would quit the League if it did not condemn the Syrian charge. The League Council then passed a non-committal resolution which suspended the Syrian complaint so long as the UAR did not attend League meetings.

The Chtaura Conference, occurring almost a year after Syria's withdrawal from the UAR, marked the first strong Syrian government stand against Egypt. This stand reflected the gathering strength of the democratic movement and the coming-together of all anti-Nasserist forces in 'a fight to the death against Nasserism'. The democratic current seemed to develop swiftly. State radio and television daily featured debates and talks by educational and other leaders on the need for democratic institutions and the virtues of the multi-party system. Leaders and politicians toured the provinces making the same points. But ominous dissensions reflecting the opposition of rightist elements to the democratic movement soon appeared.

The government invited the people to discuss a draft bill on political party organization which proposed to ban any party that broke with Arabism, adopted illegal means, bore a religious label, or called for suppression of individual freedoms. These restrictions would outlaw the SSNP, the Communist Party, the Muslim Brotherhood, and probably Nasserism. The bill provoked the ire of most of the political parties and was subsequently shelved. But Muslim Brotherhood leader Issam Attar launched repeated attacks on what he called the government's 'concessions to communism' in seeking to ban religious parties. The Brotherhood's equation of secularism with communism did not augur well for political co-operation for national ends. The Brotherhood joined Nasserists and rightists in a violent anti-communist campaign, and also waged war against the Hourani socialists because they considered Nasserism, not communism, the main danger. The Ba'th through its weekly, *Al-Ba'th*, attacked 'secessionists', especially Hourani, and called for reunion with Egypt.

THE AZM GOVERNMENT

Efforts to restore the dissolved National Assembly, suspended during the Chtaura Conference, now resumed. On 14 September, the assembly met, amended the 1950 Constitution as proposed, and gave a vote of confidence to Khalid Al-Azm, who had been named premier because he was the only political figure acceptable to both Right and Left. Qudsi then dissolved the assembly as promised. Azm with great difficulty managed to form a National Union Cabinet representing all trends, except the Ba'th which refused to serve, the Nasserists, and the Communist Party. (The communists, however, supported the new government.)

The Azm government was undermined almost from its inception by Muslim Brotherhood pressures. The Brotherhood and the big landlords and capitalists, represented in the government, tried to sabotage its attempted reforms and to prevent it from carrying out its mandate. The government was also weakened by its lack of control over the security forces, by the fact that army officers were soon busy weaving new conspiracies, and by Cairo's indefatigable efforts to subvert it. However, Azm and some of his ministers made a valiant attempt to carry out the government's mandate. This was to cancel the emergency laws, restore democratic institutions, hold parliamentary elections, lift the standards of workers and peasants, and encourage private capital to participate in development.

Under the circumstances the government's achievements were remarkable. One of its first acts was to exempt beneficiaries of the land reform from the 10 per cent service fee and to halve the price they had to pay for the land. The new Agrarian Reform Minister, Amine Nafouri, an ally of the Hourani socialists, began an intensive campaign to speed the land reform. In less than ten months, Nafouri and his predecessor (in the Azmeh government), Ahmed Abdel Kerim, managed to distribute more land to peasants than had been distributed by the UAR regime in 36 months (and more than was to be distributed in the first 24 months of the Ba'th 'socialist' regime that took power in 1963).[10] The Azm government took a number of measures to restore business confidence. Azm promised that—so long as workers' rights were maintained—there would be no further nationalizations. Private capitalists appeared to be satisfied: in one month alone thirty demands were made for licences to start new industries.

Over the powerful opposition of Cairo, which maintained that the Syrian government was not the legal successor to the UAR and could not therefore benefit from the 1961 Bonn-Cairo protocol concerning the Euphrates dam, the government opened negotiations to persuade Bonn to fulfil its commitment to finance the dam. But the West German government was in no hurry, since it lacked confidence in Syria's political stability and also wanted to obtain, in return for building the dam, an oil concession in the Jazira for the West German Concordia Company. Azm did not heed the demand of the socialists and communists to seek Soviet aid for the dam. In January 1963, Bonn agreed to build the dam, but the sum involved was only three-fifths that promised Cairo and the projected dam smaller. A ministerial committee began to study creation of a National Oil Company to exploit the oil discovered in the Jazira. Preparations were made to construct a port at Tartus to serve central Syria. Aid agreements were signed with the United States for the construction of grain silos and with Poland for the purchase of industrial machinery. China, France, and Czechoslovakia offered development credits.

Pressures from the army and the rightists succeeded in delaying the lifting of the emergency laws. As a result, trade union elections were held while these laws, which worked to the advantage of anti-democratic elements, were still in force. Nasserist-Muslim Brotherhood coalitions opposed the socialists and the communists, who, for the most part, did not make common fronts. The Nasserist-Muslim Brotherhood coalition achieved a victory in the Homs Oil-Workers' Union, but won less than half the contests in Damascus and took only about 25 per cent of union posts in Aleppo. The socialists made a good showing, and a number of communists were elected in Aleppo unions either alone or on coalition tickets. Independent trade union leaders maintained that perhaps 20 to 25 per cent of politically conscious workers were Nasserist in sympathy. The Muslim Brotherhood was influential in a number of unions, especially the Teachers' Union. A teacher's strike in December, instigated by the Brotherhood and supported by the Nasserists, was called off when fewer than half the schools in the main cities responded.

As 1962 drew to a close, the political horizon was clouded by dissension between the Muslim Brotherhood and the socialists, the Brotherhood's campaign against secularism, Cairo's continuing cold war, and sporadic Nasserist disruption. Yet on 22 December the Azm government ended the state of emergency. For two weeks thereafter Syrians enjoyed political freedoms. Politicians began to reconstitute old political parties or to form new ones. The government promised new political party legislation and national elections by July at the latest.

COUNTER-ATTACK

The formation of the Azm government was a direct blow to ambitious officers and ex-officers. Azm, firmly opposed to the army's intervention in politics, was determined to put an end to it. He had always refused to build his own coterie in the army and now declined to deal with officers other than on a constitutional basis. The counter-attack was not long in coming. It appeared to be linked to larger pan-Arab plans to topple governments unfriendly to Egypt, which now enjoyed American favour.

Early in January 1963, Nahlawi and his fellow-exiles returned to Syria, made contact with their former units, and–backed by a number of supporters–demanded reinstatement in the army, a ban on all communist activities, reorganization of the High Command, and an immediate plebiscite on union with Egypt. Simultaneously, Nasserist-Muslim Brotherhood outbreaks occurred at Damascus University and in the Hawran, where secondary-school children stoned fellow-pupils who refused to join them in anti-communist demonstrations. However, the government stood firm and sent Nahlawi and his companions once more into exile.

Coincident with this affair, Arab nationalist outbreaks against the governments in Iraq and Jordan also occurred. The Cairo press, predicting the imminent overthrow of the governments in Baghdad, Damascus, Amman, and Riad, wrote that 'winds of revolution are blowing across the Arab World' and that 'blood will be shed on the Arab land . . . in the battle against reactionary and secessionist elements'. Both the Arab and the American presses now spoke of an American *rapprochement* with President Nasser and American acceptance of pan-Arab nationalism as 'the wave of the future' in the Arab East. So widespread was the belief in the existence of a kind of Kennedy-Nasser alliance that the State Department felt compelled to deny that Nasser was serving as 'a chosen instrument' of American policy.

In Syria dissension and confusion mounted. The Military Command was divided over proposed transfers, dismissals, and promotions of officers. Soon the socialist and Muslim Brotherhood ministers, in violent conflict with each other, resigned. The arrest of bomb-carrying infiltrators from the Lebanon and Syrian destruction of a clandestine Nasserist radio station operating from just over the Lebanese border sparked a crisis in relations with Beirut.

On 8 February a Ba'th-Nasserist *coup* in Iraq brought down the Qasim government and so removed Syria's strongest support. The *coup* found Syria virtually without a government. Azm was seriously ill. Six ministers had left the Cabinet. The Hourani socialists now turned against the Azm government to call for a 'responsible progressive government to stand beside the progressive regime in Iraq', choosing to ignore the widespread reports that the United States Central Intelligence Agency had a directing hand in the Iraqi *coup*.[11] Many Syrian politicians tried to woo the new Iraqi government, but the new leaders in Baghdad spurned these appeals. On 22 February, the Iraqi leaders journeyed to Cairo to celebrate the anniversary of the Syrian-Egyptian union and with President Nasser to proclaim in scarcely veiled terms the imminent overthrow of the Damascus government.

To meet this threat, patriotic elements of all political shades – businessmen, trade unionists, religious leaders, politicians – came together to form a National Rally. The socialists, however, refused to participate and ignored the Rally's appeals to return to the government.

Three main officer groups were then preparing *coups*. They were the Arab nationalist and other Nasserist officers, the Ba'thists, and a group led by Major Ziad Hariri, Hourani's brother-in-law. Hariri assured the anti-Nasserists that his *coup* would be 'one hundred per cent anti-Nasser', but he was also in touch with the Nasserist and Ba'thist officers. Nasserist hesitations permitted Hariri to take the lead and stage his *coup* with the help of the Ba'thists on 8 March.

The easy success of the *coup* was not due to the absence of opposition but to the confusion engendered by its dual character, at once pro- and anti-Nasser, and to betrayal in high places. After the Iraqi *coup*, Army Commander-in-Chief Zahr Al-Din, backed by President Qudsi, purged the army of more than a hundred anti-Nasser officers. In line with the demands of the conspirators, Zahr Al-Din transferred other officers and named Rashid Qutayni, a Nasserist leader of the conspiracy, head of the Second Bureau (Intelligence).

A National Council of the Revolutionary Command (NCRC) became the supreme authority. The NCRC immediately reimposed the emergency laws, prohibited the assembly of more than five persons, shut down all but three newspapers and periodicals, subjected nearly all politicians, journalists, and intellectuals who had been active since the separation from Egypt to 'civic isolation', and arrested hundreds. But there was no bloodbath such as had occurred in Iraq.

The great majority of the people saw the *coup* as just one more act in an infernal cycle of army interventions and showed their disdain by completely ignoring the new regime.

[1] See Cairo Unity Talks, BBC *Summary of World Broadcasts*, Part IV, 1963, ME 1285.

[2] Of the Military Committee only Muhammad Umran proposed action against 'secession'. See Sami Jundi on the Military Committee in *Al-Ba'th*, Beirut, 1969, pp. 85–6, 89, 91, 97, 99.

[3] Assad Kourani, a conservative National Party politician from Aleppo, and Dr Izzat Trabulsi, Governor of the Central Bank until dismissed in 1961, were in turn approached, but both refused.

[4] The politicians were not allowed to leave the Officers' Club, to which they had been convoked by the Army Command, until they had agreed on the terms of the pact. The 'rightist' trend of the original army draft was modified, and the plank on socialism included, as a result of the forceful intervention of Akram Hourani. Azm, op. cit., 1 July 1972.

[5] Abdel Kerim Zahr Al-Din: *Mudhakkirat* (Memoirs), Beirut, 1968, pp. 188 ff.

[6] ibid.

[7] Testimony at the 4th Public Session of the Military Tribunal dealing with the 18 July 1963 Nasserist revolt. See *Daily Star* (Beirut), 13 September 1963.

[8] Zahr Al-Din, op. cit., p. 208.

[9] Colonel Bah Al-Din Daghestan to the military court conducting the trial of the leaders of the Aleppo revolt, 22 October 1962.

[10] SAR Central Bureau of Statistics: *Statistical Abstract* 1968, p. 113.

[11] Jordan's King Husain later confirmed this. See his interview with Hassaneen Haykal. *Ahram* Weekly Supplement, No. 28047, 27 September 1963.

[12] Zahr Al-Din's role throughout the so-called 'secession' period was ambiguous. He apparently had the confidence of the conspiring officers although as commander-in-chief his responsibility was to defend the existing regime. Azm accused him of trying to undermine the authority of the civilian government and maintaining unauthorized contacts with Nasserist personalities in the Lebanon. Azm, op. cit., 20 June 1972.

Chapter 9

The Ba'th in Power

THE 'BA'TH REVOLUTION of 8 March 1963' was neither wholly Ba'thist nor could it have looked less like a revolution. The traditional Ba'th leadership played no significant role in the *coup*. Still struggling to reorganize after its dissolution under the UAR regime, the party then had fewer than 500 members. The real author of the *coup* from the Ba'th side was the Military Committee, not at the time organically a part of the party. The committee was only one of three military factions compelled by common weakness to act together to overthrow the Azm government. Yet the Ba'th officers soon won dominance. The *coup* did open the road to radical social change, a road that passed through many conflicts.

Contradictions were inherent in the very structure of the *putsch* since each faction had its own goals. Ambitious, lacking any politically precise strategy, the newly-promoted General Ziad Hariri, although the strongest, was condemned to lose the course for power. He was neither a real Nasserist to push Syria back into union nor a Ba'thist to propose a new Ba'th alternative. The Nasserists played their cards so precipitously and so maladroitly that they lost their chance to their tactical allies, the Hariri and Ba'th officers, who were reinforced by the continuing strength of anti-Nasserism. The Ba'th Military Committee had the double advantage of being well organized and skilled in a secretive method of operation. It succeeded in eliminating the Nasserists through Hariri, shouldered passively by the separatists, and then, in turn, Hariri himself. A minority among minorities, the Ba'th officers became masters of Syria. They were then ready to challenge the party's traditional leadership from which they had always remained apart.

On the morrow of the *coup*, however, these officers needed the traditional Ba'th leadership because they had no organization of their own outside the army and also wanted a link to the Ba'th in Iraq. They therefore called on the Ba'th to become their front. The Ba'th leaders now accepted the officers as fully-fledged party members and integrated the Military Committee into the party structure as the exclusive party military organization. The Military Committee was also allowed to retain its autonomous status. The dual power-structure thus created underscored the civilian leadership's weakness in face of the military contingent.

Ba'th leaders participated in the NCRC, which under the new Provisional Constitution exercised real power. The NCRC named Salah Bitar, who had failed miserably in the December 1961 elections, to form a Cabinet. Represented in the NCRC and the Cabinet were the Ba'th, Hariri's officers, and three small pro-Nasser groupings: Hani Al-Hindi's Arab National Movement, Nihad Al-Qasim's United Arab Front, and Sami Sufan's Socialist Unionist Movement of former Ba'thists. The NCRC presidency and the post of Commander-in-Chief of the Army went to the insignificant Luay Atasi, brother-in-law of the Nasserist Jasim Alwan. Ziad Hariri became chief-of-staff. Colonel Amine Al-Hafez, who had been exiled to Argentina as a military attaché by Nahlawi, was brought back by the Ba'th officers to assume the key posts of Acting Military Governor and Interior Minister.

Nasser and the Nasserists

Nasserist demonstrations calling for immediate union with Egypt began three days after the *coup*. They were met by Ba'th counter-demonstrations. Demonstrations in this period lacked spontaneity. Army trucks went to the villages and, in the case of the Nasserists, to the Palestine refugee camps to recruit demonstrators who were transported to the scene of action and suitably remunerated. Continuing Nasserist agitation in defiance of a ban on all demonstrations posed a direct challenge to the Ba'th, which was committed to a gesture towards union with Egypt by the *coup*'s unity slogans as well as by the party's condemnation of secession. The Syrian and Iraqi Ba'th therefore proposed to Nasser a tripartite federal union, hoping to prevent Nasser's return to Syria by placing him in the dilemma of having to accept union on equal terms or bear the responsibility of failure. They knew that Nasser would not agree to any union in which he did not hold supreme power. The union negotiations, held in Cairo in March and April, were not to be taken seriously. The Ba'th officers didn't even bother to participate.

The originally secret talks (their text was later published by Cairo) were devoted mainly to mutual recriminations between Nasser and the Syrian Ba'th over the failure of the 1958–61 union. The discussions were marked by extraordinary pettiness, mutual charges of corruption, treason, and opportunism, and a conspicuous poverty of thought on the part of all participants. Nasser flatly declared that he was prepared to unite with a 'representative Syrian government', but not with the Ba'th. Simultaneously he ordered his propaganda machine to make savage attacks on the Syrian Ba'th and its leaders. To Nasser's often brutal browbeating, Aflak and Bitar replied with evasions and embarrassment. Since they had condemned 'secession', they had no case against the UAR President.

Although none of the issues at stake were resolved, a Charter for the new UAR was finally drafted. It gave the President of the new UAR (Nasser) almost unlimited power behind the façade of a parliamentary regime which would in any case be dominated by Egypt owing to its larger population. The Charter, moreover, would require the Ba'th in Syria and Iraq to share power with the Nasserists. The Ba'th, however, won a 25-month delay in its application on the grounds that if parliamentary elections were held immediately, 'we would have to rig them' to secure a vote for unity.[1] The Charter was never meant to be applied.

Publication of the Charter on 17 April–hailed in Syria by rowdy and mutually hostile Ba'th and Nasserite demonstrations–left most Syrians reserved and on the sidelines. The bitter experience of the union with Egypt was too close; the March *coup* had produced a disorganization of painful dimensions. 'Isolation decrees' deprived Damascus University of much of its teaching staff. Fear of student agitation closed the university off and on for the rest of the academic year. The *coup* and the extensive purges that followed prompted the emigration in great numbers of businessmen, professionals, technicians, and even workers who saw no end to a seemingly endless succession of *coups* and counter-*coups*.

Against this troubled background the battle between the Nasserists and the Ba'th was joined. When Nasserist officers in Aleppo revolted in late April against the delay in the union, the Ba'th and Hariri officers purged the army of forty-seven Nasserists, including the Defence Minister and the chief-of-staff, both NCRC members. The resignation of Nasserist ministers in protest allowed Bitar to form a new government with Hariri as Defence Minister. Arrests of leading Nasserists soon began.

Ziad Hariri was the next to go. During his absence in Algeria, his leading supporters were dismissed from the army and he was ordered to report to Washington to assume the post of military attaché. His attempt to defy this order collapsed when the Iraqi Ba'th threatened to intervene. Amine Al-Hafez, Interior Minister, Deputy Premier, and Acting Military Governor, became chief-of-staff and Acting Defence Minister as well.

With their hopes rapidly vanishing, Nasserist officers, backed by Syrian political exiles in Cairo, decided on a major gamble. On 18 July, under Jasim Alwan's leadership, they attempted a *coup* in Damascus in broad daylight. One of their number later testified that the Egyptian Air Force was to have intervened. The Ba'th, led by Amine Al-Hafez, sub-machine gun in hand, stood and fought. Loyal army units and the National Guard, a party para-military force organized only a few weeks before, eventually imposed control. Some 800 people, mainly innocent bystanders, were killed or wounded, twenty insurrectionists were promptly executed, hundreds were arrested, and the office of Egypt's Middle East News Agency was closed.

A week after the failure of the 18 July revolt, President Nasser denounced the 17 April union agreement and in effect declared war on what he called 'the fascist Ba'th regime'. Partly to protect itself from the blasts coming from Cairo, the Ba'th in Syria and Iraq began to prepare a bilateral union between the two countries. An economic union was concluded in August; a military union in October. General Umran later explained[2] that one purpose of the military union was to permit Syria to participate in the Iraqi Ba'th's war against the Kurds. Syrian Air Force units and a 5,000-man Syrian brigade joined the war, he said, because Baghdad could not rely on Iraqi troops. (Hundreds of Iraqi soldiers had been killed at Camp Rashid near Baghdad in July when they revolted against being sent to the north to fight the Kurds.)

MONOPOLY OF POWER

Suppression of the Nasserist revolt gave the Ba'th a monopoly of power and marked the emergence of General Hafez as the apparent strongman of the regime. Without relinquishing his other posts, General Hafez now replaced Luay Atasi as NCRC president and Army Commander-in-Chief. A Sunni from Aleppo of lower-middle-class origin, General Hafez had originally been drawn towards the Ba'th by his admiration for Akram Hourani. His rise in the Ba'th regime was not due to party affiliation but to his reputation for honesty and straightforwardness and his stubborn courage. From the beginning he made clear that he personally favoured national con-ciliation with all patriotic elements, among whom he included the Hourani socialists and the communists. He paid more than one friendly visit to 'secessionist' politicians and journalists in Mezza prison. By his commonsense and apparent understanding of the need to compromise with the country's diverse social and political forma-tions, General Hafez won respect and a large measure of confidence from the people, who began to call him 'Abu Abdo' (father of Abdo, his eldest son, the familiar form of address among Arabs). Although he had not been a member of the Military Committee before the March *coup*, the committee encouraged his rise to power apparently in the belief (which proved mistaken) that he would be easy to control. General Hafez was, in fact, not at all politically-minded. Through his person and the respect he commanded, however, he managed to protect Ba'th rule from the dissensions that rent the party in its early years in power and to give its rule a stability and continuity it might not otherwise have achieved. Since he was not identified with either the party's old guard or its younger militants, he could work with both as well as mediate between rival military blocs.

The Military Committee

The Military Committee established a tight grip on the army. One of its most able members was Salah Jadid, a younger brother of Ghassan Jadid, the SSNP militant involved in Malki's murder, who had since been assassinated in Beirut. An Alawi from the *Haddadun* (blacksmith) tribe of Latakia and from a local notable family, Salah Jadid remained out of the limelight. He became head of the Officers' Affairs Bureau and of the Personnel Branch of GHQ, posts that gave him control of dismissals, appointments, and transfers of officers. Step by step the Military Committee took command of all the military units essential for making and breaking *coups*. Lt-Col Hafez Assad, an Alawi, commanded the Air Force; Major-General Muhammad Umran, also an Alawi, the 70th Armoured Brigade, stationed in Damascus, the strongest unit in the Syrian army; the Druze officer Hamad Ubayd commanded the 5th Armoured Brigade; the Druze Selim Hatum the army's élite commando battalion which then guarded GHQ and the Broadcasting Station; the Isma'ili Abdel Kerim Jundi the Artillery; and the Sunni Ahmad Sweidani Military Intelligence, to name only the most important.

The Military Committee used its position as the autonomous and exclusive representative of the party military organization to build an 'ideological Army'. Since the Ba'thists in the army were relatively few in number, this effort involved not only intensive indoctrination but also extensive purges, mainly of Sunni officers from the cities. To fill the vacancies, the Military Committee recalled to active service all Ba'thist reserve officers and all officers with whom it was connected by family, clan, or sectarian relations. This brought an influx of Alawi, Druze, and Isma'ili officers, since both traditional army recruitment and Ba'th party membership drew largely on the rural areas where these minorities live. The committee's enemies inevitably accused it of sectarian discrimination in promotions and transfers, and in acceptance of students in the Military Academy and of officers and NCOs in the party.

EMERGENCE OF THE NEO-BA'TH

Holding power alone, the Ba'th was now compelled to define a programme. Hitherto, Ba'th slogans – unity, freedom, socialism – had not required definition. Now they had to be given content. The party had promised a revolution but admittedly had no revolutionary programme. The failure of the Egyptian-Syrian union called in question the priorities and most of the assumptions of traditional Ba'th ideology, but no re-examination of these questions had been made.

Two tendencies appeared in the Ba'th in 1963, as it struggled with these problems, and developed more clearly in 1964. The tradition-ally reformist and historically anti-Marxist and anti-communist tendency represented by the old-guard leaders, Aflak and Bitar, still gave overriding priority to pan-Arab unity. A new tendency repre-sented by younger and definitely rural elements revealed a growing concern with social and socialist ideas. These elements were influ-enced by various ideologies including Marxism. Although their ideas remained confused, they accepted the theme of class struggle. Adoption of this concept had the (unacknowledged) effect of reversing the order of priorities always maintained by the traditional leader-ship. Once the class-struggle concept is admitted, the rich classes are excluded from Arab national action for liberation and promotion of the Arab nation. In day-to-day practice and within each Arab country, this meant abandoning the overriding unification priority in favour of social and economic objectives. For unification cannot be undertaken if it does not isolate the Right from the Arab front of action. This was the sense of the policies now advanced by the young militants. But their ideas about the positive and negative roles of different social classes and political forces remained ambiguous. Although they rejected union with openly reactionary regimes, they also maintained the taboo on Arab unity; unity remained an article of faith not to be critically examined.

The new tendency in the party was represented by the second civilian generation. Its leaders were the 'three doctors', Yusef Z'ayyen, Ibrahim Makhous, and Nur Al-Din Atasi, all of whom had been greatly influenced by the Algerian revolution, in which they had served as medical volunteers. Gradually an alliance developed between this second civilian generation and some of the officers of the Military Committee and their followers. Both groups were in the main of rural and Shi'a minority origin – Alawis, Druzes, and Isma'ilis traditionally rejected by the city and the Sunni majority; both groups contained a sprinkling of Sunnis, chiefly from Deir Ezzor and the Hawran.

The new leftist tendency made its first formal appearance at the Syrian Ba'th's Regional Congress in September 1963. Under the leadership of a Druze, Hamoud Shufi, the leftists won a majority in the new Regional Command. A somewhat similar leftist grouping was elected to the Iraqi Ba'th's Regional Command. The Ba'th's sixth National Congress, held in Damascus in October, was historically the point of departure of the new tendency. The Syrian and Iraqi Regional Commands here joined forces to fight for a radicalization of party ideology and programme. Their chief achievement was to win the National Congress's acceptance of the concept of class struggle as one of the principal laws of social evolution, although its place in the Arab revolution was not defined. The old guard, alarmed by what it considered to be 'communist infiltration', largely succeeded in deforming and denaturing the Left's programme, although subscribing to its phraseology. 'Scientific socialism' was accepted but subordinated to Arab unity. 'Popular democracy' was defined in effect as 'the organic incorporation of the revolutionary and military vanguard' to form the basis of 'socialist effort', a definition reflecting the fact that the Ba'th revolution was imposed from above. Although the ideas of class struggle and scientific socialism were not developed, the congress revealed the growing role of new elements in the party much more influenced by the social aspect of Arab political action than were the traditional leaders. These elements, identified as the regionalists, later became the neo-Ba'th.

The Sixth Congress decisions—with their references to 'scientific socialism' and 'collective farms' and their dismissal of the bourgeoisie as 'an ally of the new colonialism'—provoked a near panic among the Syrian bourgeoisie, the disappearance of consumer goods from the *suqs*, and a new wave of opposition to the regime. A direct army takeover shielded the government from this crisis. General Hafez became premier in place of Bitar, whose bid for re-election to the Regional Command had been defeated by the leftists. (Hafez now held seven top government and army posts.) General Umran became Deputy Premier and Deputy Chief-of-Staff, and General Salah Jadid chief-of-staff. Hafez's government included members of both the National and Regional Commands, among the latter the 'three doctors' and long-time party militants—Ibrahim Makhous, an Alawi from Latakia, and the Sunnis Dr Nur Al-Din Atasi of the influential Homs family, and Yusef Z'ayyen, from a small town on the Iraqi frontier.

The fall of the Ba'th in Iraq in November, following on a split in the party there, precipitated a new crisis within the Syrian Ba'th. To the young militants the Iraqi defeat demonstrated the inconsequence of Aflak's ideology and slogans. Aflak, in turn, blamed the defeat on the young militants, many of whom he considered to be 'crypto-communists'. With the overthrow of the Ba'th in Iraq, the Syrian forces fighting the Kurds had to be brought home. The heavy losses these forces had suffered could no longer be kept secret. The Kurdish expedition had a bad effect on army morale. The Ba'th officers were more than ever determined to keep their hands on the helm.

Hamoud Shufi and certain of his followers, including a number of ex-communists, naïvely thought that, although brought to power by the military contingent, they could now dispense with it. They began a campaign against Aflak's 'right-wing military regime', accusing him of co-operating with 'certain militarists' to 'deviate' from the Sixth Congress resolutions and introduce into the party 'non-socialist positions' and 'non-democratic situations'. The predictable result of this campaign was a (temporary) alliance between Aflak and the officers to remove Shufi and his followers from the Regional Command and later to oust them from the party. Less naïve leftists, including the 'three doctors', did not attempt to challenge the Ba'th military contingent, but sought to enlist its support for the more radical programme of the Sixth Congress.

An Emergency Regional Congress, held in February 1964 to discuss the reasons for the Ba'th's defeat in Iraq, elected a new Regional Command in which the Military Committee demanded and secured seven of 15 seats. Amine Al-Hafez was now a member of both the National and Regional Commands. Frightened by the fate of the party in Iraq, the National Command granted the Regional Command wide powers to appoint the leaders of the party branches and make a new purge. The Regional Command used these powers to get rid of supporters of the old guard and bring in its own men. In this way the regionalists acquired a firm organizational base. Continuing differences between the Regional and National Commands led Aflak to depart for Bonn in an effort to dramatize his disapproval.

SOCIAL MALAISE

Preoccupied with the effort of establishing its rule, the Ba'th had neglected social and economic problems which were daily becoming more critical. The government's failure to define an economic policy and the passive resistance of businessmen aggravated economic difficulties. Despite the restoration of exchange controls, the flight of capital continued. Private investment declined. Not a single industrial firm was established in the year after the *coup*. Renationalization of the banks in May 1963 dried up bank credit and compelled industrial cutbacks, especially in the textile industry, and so created unemployment. Factories, forbidden to dismiss workers, often could not maintain full production for lack of raw materials, and some were bankrupted. Declining government receipts forced reductions in the ordinary and development budgets, a 25 to 40 per cent slash in civil service salaries, and many dismissals; this provoked a new exodus of technicians and skilled workers. Foreign exchange reserves became dangerously short. Although the Ba'th had legally radicalized the land reform, its execution was almost paralyzed. The traditional Ba'th leadership did not want to follow a rightist policy. But it had no political allies on the Left and wanted still less to provoke a political battle with the landlords and the powerful shaikhs of the tribes. Therefore it made no effort to carry out the reform and did the utmost to maintain friendly relations with the tribal shaikhs. Waxing confident, landlords multiplied their attacks on peasants, especially in the Jazira, Homs, and Safita regions where peasants became active in demanding their rights. In the Safita region the Ba'th's National Guard joined in attacks on – and murdered a number of – militant peasants.

By early 1964, the country was suffering economic paralysis, soaring prices, growing unemployment, and a deep malaise. And the government was completely isolated. For the new Arif regime in Iraq was attacking it almost as violently as was the Cairo government. Within Syria the Ba'th's opponents of both Right and Left became more active.

Confessional clashes between Sunnis and Alawis in Banias necessitated army intervention. Riots erupted in Homs. Police stations were assaulted in Aleppo. A drumfire attack came from Cairo and Baghdad radios. Cairo's denunciation of the Ba'th as 'atheist', its leaders as 'non-Arabs and non-Muslims', and Cairo's contemptuous dismissal of Michel Aflak as a 'Cypriot Christian' fanned the flames of right-wing Sunni antagonism to the Ba'th's 'rule of minorities' – that is, to the Ba'th's secularism. The Muslim Brotherhood and the Nasserists, both influential among the Sunni *petit bourgeoisie* of the cities, joined forces against the government.

Early in April anti-government demonstrations and riots broke out in Hama. Calm was restored by General Hafez's personal intervention, only to be shattered on his departure when *muezzin*, carrying the winding sheet which signifies the launching of a holy war, mounted the minarets to declare war on the Ba'th. The war cry 'Islam or the Ba'th' was beamed throughout the night over loudspeakers in every corner of the city, while shaikhs. Muslim brothers, and big landowners transported weapons into the Al-Hader quarter and Al-Sultan mosque. Next morning, government forces, unable to penetrate the narrow alleyways of the quarter, responded to gunfire from the mosque by shelling it and destroying its minaret. This incident was exploited all over the country by right-wing and Nasserist elements which had long been trying to provoke trouble between Sunnis and the Shi'a minorities.

The protest movement, changing in character, then spread to all the main cities where small and middle businessmen, striking for specific economic demands, were joined by engineers, lawyers, magistrates, students, teachers, and workers. These groups called for restoration of public liberties, release of political prisoners, termination of the state of emergency, and immediate restoration of democratic life by free elections. By 20 April, all the main cities were on strike. This spontaneous, unco-ordinated nationwide popular uprising, however, could not long withstand the coercive power of the government. The democratic protest movement, in which the Hourani socialists played a large part, was also undermined by its unwitting association with the Muslim Brotherhood.

The April uprising marked the first appearance of the Workers' Militia, organized by the Isma'ili trade union leader Khalid Jundi, and armed by the government. The militia's administration of what Jundi called 'workers' justice' – especially against the Muslim Brotherhood in Damascus – contributed to saving the regime and became the basis for his rising political influence.

The April events left the Ba'th, as Michel Aflak later admitted,[3] in 'horrible isolation'. Both Cairo and Baghdad (accused of having supplied arms and funds to the insurrection) now openly proclaimed their determination to bring down the Syrian government. The shock of the revolt strengthened the conviction of the left regionalists of the need for a more left policy. It also sharpened internal party conflicts on another level. This became apparent when General Umran tried to pin responsibility for the religious strife in Hama on Akram Hourani. General Hafez ordered the party and government newspapers which repeated this charge to publish a retraction and publicly lauded Hourani as 'a man of integrity above all suspicion'. This dispute marked the beginning of a behind-the-scenes conflict between Umran and Hafez. Umran, an Alawi member of the Military Committee hostile to the emerging neo-Ba'th trend, was accused of building a confessional bloc in the army and seeking a *rapprochement* with the Nasserists. He now moved into the old-guard camp.

The April uprising compelled the party to try to break out of its isolation. General Hafez attempted to conciliate the disaffected population. Hinting again at the need for a Government of National Union, he introduced a new constitution. It provided for the enlargement of the NCRC to include representatives of 'fellahin, workers, military intelligentsia and non-exploiting capital' and transformed the NCRC into a National Revolutionary Council (NRC) with legislative authority. Hafez promised that non-Ba'th elements would be invited to participate in the NRC. The constitution vested executive authority in a five-man Presidium and the Cabinet. General Hafez became President of the Presidium and Bitar once again became premier. His government made a gesture towards answering popular demands in cancelling civic isolation decrees, granting an amnesty to the fomenters of the April rebellion, and releasing the July 1963 putschists. It also outlined an economic policy.

The new constitution provided for public ownership of the means of production and of mineral resources. Defining three forms of property–state, co-operative, and private–it guaranteed that private property could be expropriated only for compensation and in the interests of public utility. Seven major textile firms were then nationalized, and the state acquired a 25 per cent share in fifteen other industrial firms. Policy statements emphasized the need for co-operation between the public and private sectors, especially in the mixed sector created by the partial nationalizations, and a number of concessions were made to the private sector. Response to the Bitar government's more conciliatory policy towards the bourgeoisie proved disappointing. Believing the government to be weak, business-men remained uncompromising.

Hourani's socialists continued their underground campaign for democratization. In widely distributed leaflets in August, Hourani called on the government to nationalize Syrian oil, to exploit it with the help of friendly countries, and to seek Soviet aid in building the Euphrates dam. The broad support these demands won, especially among rank-and-file Ba'thists, provoked the authorities, in defiance of Hafez, to put Hourani and his principal lieutenants under house arrest in September. (Hafez released them eight months later.) The communists, who had hitherto co-operated with Hourani, now turned in another direction. The emergence of the neo-Ba'th trend led the Communist Party to speculate on the contradictions within the Ba'th. It tried to open a dialogue with the more 'progressive' trends within the party–the Hafez group, on the one hand, and the younger regionalists on the other.

REGIONALIST ADVANCE

In October 1964, these two groups joined forces to compel the resignation of the Bitar government and of Bitar and Mansour Atrash (son of Sultan Pasha Atrash, and also of the old guard) from the Presidium. Again becoming premier, General Hafez constituted a government dominated by the regionalist militants. Regionalist leaders General Salah Jadid and Dr Yusef Z'ayyen took the vacant seats on the Presidium. Outraged, the National Command brought Aflak back from Bonn for a confrontation. But the National Command's attempt to oust the regionalist officers from the government and the party and to dissolve the Regional Command failed; all party organizations outside Syria supported the regionalists.[4] The Regional Command stripped General Umran, who had associated himself with the National Command, of his party posts and sent him to Spain as ambassador.

One of the issues at stake between the traditional leadership and the regionalists was whether Syria should seek West German or Soviet aid to build the Euphrates dam. The traditionalists in the main wanted West German aid even at the price of an oil concession in the Jazira for the Concordia Company. Another issue was the land reform. Although Yusef Z'ayyen had been Agrarian Reform Minister in Bitar's government, he had been able to accomplish little in the face of its general policy and of an agrarian reform department staffed by persons hostile to the reform. The regionalists wanted to speed execution of the reform. The flight of capital out of the country had reached staggering proportions. The regionalists intended to stop it, if necessary, by draconian measures.

The Hafez government began to implement regionalist policies. Colonel Abdel Kerim Jundi, a radically-minded Isma'ili, became Minister of Agrarian Reform; for the first time since 1962 a determined effort was made to carry out the reform. In December 1964, a new kind of decree law in the Middle East prohibited the granting of any oil concessions and provided for Syria's own exploitation of its oil resources. This first oil nationalization decree in the Arab world followed to the letter the policy earlier advocated by Akram Hourani, who remained under house arrest. In putting an end to the activities of the West German Concordia Company, oil nationalization indirectly rejected the conditions Bonn had tied to its offer to build the Euphrates dam and cleared the way for an approach to the USSR on this question.

The rural-based regionalists had no inhibitions about attacking the entrenched interests of the city bourgeoisie. By this time, private capitalists had smuggled nearly one thousand million Syrian pounds out of the country while they borrowed heavily from state-owned banks to maintain their operations. The dimensions of capital flight become clear when one considers that total capital investment in the industrial sector in 1965 was just over £S500 million and that the Euphrates dam would cost not much more than a thousand million Syrian pounds.

On 1 January 1965, the regionalist-dominated government launched a sweeping nationalization programme which ended the economic, social, and political power of the city bourgeoisie and put nearly all modern industry in the hands of the state. Industrial companies, 25 per cent nationalized in 1964, were now nationalized 75 to 100 per cent. Altogether 106 private firms were taken over. They had a total capital of £S243 million and about 12,000 workers. The nationalizations affected not only the big bourgeoisie but also the middle bourgeoisie and even small shareholders. Among the firms nationalized were a number of artisan workshops. These were later returned to private ownership.

Throughout the early months of 1965, nationalization was extended to cover private electricity firms, oil-distributing companies, cotton-ginning companies, and about 70 per cent of export and import trade. The government thus assumed the directing role in the country's non-agricultural economic activity. At the same time, fiscal and tax laws were modified in favour of the less well-to-do and rent reductions were decreed.

Expecting a reaction from the bourgeoisie, the government restored martial law and exceptional tribunals. In late January, a civil disobedience campaign incited by Muslim religious leaders, the Muslim Brotherhood, and merchants took on the character of a *jihad* (holy crusade) against the 'godless' Ba'th. The National Guard, the Workers' Militia, and communist militants descended into the streets to break the strike. With army help, they succeeded.

The regionalist officers took a firmer hold on the army by dismissing many Sunni officers and replacing them mainly by their Alawi and Druze followers. The government also tried to broaden its political base. General Hafez promised that the NRC, 60 per cent of whose members would be workers and peasants, would soon be established and would decide on the lifting of martial law. The Syrian Communist Party and the USSR hailed the nationalizations as putting Syria 'on the road to non-capitalist development'. The regionalists now invited communists and other left-wing groups to co-operate with the regime as individuals; some communists responded to this appeal.

The nationalizations offered numerous opportunities in managing posts to a new staff coming from rural society. The nationalizations also destroyed the economic basis of the tactical collaboration of the Ba'th's traditional leadership with conservative forces. Aflak and Bitar, however, did not openly attack the nationalizations. They issued formal statements of support. Within the party, however, they condemned the nationalizations as 'a manoeuvre' to cover a party crisis. Behind the scenes the internal party conflict became explosive.

Aflak formulated this conflict in terms of a struggle between the military and the civilians. The role played by the military within the party was an important question. But Aflak's anti-militarist crusade was equivocal, since the National Command itself had been brought to power by the military and relied on its own military clan. An effort to resolve the conflict at the party's eighth National Congress in April 1965 succeeded only in temporarily papering over differences. Through Aflak's resignation as Secretary-General and his replacement by the Jordanian Munif Al-Razzaz, the traditional leadership hoped to maintain the Aflak line by making limited concessions to the Left. The most significant result of this move was that it enabled Razzaz to win General Hafez's support for the old guard, and Hafez for a time managed to save it.

The isolation of the party leadership (both national and regional) from the Syrian people and the party bases—a situation admitted by the new Secretary-General—encouraged new splits. A power struggle now developed between Generals Hafez and Jadid. An Emergency Regional Congress, held in July to settle this conflict, elected a new Regional Command, seven of whose members were officers. Since half the new Command supported Hafez, and the other half Jadid, nothing was settled.

The congress, however, again radicalized the party programme. A 'phased' programme defined the stages by which the country was to be placed on the road to 'socialist transformation' and 'people's democracy', with the Ba'th as the vanguard party working through the 'popular organizations'. The promised NRC was established on 23 August and empowered to act as a legislature and to draft a constitution. Its 95 members included the two party Commands and handpicked representatives of the army, peasants, workers, women, the liberal professions, teachers, and 'progressive citizens'. One of these 'progressive citizens' was a communist. The NRC, meeting for the first time on 2 September, elected a new five-man Presidium headed by General Hafez and containing three regionalists. Thirteen members of the NRC, including Aflak, Bitar, Jadid, and his right-hand man, Major Selim Hatum, boycotted this meeting, a clear indication of unabated party strife.

Under pressure from Hafez, General Jadid resigned as chief-of-staff. Elected Assistant Secretary-General of the Regional Command, he won over a number of Hafez's supporters to achieve dominance in the Command. The Command then began a furious attack on Hafez, ostensibly for the more friendly attitude he had adopted towards President Nasser in an effort to end Syria's isolation, but in fact because he had begun to stand with the National Command. On Hafez's return from the Arab Summit Conference held in

Casablanca in September 1965, he was replaced as premier by Yusef Z'ayyen.

In an effort to strengthen his position, Hafez tried to reinstate some of Hourani's men in the army. The Jadid-dominated government then arrested Hourani and his leading partisans on charges of 'collusion with a foreign power'. The reason for these arrests–aside from striking at Hafez–was a campaign that Hourani had been waging against a contract negotiated by certain regionalist officers with a British consortium; the contract dealt with the construction of an oil pipeline from the Jazira oilfields to the coast. Analyzing the contract in detail, Hourani claimed that its terms were even worse than the terms of the contract concluded with IPC during the Mandate. His campaign provoked wide discussion and opposition to the contract within the Ba'th itself. But the contract was signed, difficulties of the kind predicted by Hourani soon developed, and the British consortium eventually withdrew. (In December 1965, Hafez released Hourani, who was ill, so that he might go to Paris for medical treatment.)

Regionalist attacks drove Hafez closer to the National Command. Mounting conflicts created a crisis atmosphere. Early in December the National Command decided to require officers in the Regional Command (but not in the National Command) to resign from the army. But the Regional Command controlled Syria and most army bases now supported the regionalist officers. Except for Hafez's popularity with the people, the National Command was isolated. In answer to the National Command's order, the chief-of-staff of the Armoured Brigade stationed in Homs–Lt-Col Mustafa Tlas, then a Jadid partisan–arrested its three commanding officers who were loyal to Hafez and took over the brigade for the regionalists. Considering this act tantamount to a *coup*, the National Command decided to take over all authority, dissolving the Regional Command on the grounds that it had violated party statutes. But the National Command itself violated party statutes in taking this action without holding a party congress.

Assuming the functions of the Regional Command, the National Command named Salah Bitar to form a government. In the hope of avoiding a confessional aspect to the conflict, he brought General Umran, an Alawi, back from Madrid to serve as Deputy Premier and Defence Minister. The National Command mounted a campaign in the party branches against the regionalist officers, but was itself hopelessly divided by conflicts between Amine Al-Hafez and Hafez Assad, between both of them and Umran, between Bitar and Hafez and so on.

The Bitar government, declaring its intention to end the party's isolation at home and abroad, released political prisoners (including Hourani's followers), invited discussions with the discontented, and appointed a committee to study the nationalized industries, thereby provoking rumours of denationalization. But the major preoccupation was to consolidate the National Command's position. The National Command purged the NRC, enlarged it to 134 members, bringing in its own partisans, and prepared for a Regional Congress to elect a new Regional Command. The congress was postponed when the National Command realized it could not get its people elected without a purge of party branches. Decisions were taken to dissolve the National Guard and transfer a number of Jadid's partisans in the army.

THE 23 FEBRUARY 1966 COUP

These decisions provoked Syria's thirteenth and bloodiest army *coup* in seventeen years on 23 February. Its success was assured by the switch of General Hafez Assad, the Alawi Commander of the Air Force and a former supporter of Hafez, to the side of the insurrection. Hafez, Umran, Bitar, and other members of the National Command who did not manage to escape were imprisoned; Bitar, Aflak, and others were subsequently excluded from the party as 'imperialist agents' and 'traitors', and later the two historic leaders of the party were condemned to death. From this time, two Ba'th parties existed: the neo-Ba'th centred in Damascus, which soon built up branches in other Arab countries, and the old Ba'th based for the time being in Beirut.

The neo-Ba'thists, making their *coup* in the name of legality (the National Command having illegally dissolved the Regional Command), scrapped the 1964 Constitution and did away with the complicated structure which had fragmented power in rival party and government institutions. All power was then vested in the Regional Command. The Head of State, the premier, and the Cabinet, all appointed and dismissed by the Regional Command, were to exercise legislative and executive power, and later a new National Command was installed. General Jadid, the strongman of the new regime, chose to rule from behind the scenes as Assistant Secretary-General of the Regional Command. General Assad remained Commander of the Air Force and became Minister of Defence. Ahmad Sweidani, a Sunni, was promoted to major-general and named chief-of-staff. The most prominent civilians in the new regime were the three doctors, Chief of State Nur Al-Din Atasi, Premier Yusef Z'ayyen, and Deputy Premier and Foreign Minister Ibrahim Makhous.

The new rulers of Syria were mainly of peasant origin and of Alawi, Druze, and Isma'ili religious and cultural affiliation. This was the source of their radicalism *vis-à-vis* the city, especially the city merchants who dominated the agricultural economy, and the urban Sunni establishment. In the countryside their radicalism did not reach very deep. For they were not of the poor peasantry; they came from small and mainly middle landowning families and sometimes from families of local notables. Their dispossession of the bourgeoisie in the cities contrasted with their willingness to coexist with the countryside bourgeoisie and even–although on a basis of rivalry– with the big landlords once their political teeth had been pulled.

Changes in the land reform made by the neo-Ba'th soon after it took power give an insight into the nature of the regime. One amendment provided that in the case of planted land reclaimed through an irrigation project, state or private, the land reform law would not be applied to reduce the size of the landholding which was converted from non-irrigated to irrigated land. This amendment, designed to encourage extension of irrigated land, could open the way for the reinforcement of capitalist agriculture and would encourage mainly well-to-do landlords. In areas where state dams have been or are being constructed–notably the Euphrates and Latakia provinces where the regime had its social and political base–landlords could perhaps acquire several times as much irrigated land as could be owned elsewhere. A crucial question is whether or not this amendment will be applied to land reclaimed as a result of the construction of the Euphrates dam. So far, in the Euphrates area where middle land-ownership prevails, middle landlords not originally affected by the land reform law have been the main beneficiaries of this change in the law. But landowning peasants have also enjoyed the chance to become important exploiters.

The neo-Ba'thists did not reduce the ceilings on landownership, although these ceilings left less than one per cent of landowners in possession of more than 15 per cent of the cultivated land and the majority of peasants landless. The wide disparity between the size of the landlord's holding and the peasant's did not trouble the neo-Ba'th's dominant trend, best personified in the Deir Ezzor Ba'thists, themselves middle landowners. It did disturb a minority, represented by Colonel Abdel Kerim Jundi, of an Isma'ili local notable family of Salamiyah, who wanted to carry the reform further and develop collective ownership and state farms.

The neo-Ba'thists had the peasant's instinctive conservatism, fearing communism, distrusting popular movements, revealing a distinctly paternalistic attitude to the underprivileged classes. They accepted communist support because they were weak, especially in the cities, and the Communist Party was the only organized force physically present in almost every city. Moreover, they considered the communists less dangerous than the Nasserists and believed that collaboration with the communists would open the door to Soviet aid and support. The new regime therefore appointed the first communist minister in Syrian history, as well as two progressive ministers friendly to the communists. (All non-Ba'thists served as individuals, not as party representatives.) When Khalid Bagdash returned to Syria after eight years of exile, the neo-Ba'th reluctantly accepted the *fait accompli*. The Communist Party newspaper remained illegal, but its clandestine distribution was permitted. Co-operation with the communists, however, was strictly limited and did not prevent the government from periodically arresting–and sometimes torturing and killing–Communist Party members.

The new government acted quickly to end Syria's isolation internationally and in the Arab world. To Premier Z'ayyen's declaration that 'the support of the USSR is a vital necessity for Syria', Moscow responded by finding the new rulers 'resolved to apply socialist principles in industry and agriculture'. Invited to Moscow, Z'ayyen there won a Soviet commitment to build the Euphrates dam, a project Syria and the USSR had been discussing intermittently since 1963. The Soviets also promised an acceleration of aid in other fields. When Moscow warned other powers against attempts to overthrow the new Syrian regime, it was clear that the government had consolidated its position internationally.

Once in power, the neo-Ba'thists cast aside the anti-Nasser card they had used against Amine Al-Hafez and set out to mend relations with Cairo. Trade talks led to a trade and payments agreement, the first Syrian-Egyptian agreement since 1961. Moscow's prodding encouraged the Damascus-Cairo reconciliation. Soviet Premier Kosygin, during a visit to Cairo in May, urged Nasser to co-operate with the new Syrian government as a first step towards a 'united front of Arab progressive states'. The two countries gradually moved towards restoration of diplomatic relations and Cairo at last–after five years–recognized Syria's independence. The neo-Ba'th government advocated 'co-ordination' of policy among progressive Arab states, wooing Algeria and the Yemen as well as Egypt. Premier Z'ayyen stated the neo-Ba'th's order of priorities. 'The point of departure for the fulfilment of unity', he said,[5] 'is the struggle for socialism at home and the revolutionary struggle against imperialism and reaction abroad'.

The government launched its 'revolutionary struggle' by opening the 'battle against the oil trusts'. Under the imperative of securing hard currency for development needs, it demanded from IPC substantial increases in oil dues and £40 million sterling in retrospective payments. The government claimed this sum was owed for the

1956–65 period under the 50–50 agreement of 1955 because the company had 'fraudulently calculated its profits'.[6] As part of its 'revolutionary struggle', the government adopted a new policy towards Palestine by calling for 'mobilization of the masses' for a popular liberation war.

Eruption of a new conflict within the regime encouraged Syria's enemies. Major Selim Hatum, the influential Druze leader of the army's élite commando battalion–al-Maghaaweer (singular: mighwaar –'very courageous')–was the key figure in the new split. Ambitious, adventurous, and arbitrary, Hatum ruled this battalion like a feudal chieftain, considering it his private domain, and manipulated his men at will. The confessional and regional allegiances he could command enabled him to consolidate to a maximum his individual authority. Major Hatum, one of the most leftist officers, had taken a leading role in the February 1966 coup. He was excluded from the Regional Command soon after because the party could not tolerate his attempts to widen his control over the state institutions. In reply, Hatum multiplied his leftist speeches, proclaimed his admiration for Che Guevara, and (unsuccessfully) sought communist support. Jadid's dismissal of a number of Druze officers after Salah Bitar's escape from prison in August fed Hatum's and Druze resentment.

Early in September–a few days after the old National Command from Beirut called on Syrians to overthrow the government–Major Hatum attempted a coup by luring government and party leaders to the Jebel Druze, where he seized them as hostages. During these tense days Amman Radio repeatedly interrupted its programmes to call on Syrians to revolt. The government rearmed the Workers' Militia, which it had disarmed on seizing power, and sent it with the National Guard into the streets. Hatum fled to Jordan when the army besieged the Druze capital, Suwayda, and threatened to bomb it. In Jordan, he accused the Syrian government of being controlled by 'Alawis and communists'. (During the June 1967 war Hatum returned to Syria, apparently believing conditions then existing would permit him to recover power. Whether or not he returned at King Husain's instigation, his intrusion into Syria offered the regime the chance to finish with a rebel. He was executed on 25 June 1967. His career, with its wide swings between Left and Right, illustrates the political instability which characterized some army officers.)

Once the danger was past, the Workers' Militia–on the initiative of its ambitious leader, Khalid Jundi–began at gunpoint to purge state enterprises of 'reactionaries' and 'imperialist agents'. No doubt some rank-and-file members of the militia saw themselves acting 'in defence of the revolution'. But Jundi was opportunistically using the militia to establish his political influence. Never a worker, he was vulnerable because he presented the worst possible image of a popular leader. Demagogic and corrupt, he regularly spent in one night's entertainment the equivalent of a worker's monthly salary. General Jadid quickly put an end to the militia's purge, and compelled workers to turn in their arms and Jundi to renounce his mission. The neo-Ba'th was no more prepared than the old Ba'th to tolerate a movement that might escape its control.

Syria's dispute with IPC reached a climax in December 1966 when, with negotiations deadlocked, the government seized all IPC properties in Syria and cut off the flow of oil from Iraq. This action drastically reduced Iraq's oil income and Lebanese and Jordanian oil-transit revenue. A Syrian campaign calling on Iraq to nationalize its oil, coupled with Iraq's loss of oil revenue, threatened political repercussions in that politically unstable country; IPC decided to compromise. A settlement in March 1967 gave Syria a more than 50 per cent increase in oil dues, but shelved its demand for retroactive payments pending a review by both sides of their accounts for the 1956–65 period. The increase in dues won by Syria was passed on by IPC to Jordan and Lebanon. For the first time the neo-Ba'th government was accorded a certain grudging respect by other Arab governments.

The government's victory in the oil battle came at a time of mounting tension on the Syrian-Israeli frontiers and of growing Arab disarray. The Middle East was already on the road to war.

[1] BBC *Summary of World Broadcasts*, Middle East and North Africa, 1963, Part IV, ME/1343/E10.
[2] At the Ba'th Party Congress of February 1964, *Arab World*, 25 March 1964.
[3] Speech to National Command in December 1965, *Arab World*, 25 February 1966.
[4] Munif Al-Razzaz: *Al-Tajriba Al-Murra*, Beirut, 1967, p. 112–17.
[5] *Arab World*, 20 July 1966.
[6] According to the Lebanese economist Dr Nicolas Sarkis, Syria had received not the 50 per cent to which it was entitled, but only 17·5 per cent.

Chapter 10

The June 1967 War: Prelude and Aftermath

THE ARABS CANNOT DIVORCE the June 1967 war from its root causes: the forcible dispossession of the indigenous Palestine population by an alien people and the inherently expansionist character of the state of Israel. This character is evident in Israel's mission to 'ingather' all the Jews in the world,[1] in its *de facto* step-by-step expansion, and in long-held Zionist territorial ambitions, often frankly avowed by activist Israeli leaders and even now not yet fulfilled.[2]

The mechanics of the continuing conflict have been largely determined by Israel's permanent military superiority over all its Arab neighbours combined and by the efforts of Arab leaders to hide their impotence behind verbal violence and threats of war. Two major developments provided the immediate political dynamic of the 1967 crisis. One was the emergence in the mid-1960s of an organized Palestine resistance movement. The other was Israel's diversion of the waters of the Jordan to irrigate the Negev.

Israel's Jordan diversion, whose first stage was completed in 1964, was for the Arabs as serious as the original establishment of Israel since it consolidated a decisive step in Israeli expansionism. Much of the land on which the diversion is constructed is Arab-owned land, seized in violation of the Partition Resolution which guaranteed Arab rights and property within the Jewish state. Parts of the project involve land outside the territory allotted the Jewish state in the Partition Resolution. As Israeli leaders did not conceal, the aim of the diversion was to enhance Israel's military, economic, and human potential, to facilitate the settlement of Jewish immigrants, and to bar forever the return of the Palestinians. The diversion project was predicated on taking as much as possible of the fresh water of the Jordan for use outside the watershed. The Jordan, however, is an international river in which other riparian states have rights. Only 23 per cent of its waters originate in Israel. Seventy-seven per cent come from tributaries – the Hasbani, Banias, and Yarmuk – which rise in Syria and Lebanon. (The Yarmuk for part of its course forms the boundary between Syria and Jordan.)

CONFLICT OVER THE JORDAN

The Demilitarized Zone

The conflict over the Jordan waters closely involved Syria and was played out in and near the Syrian–Israeli demilitarized zone, whose central sector lies on both sides of the river between Lake Huleh and Lake Tiberias. The 1949 Armistice Agreement, as we have already noted, gave the zone a 'special status', in which neither side exercised sovereignty; it excluded the armed forces of both sides and provided that 'no military or political advantage should be gained under the truce'.

In breach of the Armistice Agreement Israel refused to allow Palestinian Arab civilians who had fled during the 1948 war to return and expelled other Palestinian Arabs from the zone, appropriating their land. Thereafter, Israel systematically tried to take over the zone. U.N. authorities attributed continuing difficulties in the zone to a number of factors. These included Israel's claim to sovereignty and denial of any Syrian rights, and the fact that after 1951 it boycotted all regular meetings of the Mixed Armistice Commission (MAC). Israel also constructed fortifications and introduced border police into the zone. Annual Israeli attempts to expand cultivation into–and so gain control of–Arab-owned land in the zone always provoked troubles. Another recurring source of tension was Israel's refusal to respect the Anglo-French accords of the 1920s which had acknowledged Syria's traditional fishing rights in Lake Tiberias. On occasion, the United Nations complained of Syrian breaches of the Armistice Agreement, and it denied Syria's claim to a right to be consulted on all activities in the zone. But, in general, U.N. interpretations of the legal status of the zone differed little from Syria's.[3]

Israel's drainage of the Huleh marshes, started in 1951, encroached on Arab-owned land in the demilitarized zone. When Palestinian Arabs resisted Israeli occupation of their lands, serious clashes developed. In response to Syria's complaints the United Nations ordered the work suspended until agreement could be reached. Later, over Syrian objections, the United Nations permitted Israel to resume work on non-Arab-owned lands, and the project was completed in 1956.

THE JOHNSTON PLAN

On 2 September 1953, without informing the MAC chairman, Israel began to work 24 hours a day on the Negev diversion canal at the Bridge of Jacob's Daughters in the demilitarized zone, claiming the canal was only a small one intended for local use, a deception later admitted.[4] The Israelis apparently hoped by a *fait accompli* to frustrate American plans for joint Arab-Israeli water development then in preparation. Although the United Nations held the diversion to be a violation of the Armistice Agreement, Israel did not heed the Security Council desist order until Washington suspended American economic aid. American pressures restrained Israel from carrying out a unilateral diversion of the Jordan for the next two years, during which the United States tried to win consent for a joint water project. A study of unified Jordan water development, already made at UNRWA's request, formed the basis for the proposals for joint water development presented to the Arab states and Israel by United States presidential envoy Eric Johnston, late in 1953.

The American initiative in attempting to remove the question of the Jordan waters from the overall political context of the Palestine problem ran directly counter to the recommendations of the U.N. Economic Survey Mission which in 1949 pointed out that in the absence of a general settlement

> on outstanding issues involving repatriation and compensation of Arab refugees and territorial boundaries, it is unrealistic to suppose that agreement on the complex question of international water rights could be negotiated among the parties . . .

In this sense, the Johnston proposals were probably doomed to failure from the start. They threatened Israel's plan to take the lion's share of the waters for itself. Leading Israeli officials and journals denounced the proposals as designed 'to rob Israel of its water' and 'sabotage' its water plans. To the Arab states, acceptance of the proposals would mean renouncing the rights of the displaced Palestinians to return to their homes and lands, rights annually reaffirmed by the United Nations, and implicit recognition of the Armistice demarcation lines as the boundaries of Israel. But, defying popular protests (led in Syria by the Ba'th), Arab governments agreed to negotiate on a technical level.

The Johnston proposals provoked political conflicts in each of the states concerned. Egypt alone consistently supported Johnston's mission. Although not directly concerned in the Jordan River plan, Egypt was much interested in a parallel proposal, brought by Johnston, to use Nile water to irrigate a part of western Sinai for resettlement of Palestine refugees. (The Cairo regime crushed with great harshness a week-long uprising of Palestine refugees in Gaza against this plan.) Egypt therefore used its influence to try to persuade other Arab states to accept the Johnston proposals. And, in June

1954, Johnston and the Arab representatives reached agreement 'on the general lines of an overall plan for development of the Jordan Basin and on the need for immediate implementation'.

Israel, however, continued to reject the proposed water allocations and the idea of international supervision. Israel also refused to waive its demand for inclusion of the wholly Lebanese river, the Litani. Only early in 1955–after Johnston had threatened to break off negotiations and blame Israel for their failure[5]–did the Israeli government adopt a less rigid position. But sharing the Jordan waters was no part of the programme of David Ben Gurion, who became Israeli Defence Minister on 17 February. The Gaza Raid and three other large-scale Israeli attacks on Egypt in 1955, and a big Israeli assault on Syria in December, scuttled Johnston's mission and left Israel free to proceed with its unilateral plan.

American Secretary of State Dulles also contributed to Johnston's failure in specifically tying the proposals to resettlement of the refugees and so strengthening Arab opposition, especially in Syria. The Syrian, Lebanese, and Jordanian premiers, meeting in Damascus in October 1955, called for rejection of the proposals. The Arab League, rather than comply, referred the proposals back to its technical committee for further study. Although Israel bore a large share of the responsibility for the failure of Johnston's mission, it claimed the Arabs had 'vetoed the Johnston plan'. Around this theme it organized a vast and continuing campaign to mobilize world opinion behind its unilateral water programme.

THE JORDAN DIVERSION

In 1956, the Israelis moved the site of the Jordan-Negev diversion to the north-west corner of Lake Tiberias and in 1958 resumed work. From the heights above Lake Tiberias, Syrians could see this project going forward. Tensions inevitably mounted. Syria was then the Northern Region of the UAR, and Syrian Ba'th leaders urged President Nasser to take some action to halt the Israeli diversion. His contention that nothing could be done was the more difficult for Syrians to accept because, after 1956, Syria had become the focus of Israel's attention and the only victim of its 'reprisal' raids.

Beginning in 1957, provocative Israeli encroachments on Arab lands in the demilitarized zone gave rise to ever more serious clashes. Early in 1960, a heavy Israeli attack on the Arab village of Tawafik drew severe censure from the Mixed Armistice Commission. A crisis developed as both Israel and the UAR concentrated troops. President Nasser denounced the 1950 Tripartite Declaration and threatened to cut off oil in the event of a new Western aggression against the Arabs;

Ben Gurion visited Western capitals to secure more arms. This theatrical commotion served the aims of the Arab cold war, in which Nasser, Husain, and Qasim tried to outbid each other on the Palestine question; it also assured the success of Ben Gurion's mission; with United States help, he concluded a secret arms deal with Federal Germany.

After regaining its independence in 1961, Syria repeatedly pressed for action against Israel's Jordan diversion. In mid-March 1962, the Israelis directed a big attack against Syrian villages on the eastern side of Lake Tiberias, and jet planes fought over Syrian territory. The United States warned Israel against any further 'retaliatory' raids. The Security Council censured the attack. Syrian and Arab fears were further inflamed at this time by reports that Israel's Jordan diversion would soon be completed and that the capacity of the Israeli diversion plant far exceeded what the Johnston proposals had envisaged.

In 1963, following the Ba'th's seizure of power in Baghdad and Damascus, the party's sixth National Congress resolved that Israel's Jordan-Negev diversion 'must be prevented by force' and that a Palestine entity should be created. Under Syrian pressure, Arab chiefs-of-staff met in December to consider what could be done. The approaching completion of Israel's Jordan-Negev conduit placed Arab governments in a painful dilemma. If they did not assert their rights to the waters of the Arab tributaries of the Jordan, Israel could enter a claim of 'prior appropriation' and deprive them of any legal recourse. [6] If they did assert Arab rights, they ran the risk of military attack which they knew they were too weak to withstand.

SUMMIT DIPLOMACY

The Ba'th's call for war to halt the Israeli diversion compelled President Nasser to find a way around this dilemma and to make other Arab states share responsibility for whatever action or inaction followed. His solution was to call off the Arab cold war and inaugurate his summit diplomacy. At his bidding, a conference of Arab heads of state convened in Cairo in January 1964 to unify Arab action on Palestine on the premise that the Arabs could not for the time being go to war. As a 'national duty' Syria reluctantly attended the conference, where it made common cause with Algeria in proposing an Algerian-type war against Israel. This proposal received short shrift. Syrian 'adventurism' drew severe criticism. Syria's scepticism about the proposed alternatives, however, served to expose the element of sham in the summit conferences. For these conferences were not devised to take any real action. Their purpose was to convince the restive Arab peoples that something effective was being done against the Israeli diversion and to persuade the United States to compel Israel to abandon its unilateral diversion. The Summits failed in both aims and played into the hands of the activist clan in Israel.

The Cairo Summit decided on two major lines of action: creation of a Palestine entity, and diversion of the Arab tributaries of the Jordan for irrigation of Arab lands. The Arab diversion would not affect Israel's water supply in the Jordan valley because Israel's needs within the watershed are more than fully met by the Dan tributary. Its aim was to prevent Israel from capturing the waters of the Arab tributaries for use outside the watershed in the Negev. A Unified Arab Command was established to protect the diversion, but the plan faced many technical and other obstacles. According to an Israeli source, the Arab diversion would at most have deprived Israel of only 5 to 6 per cent of its allocations under the Johnston proposals.[7]

Arab Foreign Ministers were sent to world capitals to explain the Arab project, the defensive character of Arab military preparations, and the decision of Arab governments to continue, as they had since 1949, to stand on the U.N. resolutions (the Partition Resolution and the December 1948 Resolution demanding that all refugees who wished to return home be allowed to do so). But Arab propaganda to the Arab peoples was full of extravagant and braggart claims about the harm the Arab diversion would inflict on Israel. This propaganda only served to facilitate an Israeli propaganda campaign which presented the Arab diversion as an 'act of aggression' justifying a military response. Golda Meir affirmed that the Arab diversion 'constitutes a direct menace to Israel's existence'. Yigal Allon added that it would be considered 'a hostile act', and so on. Although what was at stake was not Israel's existence but its unilateral water programme–which did not allow fair shares to the Arabs and contravened the rights of the Palestine people–the activist clique in Israel had found its war cry. Israeli propaganda evoked a sympathetic response in the West. A new Western arms build-up of Israel's offensive military potential began at this time.

In accordance with the Summit decision to form a Palestine entity, a National Palestine Congress was held in May 1964 to set up the Palestine Liberation Organization (PLO) and a Palestine Liberation Army. Arab opinion considered PLO just another device by which Arab governments hoped to control the impatient Palestinians and saw in the choice of Ahmed Choukeri as its leader and of Gaza as its headquarters clear evidence that PLO would be under Cairo's direction. But Palestinians, long since disillusioned by official

Arab inaction, seized on the chance to organize and voice their political demands, and so made PLO–to an extent–a political force in its own right. Creation of PLO and its army, and the appearance at this time of other Palestinian fighting organizations, marked the exiled Palestinian's first direct and organized political intervention in the Palestine problem and Arab political life.

In the interval between the first Summit and the second, held in Alexandria in September 1964, Israel's Jordan-Negev diversion went into operation. Work on the Arab projects, however, had not started because the Arab states concerned, while fearing an Israeli attack, also feared Egyptian interference and so refused to permit the Unified Command to move in Arab units to protect the projects. The Alexandria Summit therefore gave priority to a dam on the Yarmuk which would not affect Israel's diversion and could thus hope to escape attack. But Israeli war threats multiplied, and General Dayan declared:[8] 'The Army's force of persuasion will not be sufficient. Its entry into action will be necessary as it was in 1956 to open the Port of Elath'.

Israel's threats, an increasing flow of Western arms to Israel, and reports of Bonn's intention to establish diplomatic relations with Israel contributed to mounting anxiety and frustration in Arab capitals. The first cracks in the Arab consensus achieved at the Summits appeared when the Arab states failed to reach a common stand towards Bonn's diplomatic initiative *vis-à-vis* Israel. The cracks widened when Tunisian President Bourguiba called for negotiations with Israel on the basis of the U.N. Resolutions. Israel had since 1949 consistently rejected these resolutions; Bourguiba's intervention therefore seemed at best gratuitous. The failure of most Arab states to assign the Unified Command any troops, and their reluctance to permit entry of Unified Command units into their territory, brought the Command to a standstill.

On 31 May 1965, President Nasser acknowledged that the Arab diversion plan could not be carried out and that the Arabs could not go to war in the foreseeable future. In August, military reverses in the Yemen and a major domestic crisis compelled Nasser to negotiate with Saudi Arabia a truce in the Yemen war. His concessions drew sharp attacks from the Syrian Ba'th. During a visit to Moscow soon after, Nasser vented his exasperation with the Ba'th in a speech to Syrian and Egyptian students. Accusing Syrian Ba'thists of recklessness and of trying to 'create embarrassing situations', he warned that they would destroy his summit policy and that distrust between Syria and Egypt would render the Unified Command impotent.

Two weeks later the third Summit met in Casablanca, but only to acknowledge failure on every front. Arab governments had not

carried out earlier summit resolutions concerning assistance to PLO
and now rejected all PLO demands. Syria had temporarily suspended
work on its part of the Arab diversion – an irrigation canal from the
Banias – after Israeli attacks in March, May, and August which
destroyed its equipment and twice compelled it to change the site of
the work. General Ali Amr, Chief of the Unified Command, estimated it would take four years and £150 million (sterling) to build
Arab strength to the point where it could stand up to Israel. Even the
Ba'th had retreated. Its Secretary-General, Munif Razzaz, who had
accompanied President Hafez to Casablanca, declared that Syria did
not consider war with Israel either desirable or possible and that
Arab attempts to divert the Jordan were not worth the candle. As a
face-saving gesture, the conference adopted an Arab Solidarity Pact
in which, among other things, the Arab states agreed to stop interfering in each other's affairs and using their information media to
attack each other.

The pact did not long paper over inter-Arab tensions. With the
breakdown of the Yemen truce, the Saudi-Egyptian conflict resumed.
King Faisal set out to rally pro-Western Muslim states in an Islamic
alignment to 'contain' progressive Arab regimes and for this project
won King Husain's support. President Nasser then declared war on
the Islamic Pact as a 'turbanned' version of the Baghdad Pact. The
left Ba'th regime that took power in Syria in February 1966 renounced
the Casablanca Solidarity Pact and called on all 'progressive Arab
states' to form a common front against imperialism and reaction.
Moscow endorsed this appeal. Syria then tried to manoeuvre Nasser
into discarding his summit diplomacy in favour of a counter-Summit
of Arab progressive states. In July, Nasser moved closer to the Syrian-
Soviet line when he announced the end of his summit diplomacy.

Neither the progressive anti-imperialist front nor the Islamic Pact
materialized, but the leading Arab states were split into two
venomously antagonistic camps: the progressive led by Nasser and
the pro-Western led by Faisal. The major propaganda theme of the
pro-Western camp was Nasser's 'inaction' on the Palestine question.

THE PALESTINIANS

The virtual abandonment of the Arab diversion plan did not halt
Israeli preventive-war talk. The Israeli activist clan had failed to win
all its objectives in the 1948 war (when it sought control of all
Palestine) and in the 1956 war (when Ben Gurion announced Israel's
intention to remain in Gaza, Sharm Al-Sheik, and Sinai). The
activists had not renounced these aims. Moreover, developing financial and economic crises within Israel, coupled with rising emigration

and falling immigration, made a war atmosphere seem desirable to the activists. They acquired a new pretext for creating a situation favourable to war when Palestinians, having finally lost hope in justice from the United Nations, decided to take into their own hands the task of liberating Palestine.

Palestinian workers and students in the Gaza refugee camps began organizing their own liberation movement, Al Fatah, during the Israeli occupation of the Gaza strip in 1956. But Fatah launched its first commando attack inside Israel only on 1 January 1965. Although mere pinpricks, Fatah's attacks posed a real political threat to Israel which has always denied the existence of the Palestine people. To counter the political threat and divert attention from the Palestinians, Israel held the Arab states, in particular Syria, responsible for the commandos. Actually—with the exception of Syria—the Arab states bordering Israel persecuted and arrested the commandos and Jordan did not hesitate to kill them. Syria alone allowed the commandos relative freedom of movement, broadcast their communiqués, and gave them financial assistance and arms. The commandos made almost all their attacks, however, through Jordan or Lebanon.

THE RADICAL BA'TH REGIME IN SYRIA

Because of its stubborn efforts to divert the Banias and its rejection of the role of 'guardian or protector' over Israel's frontiers, Syria was already the chief target of the Israeli activists when the neo-Ba'th took power in February 1966. Soon after, the new government called for a 'popular liberation war' to liberate Palestine and rid the Arab world of imperialism and reaction. The neo-Ba'th government's assistance to the Palestine commandos and its popular war slogans obeyed a double imperative: to apply the nationalist themes of Ba'th ideology and—more concretely and tactically—to pull the Palestinians out from under Nasser's influence. Although neo-Ba'th sincerity about the Palestine cause is not in doubt, Ba'th-Nasserist rivalry was at the origin of its 'extremist' propaganda on this as on other questions.

The popular war theme also brought to the fore the colonialist aspect of the Israeli state and so posed a potential political threat to Israel. However, since the regime was unable or unwilling to take the (potentially revolutionary) measures required to wage a popular liberation war, the new policy became one of revolutionary and bellicose verbalism. The Syrian popular war threat was empty. But the increasing violence of Syria's verbal aggressiveness more and more assumed the character of a calculated provocation, as the neo-Ba'th came to believe that the time had come to engage Israel in decisive battle. This provocative policy gave the Israeli activist clan precisely the pretext it needed to go to war to fulfil its territorial ambitions.

Syria's political radicalization after February 1966, its vanguard anti-imperialist stance, and close ties with the USSR provoked the United States and frightened pro-Western regimes in the area. These factors also became important in precipitating the 1967 crisis.

Within two months of the neo-Ba'th's advent to power, Israeli activists began a systematic escalation of threats and attacks which aimed – as General Rabin declared in a moment of frankness[9] – to bring down the Damascus government. The escalation was pegged first on Syria's continuing efforts to divert the Banias, although Israel knew that this diversion could not significantly affect its water supply (because much of the river's annual flow is flood water which cannot be dammed outside Israel); and, secondly, on Syria's alleged responsibility for the Palestine commandos. Parallel with the escalation of Israeli threats, Jordan's King Husain tried to subvert the Syrian government.

Israeli threats remained verbal until 14 July when the Israeli Air Force heavily attacked the Banias diversion site. In mid-August, Israel and Syria fought a major air and artillery battle near Lake Tiberias. Israeli planes, exercising what Premier Eshkol called 'the right of pursuit' in imitation of the United States in Vietnam, chased Syrian MIGs deep into Syria.

Three weeks later, just after Major Hatum's abortive *coup*, Jordanian troops massed on the Syrian frontier. The Israeli chief-of-staff, General Rabin, chose this moment to assert[10] that 'the combats Israel must wage against Syria . . . aim at the regime in Syria'. Premier Eshkol underscored this threat in declaring that henceforth Syria would be held accountable for all acts of sabotage by 'terrorist infiltrators' wherever they originated. King Husain raised the spectre of a Soviet-Syrian-Egyptian Axis in threatening to 'resort to force in Syria if foreign [Soviet] intervention is signalled'.[11] Israeli threats hastened the conclusion of a Syrian-Egyptian defence pact early in November. To Syria, the pact brought moral support if nothing else. Egypt hoped the pact would secure it a restraining influence on Damascus.

During all this period the Security Council had been paralyzed, so far as the tension between Syria and Israel was concerned, by Soviet-American differences. Israel's attack on the Jordanian village of Samu on 13 November, however, was unanimously condemned by the Security Council. This attack also gave King Husain the pretext harshly to repress his Palestinian subjects, who demonstrated crying for arms, and to taunt President Nasser for 'hiding behind the U.N. Emergency Forces'. A 'Voice of Free Syria', broadcasting from Jordan, began at this time to incite Syrians to overthrow the Damascus government. Details about an alleged Jordanian conspiracy against Syria–involving some of the Syrian officers who had found asylum in Jordan after Hatum's abortive *coup*–came from defecting Jordanian army officers.

In early 1967 emergency meetings of the Syrian-Israeli Mixed Armistice Commission (Israel for the first time in seven years had agreed to attend) broke down. But commando forays into Israel fell off. The neo-Ba'th's internal enemies, the Muslim Brotherhood in the lead, accused the government of having withdrawn its support from the Palestinians in response to Egyptian and Soviet pressures. They also derided its slogans of popular liberation war.

Early in April, in a deliberate provocation, Israel announced it would cultivate all areas of the demilitarized zone including Arab-owned plots; on 7 April, it sent an armoured tractor to cultivate a disputed plot. When the Syrians predictably fired on the tractor, Israel responded with a major artillery, tank, and air attack on Syrian border villages and shot down six Syrian planes. This assault has been called the 'curtain-riser to the six-day war'.[12] It could only have been intended to show contempt for the Egyptian-Syrian defence pact and/or provoke Egypt into action. Following this attack, the Syrian government took the first steps to organize a 'people's army'. Through this party-controlled popular militia, the Ba'th hoped to mobilize all able-bodied citizens to defend the Ba'th revolution.

The Israeli attack emboldened the internal opposition in Syria. Clandestine radio stations operating from Jordan called for the 'overthrow of the atheist regime hostile to Arabism and Islam' and 'deliverance of the country from Marxism and communism'. On 25 April, the army's official organ, *Jaysh Al-Sha'ab* (The People's Army), published an article entitled 'The Means of Creating the New Arab Man'. In urging the need to sweep away the crippling traditions of the past, the author consigned 'God, religion, feudalism, capitalism, colonialism, and all the values that prevailed under the old society' to the 'museum of history'; he offered as the only new value 'absolute belief in man's ability'. The article provoked a storm of religious-right-wing protest and vilification of the 'godless Ba'th'. Strikes and clashes occurred in Damascus and other cities.

The Workers' Militia, rearmed by the government, played the biggest role in breaking the merchants' strike in Damascus. The ring-leaders of the agitation were imprisoned; their property was confiscated. The author of the offending article and the magazine's editor were arrested, summarily tried, and condemned to hard labour for life. (Both were later quietly released.) Charging Jordanian and Saudi complicity in the troubles, the government expelled three Saudi diplomats. Within four days, it had the situation in hand and conditions returned to normal.

ISRAELI THREATS

During this crisis Israel increased its pressures on Syria. According to a UNTSO military observer stationed on the Syrian-Israeli armistice demarcation line during the three months before the June war, movements of Israeli tanks, tank-transporters, artillery, and personnel carriers were observed near the frontier in the last week of April and the first week of May and were reported to UNTSO head-quarters in Jerusalem. But UNTSO was told by Israel that these movements were only road manoeuvres and that tanks had not entered 'the defensive area', although 'it had already been reported that they had done so from UN observation posts on the Syrian side'.[13] Reports of these movements, whatever their significance, inevitably reached the Syrian government, which could hardly consider them anything but menacing. On 8 May, Syria sent two emissaries to Cairo to warn President Nasser of Israeli troop concentrations on its frontiers.

A rising chorus of extravagant threats against Syria by Premier Eshkol and Chief-of-Staff Rabin, among others, now came from Israel. Eshkol asserted Israel's readiness to use force. A 'high Israeli source' threatened to 'occupy' Damascus. Rabin declared: 'So long as the ardent revolutionaries in Damascus have not been overthrown, no government in the Middle East can feel safe'. Israel's threats and its repeated massive 'reprisals' seem to have been devised to provoke Nasser to come to the aid of Syria, since Israeli leaders could hardly have failed to foresee that he would have to respond.[14]

Once Nasser moved his troops into Sinai in response to the menacing Israeli actions against Syria, Syria ceased to be the pretext for the march towards war and was pushed to the sidelines. The extraordinary reaction of the Arab peoples to this move compelled King Husain to fly to Cairo for a spectacular reconciliation and to put his forces under Egyptian command. Only Syria refused reconciliation with a leader regarded as an American hireling. General Rabin later admitted that the forces Nasser sent into Sinai 'were not sufficient to launch an offensive against Israel. He knew it and we know it'.[15] Nasser's closure of the Tiran Straits to Israeli shipping had little economic importance to Israel because barely 5 per cent of its commerce passed through the straits and most of this in non-Israeli bottoms. But the Egyptian blockade was a political defeat for Israel and hence intolerable. The blockade therefore became Israel's *casus belli*, although General Rabin later said that 'basically the war was provoked by a series of factors of a local and international nature' – factors which he did not specify beyond reference to the Soviet presence in the region.

THE SIX-DAY WAR

Israel's *blitzkrieg* on 5 June caught Syria unprepared. By midday Israeli raids had destroyed two-thirds of the Syrian Air Force. Otherwise–except for an unsuccessful Syrian attempt to raid Haifa on the 5th and artillery fire exchanged during the next two days–the Syrian-Israeli front was quiet. This despite Cairo Radio appeals to Syria to take the offensive. A heavy Israeli air bombardment started on the 8th. Israel began its offensive into Syria on the 9th after it had disposed of the Egyptian army and after Syria had accepted the United Nations call for a cease-fire. American and British correspondents in Washington reported that President Johnson deliberately refused to put pressure on Israel to respect the cease-fire until after Israeli conquests had been completed on all three fronts. On the Syrian front Israel seized the sources of the Jordan and–after it had agreed to a cease-fire–took the provincial capital, Qunaytra.

The Syrian army at first resisted courageously, but the Golan Heights proved as vulnerable without air support as other Maginot-line type defences. Moreover, at 8.45 a.m. on the 10th, the Syrian Defence Ministry announced the fall of Qunaytra, then still in Syrian hands, perhaps in an effort to strengthen the hand of Syria's U.N. representative who had been trying vainly for two days to get the Security Council to enforce a cease-fire. The premature report of Qunaytra's fall had a devastating effect on army morale. Believing themselves encircled, officers and soldiers began to flee. Six hours later the Israelis walked into Qunaytra almost unopposed. At 6.30 p.m. on the 10th, the cease-fire finally went into effect.

The Syrian army had suffered about 2,000 casualties, including, according to the Israelis, 361 prisoners and about a thousand dead. The Israeli army used napalm against villages as well as military positions, sacked Qunaytra, and levelled villages to the ground. Some 35,000 people, a quarter of the population, fled the Golan plateau during the fighting. In the next six months, the Israeli occupation forces expelled another 95,000 people by demolishing villages, cutting off water and food supplies, and by threats reinforced by torture and execution of those who refused to leave.[17] Expellees were compelled to leave behind everything they owned–shops full of goods, sheep and goats, clothes and household possessions, as well as lands, homes, vineyards, and apple trees. For a time they camped in open fields near Deraa, most without shelter of any kind; later they were harboured in tent encampments near Damascus and Deraa. Only about 8,000 Syrians, 5 per cent of the population, remained under the Israeli occupation;[18] most of these were Druzes. With the exception of 400 people, mainly Druzes, Israel allowed no one to return. Having cleared the area of the indigenous population, the Israelis set out to people it with Jews. Only a few weeks after the war, Israel called on Jewish people from all over the world to come and settle in the Golan and soon established a dozen or more military settlements. All these measures were in violation of international law, specifically of the Fourth Geneva Convention drawn up after the Second World War to prevent a reoccurrence of the crimes committed by the Nazis against the Jews and other innocent peoples.

In contrast, the Syrian government's treatment of its Jewish citizens was and remains correct.[19] Since 1967 they, like some Christians and Muslims, must have special authorization to travel through the country. In most cases this authorization is granted on demand. Like other Syrians, Jews must have a valid reason for going abroad and cannot take their money out of the country. Some Syrian Jews have been allowed to travel abroad. In practice Syrian Jews are not conscripted into the army. Syria is a country at war; the enemy occupies the south-west corner of the country barely 40 miles from Damascus. Given Israel's claim to the allegiance of all Jews in the world and the indirect connections maintained by some Syrian Jews with relatives who have emigrated to Israel, Syrian Jews are inevitably regarded with some suspicion by other Syrians. The Zionist campaign about the alleged mistreatment of Jews in Syria will surely increase such suspicion as exists. Yet Syrian Jews live unmolested and with full cultural and religious freedom. In Damascus, the home of more than half the Syrian Jews, there are fourteen synagogues and two Jewish schools maintained by the Jewish community (with assistance from abroad). These schools teach Hebrew. Of 900 students, a hundred are Muslims or Christians; some are Palestine refugees. There is no restriction on profession. Jews practise the liberal professions. Many are merchants, often well-to-do. The Jewish community's Religious Council has repeatedly—in messages to world organizations and in interviews—flatly denied Zionist allegations of discrimination and mistreatment. Syrians contrast the West's artificially stirred concern for the Syrian Jews with its indifference, if not worse, to the sufferings of the Palestinian and other Arab victims of the 1967 war, and to the discrimination practised in Israel against Oriental Jews.

'NO CAPITULATION OR COMPROMISES'

Syria's losses in men, arms, and land were smaller than those of Egypt and Jordan, but the traumatic humiliation of the débâcle was no less overwhelming. The defeat widened the void between the government and the people. Refusing to consider themselves in any way involved in a disaster not of their making, the people withdrew even further from any concern with the regime and how it exercised power. The conduct of the war, the premature announcement of Qunaytra's fall, and the rumours that the army's best units had been withdrawn from the front to protect the regime inspired deep misgivings and considerable hostility. Doubts and suspicions received no public airing, since the government held no treason trials and conducted no public investigations, no hunts for scapegoats, and no purges. Neither did it make any changes in its political line. Towards Israel the people remained intransigent, more committed than ever to the Palestine cause. Israel's early assertion of its intention to keep the Golan Heights dissipated any illusions about recovering the occupied land by anything but force.

Like other Arab governments, the Syrian government insisted on calling the greatest defeat in Arab history 'the setback'. Its strategy to overcome 'the setback' was to pursue an uncompromising line. During the war it had broken diplomatic relations with the United States and Britain and closed the oil pipelines. It now called for an embargo on oil shipments to Israel's supporters – the United States, Britain, and West Germany – and for a total economic, political, and cultural boycott of these states. Syria was active in the conferences of Arab foreign, economic, and oil ministers, held in summer 1967, and joined in their calls for an oil embargo and other economic measures. But it rejected President Nasser's appeal for a united Arab front against Israel because it refused to accept 'Arab reaction' as a partner in the common struggle. The Syrian government declined to attend the Khartum Conference of Arab heads of state and so did not share in the annual financial subsidies which Saudi Arabia, Kuwait, and Libya agreed to pay to Egypt and Jordan. But Syria did receive a small grant from Kuwait, apparently as an inducement to allow the reopening of the oil pipelines. The Ba'th found its views on the futility of Summits soon confirmed. The fifth Arab Summit scheduled to meet in January 1968 in Morocco was indefinitely postponed because of inter-Arab conflicts.

Syria was the only country to send its Head of State, Nur Al-Din Atasi, to the Emergency Session of the U.N. General Assembly held just after the war. But it opposed the Security Council's efforts to achieve a 'peaceful solution', and, in particular, Security Council

Resolution 242 (calling for Israeli withdrawal and Arab recognition of Israel) because, in Premier Z'ayyen's words,

> to accept it would be to relinquish all previous U.N. resolutions in favour of the Arab people of Palestine and to completely disregard the Palestine cause and the people of Palestine.

Throughout this period both the government and the party tried to consolidate ties with socialist and non-aligned countries and with France, which had opposed the Israeli aggression. That the USSR did not approve of Syria's rejection of political solutions became clear in Soviet press references to 'Arab hotheads' and 'adventurist trends'. But Syria's efforts to create a front of progressive Arab states were in accord with Soviet policy. The USSR more than made good Syrian arms losses, provided military advisers, continued its extensive economic assistance, and encouraged discussions between the Soviet Communist Party and the Ba'th. However, after prolonged debate, the government decided not to follow Egypt's example of placing its army under effective Soviet control.

The government's hard line was inspired by a number of considerations. Perhaps the most important was its desire to attract the developing Palestine resistance and to have this movement as an ally against its Arab adversaries. The very hostility of the popular reaction to the regime's performance during the war and to the present precarious military situation contributed to accentuating the uncompromising line. This line was also a response to the intransigence of public opinion itself. Moreover, a developing conflict between the Army Command and the party leadership invited the latter to insist on 'no capitulations' in face of the more supple approaches suggested by the Army Command.

One of the regime's greatest contradictions was the divorce between what it proclaimed day and night and what it really did. On the Palestine question, however, the gap between slogans and actual practice was relatively narrow, especially after the Ba'th created its own Palestine commando organization, Al-Saiqa (The Thunderbolt), made up of Palestinians from Syria, Lebanon, and Jordan. The regime also continued to help Fatah as well as other commando movements. Yet there was still a contradiction between its appeals to a generalized popular war, and to more intensified fedayin action, and the difficult military situation created by the 1967 defeat. The contradictions were aggravated by the regime's refusal to co-operate with other political forces at home and to facilitate effective popular mobilization.

For the government rejected the overtures made to it after the war

by other progressive movements. Before the war, all these movements
–except the communists and the Arab National Movement (ANM) –
had been convinced of the need to overthrow the neo-Ba'th government. The ANM, formerly Nasserist and violently hostile to the
neo-Ba'th, was then in mutation, moving through fierce ideological
conflict towards adoption of Marxism-Leninism, and incidentally
towards a new approach to the neo-Ba'th. After the war, various
progressive groups proposed formation of a national Progressive
Front including the neo-Ba'th. Involved in this effort were the
Hourani socialists (Akram Hourani had been allowed to return to
Syria just after the war), the ANM, Sami Sufan's Socialist Unionist
Movement, the Nasserist Arab Socialist Union, and other former
Ba'thists and Nasserists of various shades. All decided on a 'legal
democratic course' to persuade the regime to democratize power.

The government's answer was heavy-handed repression and mass
arrests. (Hourani managed to escape to the Lebanon.) The Progressive Front, none the less, officially came into being in May 1968 and
issued a National Charter. The Charter bluntly accused the Syrian
Ba'th of being responsible for the 1967 defeat, since its propaganda
had 'provided the pretext Israel had been seeking to wage aggression'
and its pre-war slogans 'had been way out of line', conforming neither
with Syria's preparedness to repel aggression nor Arab ability to
stand up to it. The front's programme emphasized the need for
democratization and formation of a government of national
union.

The front, however, proved ephemeral. This may be explained by
its heterogeneity and by the fact that most of the movements composing it were then experiencing important internal mutations and
conflicts. Even the Hourani socialists were divided, one tendency
following Hourani in his resolute opposition to the Jadid regime, the
other prepared to consider working with it. President Nasser's
developing co-operation with the Jadid regime weakened Nasserist
enthusiasm for the front. The government's tactic of trying to destroy
the front from within–by picking out certain people and giving them
posts–proved quite successful, given the differences within the front
and within the parties composing it. These differences became more
acute with the orthodox Ba'th's seizure of power in Baghdad in July
1968; some wanted to work with it against the regime, while others
were opposed.

In declining to work with other more or less progressive movements, the Jadid regime confirmed its isolation. Cut off from the
traditional Ba'thists, from the Nasserists, the socialists, and the
middle classes of the cities, it commanded the support only of the
communists and minor socialist elements. The fact that it did not

have any chance of survival through an immediate popular consultation may partially explain the overriding priority it gave to economic development and modernization. In a period of great difficulties, the regime succeeded in offering the Syrian people a more and more attractive realization of industrial and infrastructure projects, including the most vital projects, often advanced since independence but never before actually tackled. Yusef Z'ayyen was the architect of this grand design.

[1] U.N. Mediator Count Folke Bernadotte told the Security Council: 'It could not be ignored that unrestricted immigration to the Jewish area of Palestine might, over a period of years, give rise to a population pressure and to economic and political disturbances which would justify present Arab fears of ultimate Jewish expansion in the Near East. It can scarcely be ignored that Jewish immigration into the Jewish area of Palestine concerns not only the Jewish people and territory but also the neighbouring Arab world'. Report of the U.N. Mediator on Palestine to the Security Council, 12 July 1948, U.N. Doc. S/888. On 17 September 1948, Bernadotte was assassinated by Zionist terrorists.

[2] General Dayan, *Le Monde*, 9 July 1969: 'People abroad ought to realize that quite apart from their strategic importance to Israel, Sinai, the Golan Heights, the Tiran Straits, and the hills west of the Jordan lie at the heart of Jewish history. Nor has the "restoration of historical Israel" ended yet. Since the return to Zion a hundred years ago a double process of colonization and expansion of frontiers has been going on. We have not yet reached the end of the road: it is the people of Israel who will determine the frontiers of their own state'.

[3] For a more complete treatment of these points see Fred J. Khouri: *The Arab-Israeli Dilemma*, Syracuse, N.Y., 1968, pp. 191–7.

[4] Lieutenant General E. L. M. Burns: *Between Arab and Israeli*, New York, 1963, p. 111.

[5] Yoram Nimrod: 'L'eau, l'atome et le conflit', *Les Temps Modernes*, No. 253 Bis 1967, 887–8.

[6] Georgiana Stevens: *Jordan River Partition*, Stanford Univ., California, 1965, pp. 75–6.

[7] Nimrod, op. cit., p. 893.

[8] *Haaretz*, cited in *COC*, LVII, 1965, 24. Similar statements by Dayan were reported by the *New York Times* and *Le Monde* in 1965's first half.

[9] Interview in *Bamahane*, official organ of the Israeli army, cited in *Le Monde*, 13 September 1966.

[10] ibid. See also Rabin interview, *Le Monde*, 29 February 1968.

[11] Interview, *Daily Telegraph* (London), 7 October 1966.

[12] Charles W. Yost: 'The Arab Israeli War: How It Began', *Foreign Affairs*, Vol. 46, No. 2, January 1968.

[13] *Daily Star* (Beirut), 17 August 1967.

[14] Yost, op. cit.

[15] Interview, *Le Monde*, 29 February 1968.

[16] ibid.

[17] Testimony before the U.N. Special Committee to Investigate Israeli Practices Affecting the Human Rights of the Population of the Occupied Territories in 1971 and the U.N. Human Rights Committee in 1969. Israel has refused to permit these U.N. committees to visit the Occupied Territories.

[18] Figure given by Syrian government, generally confirmed by representatives of international agencies, like Red Cross, and foreign correspondents.

[19] See statements of Earl Ferrers, House of Lords, *Hansard*, 23 February 1972; the International Red Cross representative in Damascus in a letter to SAR Ministry of Interior (1 June 1968) in *Remarques Africaines* (Brussels), 18 November 1971; of Louis Eaks, head of a Liberal Party delegation, in *Guardian*, 21 January 1972; cables of the Jewish Religious Council in Syria to world bodies, 15 June 1972.

Chapter 11

State-Building

SYRIA IS AMONG THE MORE FORTUNATE of developing countries. Its relative underpopulation, relatively abundant resources (many only now coming to light), the outstanding advantages of its geographic and strategic position (regional commerce, oil transit), the influence of its long traditions of saving and enterprise–these factors suggest that this small country could, in certain circumstances, develop autonomously without important foreign aid. High military expenditures determined directly by the Israeli threat, as well as a weak action at the governmental level in mobilizing natural resources and human energies, underline the vital importance of the loans Syria has received from the USSR and other socialist countries. Politically and socially speaking, the dominant share of Soviet loans in the national development programme contributed to consolidating successive neo-Ba'th regimes. In this way, Soviet loans have helped to provide the stable political and economic basis needed for state-building. They have also conditioned the options of these governments in the direction of reinforcing the public sector in industry and infrastructure.

The neo-Ba'th endeavour to transform Syria into a modern state, whatever its shortcomings, became the most systematic and dynamic development effort in the entire region.

THE AGRICULTURAL SECTOR

The modest agrarian reform of 1958 was to have been completed in 1963. However, at the end of 1963, only 17 per cent of the land subject to expropriation had been distributed to 14,572 peasant families.[1] The serious attempt to carry out the reform,[2] which began under the neo-Ba'thist Abdel Kerim Jundi in 1965, succeeded by 1970 in completing expropriation of all the land subject to expropriation. And, by the end of 1971, 85 per cent of the expropriated land had been distributed.

When distribution is completed, only 60,000 (one-fourth) of the 240,000 peasant families needing land will have received land. The fact that completion of the reform will leave the peasant problem still so far from solution underscores the limited character of the reform.

Peasants who received land did not always succeed in cultivating it. In the absence of a state policy of adequately financing small peasants, giving them technical assistance, and providing state marketing facilities, poor peasant beneficiaries of the reform often did not have the resources to cultivate the land. So they rented their parcels to yesterday's landlord. The landlord, by concentrating these parcels, continued to be the real exploiter of the land, while the peasants worked as his sharecroppers. Some peasant beneficiaries use the rent money they receive from the landlord to migrate to the cities or even to the Lebanon.

The neo-Ba'th goal was to organize all peasant beneficiaries in land reform co-operatives and to spread agricultural co-operatives. These co-operatives are simple services co-operatives, providing credits and sometimes marketing facilities. Implantation of land reform co-operatives has lagged behind land distribution. Co-operatives for long proved incapable of improving methods of cultivation and increasing production. Two factors were mainly responsible. One was the low educational and cultural level of the members, many of whom were illiterate and without a co-operative conscience. The other was the state's inability to provide the necessary financial, and especially technical, assistance. The lack of technical cadres had a crippling effect on the development of the agricultural sector. In 1969, only thirty agricultural engineers worked with co-operatives; not all of these were full-time employees. Syria needs more than ten times its present number of agricultural engineers. The shortage of technical assistants is just as great.

State credits to agriculture increased after 1966 but–owing in part to the composition of Area Lending Committees–rich peasants still get the lion's share of state loans. Investigations revealed that loans to co-operatives were often used by individual members to build private houses or pursue their own private enterprises without any attempt at collective activity. This was possible because each member owned and worked his land individually. Social links between members generally remained at an elementary level, giving leeway for the continuing influence of family, tribal, and sectarian interests.

Co-operative marketing of vegetables, fruits, and other crops lacks both the necessary structure and efficient orientations. As a result, poor peasants face great difficulties, while rich peasants are able to manipulate the laws and the conditions of cultivation and sale to their own advantage. Rich peasants also profited from the long delay in carrying out the land reform. In the period between expropriation and distribution, the state rented the land; for the most part only well-to-do and rich peasants could afford the rent. The position of rich peasants has thus been strengthened; they tend to dominate the co-operatives.

In addition to speeding up the execution of the reform, the neo-Ba'thists in 1966 and after took other important and positive measures. Credit policy has been improved. The personnel entrusted with execution of the reform—formerly bureaucratic, often hostile to the peasant, and sometimes corrupt—is becoming more qualified and efficient. A serious long-term effort to provide needed agricultural engineers and technicians by expanding the facilities for agricultural education at every level got under way. Co-operatives are now growing rapidly in number. Their qualitative performance is beginning to improve. Real attention is now being paid to the technical aspects of agrarian reform with the organization of machine stations, chicken and milk farms, and efforts to develop livestock production. (Livestock production, hitherto the province of the semi-nomad, was never integrated into agriculture. The steady shrinking of pasture land and settlement of the nomad make this a critical problem. Much of the area to be irrigated by the Euphrates dam may be devoted to fodder crops owing to planned expansion in cattle-breeding.)

The attempt to establish a generalized system of co-operatives is leading the reform to develop beyond the narrow context established in 1958. The need to introduce marketing and production co-operatives is sharply realized. First efforts in this direction are now being made. A tendency to reorganize agricultural production in the direction of collective forms of rural property and scientific cultivation appeared in 1967 with the establishment of the first state farm. By 1971, state farms covered 250,000 hectares. The plan is to organize two in each district. State farms will become centres of specialization and agricultural research. Although these farms have inevitably encountered many difficulties, they offer an effective means to modernize Syrian agriculture.

Syria's agrarian reform still adheres to the capitalist model. It does not suppress individual property. Nor does it equalize land property on a national scale. The old landlords and the rich peasants retain a privileged point of departure. The middle peasants, or those to become middle peasants, are concretely offered far better possibilities than the poor peasants both in area exploited and the means of exploitation. The prevailing tendency under actual political conditions is that of developing and stimulating capitalist relations in the countryside. Moreover, since 1970 application of land reform laws has been more favourable to landlords; some seized land has been returned to former owners.

The great majority of peasants remain outside the agrarian reform. They either possess a small plot, which they cultivate with their own labour, or are landless. *Musha-a* tenure still prevails in many villages. This system, whereby small strips of land are rotated regularly among peasants of the village, blocks improvement of cultivation and aggravates inequality, since the best land usually goes to the influential people in the village. An effort to eliminate this type of tenure began in 1933. In the mid-1960s an official report estimated that—if no radical changes in method were made—another sixty-five years would be needed to eradicate this type of tenure.[3]

Agricultural workers and sharecroppers are protected by the 1958 Agricultural Relations Law, but observance of this law has been less than complete. The Special Inspection Organ for which the law provided had still not been established thirteen years later. In the provinces officials of the Ministry of Labour and Social Affairs did not acquire sufficient authority always to enforce work contracts. The law set no minimum wage; up to 1967, at least, wages tended to decline. The agricultural worker still had no protection against arbitrary dismissal. The sharecropper still had to rely on the money-lender or his landlord for credits.

Poor peasants suffer a high degree of underemployment. About 33 per cent of the agricultural population is estimated to be surplus.[4] Emigration of the rural population to the cities has become a serious problem as the gap between the average income in the agricultural and other sectors has widened.

One of the greatest lacunae in the effort to develop the Syrian countryside is the failure to make any dent in peasant illiteracy. Roughly 80 per cent of the agricultural working force remains illiterate. Up to the present time, no serious attempt has been made to eradicate peasant illiteracy.

Another great weakness in the land reform is the failure to involve the peasants themselves: that is, the absence of any democratic mobilization of the peasants. Yet peasants have not remained wholly passive. In 1969 a large-scale peasant uprising occurred in the Ghab over the question of repaying back debts to the Agricultural Bank. Peasant indebtedness stemmed largely from the state's system of exploiting the land. The size of the plot rented by the government to the peasant was too small to enable him to make a profit; the government rented the land to the peasant by the year and periodically redistributed it. This system transformed the peasants into agricultural labourers and prevented improvements in the land and in cultivation. The mainly Alawi peasants migrated to the Ghab when reclamation started and small parcels could be rented cheaply because the land was drained but not yet reclaimed. Without resources to cultivate the land they became dependent for seeds and credits on small entrepreneurs from Hama. These 'suppliers' grew rich while the peasants suffered a dual exploitation. The 1969 uprising–suppressed with violence and the arrest of some 350 peasants–finally led to a new policy. The government decided to organize co-operatives throughout the Ghab and attach them to an institute that would plan their production and sell their produce.

The bureaucratic execution of the land reform meant that the negative actions of landlords who reduced their investment in agriculture and sometimes refused to cultivate their land could not be offset. In the period 1962–71 the area of cultivated land–irrigated and non-irrigated–declined; so did the yield of cotton and cereals, the principal crops. Inability fully to use present land potentials poses sharply the need to define a policy for exploitation of the irrigated land to be made available by the Euphrates dam and other projects. A radical current favours extension of state farms, but pressures for more traditional types of tenure are strong.

PLANNING

Syria first adopted the idea of state direction and programming of economic development in the mid-1950s. In the first post-war decade, the private enterprise boom saw an accumulation of capital of some importance for a country of this size. But much of the capital was invested in building construction, especially European-type housing for the well-to-do, or spent on luxury imports. By the mid-1950s, the boom had spent itself without laying the basis for future growth and without making significant changes in an antiquated social structure or a highly uneven distribution of national income.

Successive development 'plans' adopted, beginning in 1955, consisted in no more than lists of investment projects, inadequately studied, if at all. Under these 'plans' the public sector consistently failed to fulfil its investment targets; fixed capital formation tended to be concentrated in services; public finances remained in disorder. The second plan, which started in 1966, was still a piecemeal affair without even an overall budget. The Jadid-Z'ayyen regime, however, set out to create a new planning structure. New planning authorities – a Higher Planning Council and a Planning Commission–were given vast powers. A Central Statistical Bureau was created to provide the necessary economic and social data. A Planning Institute was established to train Syrian planning experts and reduce reliance on foreign experts. The Ministry of Finance was reorganized and given extraordinary powers to control and develop state finances. Planning authorities claim that the Third Five-Year Plan (1971–75) was not borrowed but the product of the Syrian environment and that it marks the beginning of planning in a meaningful sense. They worked not in isolation but in consultation with interested groups: some 4,000 people were involved in evaluating the results of the second plan and preparing the third.

INDUSTRIAL DEVELOPMENT

The nationalizations of 1965 and after put 80–90 per cent of 'big' enterprise in the public sector. Middle and small enterprises continued to develop in the private sector. The public industrial sector suffered from a shortage of technical and managerial cadres and from the negative role often played within it by holdovers from the pre-nationalization era, who in one way or another managed to sabotage production. New managers and administrators frequently chosen for party or clan loyalty were not always competent. The bureaucracy's inherent inertia and fear of decision-making took its toll. Unable to understand their responsibility to increase production and productivity, many workers thought the time ripe to win new concessions. Others were disinterested since they enjoyed job security. In any case, as the official press admitted in 1972, workers were treated no differently by state managers and other superiors than they had been by the capitalists. Poor management, a very low level of socialist consciousness, lack of planning at the local level contributed to high production costs and failure to realize objectives.

The greatest drain on the profitability of the nationalized firms resulted from overstaffing in both the production and administrative departments. Some nationalized firms have succeeded in operating profitably. But most balance their budgets by resort to the nationalized banks. (The banks cover the deficits, but must in turn call on the Central Bank which will eventually have to issue more currency.) The notion of profitability is thus not respected. In presenting its new 'austerity budget' in December 1971, the government admitted that, although it is devoting special attention to industrial development, industrial investment last year 'did not result in any income'.

Extensive nationalization, coupled with the state's assumption of responsibility for economic development, created the basis for bringing coherence into totally incoherent economic sectors and for diversifying industry and beginning construction of a modern interdependent industrial system.

A promising oil industry is developing with Soviet help in prospecting. By 1964, when Syria nationalized its oil, oil in sufficient quantities for commercial development had been found in three fields in the Jazira. Exploitation started during the second plan and ahead of schedule. The pipeline to carry the oil to the Homs refinery and Tartus port was put into service in April 1968. The first Syrian oil was exported in July. A new oil refinery to handle Syrian crude, which presented special problems owing to its high sulphur content, now stands alongside the old refinery in Homs. Another refinery will soon be built. New oil discoveries allow hopes for a substantial rise above the 1971 production level of just over 5 million tons. But the low quality of Syrian crude compounds marketing difficulties inevitable for a small independent producer; hard currency earnings have so far been disappointing.[5]

Oil refining opens the way to development of a petro-chemicals industry. A nitrogen fertilizer complex in Homs, first projected in the 1957 Soviet aid agreement and now completed, will use light naptha produced by the Homs refinery. Difficulties with one of the three foreign contractors involved in its construction have already delayed the start of production for almost two years, at considerable cost to the state. A phosphate fertilizer plant based on important phosphate reserves discovered in the desert south of Palmyra will also be located in Homs. Availability of phosphate, a primary raw material for many chemical industries, should contribute to the development of a chemicals industry as well as provide an important source of foreign exchange.

Prospecting has confirmed the existence of considerable quantities of iron-ore. Studies suggested a metallurgical industry could be economically developed using power supplied by the Euphrates dam. Since Syria will need a million tons of iron and steel a year by 1980, the government has approved a project to construct an iron and steel factory near Hama. Other 'new type' industries have been or are being introduced. An asbestos cement factory now turns out ordinary and high-pressure pipes, needed for irrigation, drinking water, and sewerage networks, and corrugated sheets for use in factory and warehouse construction. An iron-bars factory in Aleppo produces sleepers for railroads now under construction and reinforced concrete poles for new transmission lines being laid. A factory to assemble, and ultimately to produce, tractors and diesel motors has been built in Aleppo. An industry for making machinery spare parts is under study. These 'new type' industries contribute to developing technical capacities.

These and other projects have introduced a slight modification in the structure of industry. By 1970, oil production and refining had replaced textiles as the major industry. Industry's contribution to national income had risen from 11 to 13 per cent in the mid-1960s to nearly 20 per cent by 1970. This was due, however, almost entirely to rising oil production. The contribution of industry is growing, but under conditions of backwardness and an inability to export on a significant scale. These conditions inhibit qualitative change in the sense of a major contribution by industry to economic development. Industrial projects, important as they are, are mostly infrastructure projects.

A CONSTRUCTION SITE

An orderly plan to equip Syria with the infrastructure of a modern state is well under way. Nationalization of all electricity companies in 1965 permitted organization of a centralized electricity system under one public authority and early construction of a grid linking Homs, Hama, Damascus, and Aleppo. A high-tension line to carry power from Homs to the construction site of the Euphrates dam also went into operation. Once the dam's power-station is completed, this line will distribute power in the opposite direction. Through its control of industrial investment, the government has been able to develop cable and other industries to supply the needs of its electricity projects.

Syria is being restored to its millennial vocation as a regional communications centre. The different parts of the country are being tied together in a rational communications network. Now boasting the most modern airport in the Middle East, Damascus hopes to make it the hinge of international communications in this region. The Mediterranean ports are being developed. Latakia port has been enlarged to serve Aleppo and the agricultural provinces of the north-east and to handle transit trade for Iraq, Kuwait, and Iran. However, since this port silts up easily and is costly to dredge, Tartus rather than Latakia will become the major port. Serving central and south Syria, Tartus is expected to develop as one of the most important ports in the eastern Mediterranean. The first stage of this very modern port, which is equipped with special quays for handling phosphate, sulphur, and other raw materials, has been completed. Tartus is also the terminal of the new oil pipeline from the Jazira. Through Latakia and Tartus, Syria hopes to capture from Beirut its leading position in handling the transit trade of the interior Arab countries. Transit trade using these ports is expanding rapidly, almost doubling between 1967 and 1969.

A programme of road improvement, road- and bridge-building, will facilitate connections from the Mediterranean ports to the cities of the interior, the hinterland, and also Iran, Iraq, and Jordan. New roads lead from Deir Ezzor on the Euphrates to Homs, and from Damascus to the Iraq frontier and on to Baghdad. Main arteries connecting with international highways are being asphalted and improved. These roads will contribute to the expansion of transit trade and the growth of the Mediterranean ports.

An ambitious effort to develop a rational railroad system began in 1964 with the creation of a single public authority, the General Railroad Organization. From the pre-independence era, Syria inherited three separate railroad lines without interconnections. These roads totalled 855 kilometres (of which 314 were narrow gauge) or 4·65 kilometres for every thousand square kilometres, compared, for example, to the United Kingdom's one hundred.

The railroad plan gave priority to a 755-kilometre line from Qamishli in the Jazira through Deir Ezzor and Aleppo to Latakia. This railroad will make transport of crops from the north-eastern agricultural regions to the main cities and the coast much cheaper and more efficient than their present transport by truck. Work on this line, which is being built with Soviet aid, started during the first plan, but lagged behind schedule. Since it could not be completed before the start of construction on the Euphrates dam, Tartus became the port of entry for the equipment, machinery, and materials needed for the dam. This required construction of a railway to link Tartus to the Beirut-Homs-Aleppo line as well as completion of the Aleppo-Tabqa section of the Qamishli-Latakia line. All these projects, including the first stage of Tartus port, were finished and ready for use when work on the dam was inaugurated in March 1968.

Other rail projects include a line between Damascus and Homs, another from Homs to the new phosphate mines near Palmyra, and still another from Deir Ezzor to the Iraq frontier and on to Baghdad. This last line will complete a direct link-up between the Mediterranean and the Gulf at Basra. Achievement of all these projects will mean that Syria has laid more track in a decade than the Powers did in more than half a century.

The Euphrates Dam

The Euphrates dam is the most eloquent symbol of the development and modernization effort of the neo-Ba'th regime. The dam under construction since March 1968 at Tabqa, 130 kilometres south-east of Aleppo, is one of the biggest earth dams in the world. In some respects, it is larger than Egypt's (rock-fill) High Dam at Aswan. Its first stage—a dam 60 metres high with a span of 4,500 metres containing a lake 80 kilometres by 8 and a power-station with eight generators—will be completed in 1974, a year ahead of schedule. The construction will then meet the country's immediate needs in permitting the irrigation of 640,000 hectares of land and in ultimately generating 800–1,100 megawatts of electric power. This is more than five times the power consumption of 1970. The river will be closed and its waters diverted into the electric power-station in 1973, when three generators will start producing 300 megawatts. After completion of the dam's first stage, if and when the need arises, a second stage will raise the dam by another 20 metres. Irrigation and power potentials created by the second stage – not now envisaged – are not limited.

The major problem of Syrian agriculture has always been both the insufficiency and the instability of rainfall. All agricultural development is still at the mercy of the weather. The dam represents the historic defiance of man in this small area to overcome his secular dependence on natural phenomena. Installation of irrigation and drainage systems and bringing the new land under cultivation will take time. Once achieved, however, the Euphrates irrigation project in connection with other projects, especially that of the development of the Khabur River, will more than double the land area under irrigation. The increase the dam will achieve in the ratio of irrigated land to the total cultivated area means that the structure of agricultural production and exploitation, and cultures themselves, must change. Since the soil in this region is very fertile, intensive cultivation will produce high yields. The standard of living of the inhabitants of this area will rise. The transfer here of poor peasants from other regions will contribute to enlarging the national consumer market and at the same time will accelerate the growth-rate of national income. The crucial need for foreign aid could be reduced through a better local accumulation of capital, if the transfer of the agricultural surplus is rationally assured.

From the industrial point of view, the dam will provide the power to fuel local industry. More important, it will – through the mutation in favour of irrigated land – create a potentially important market for fertilizers, pesticides, herbicides, and plastics. This means a more certain future for actual and coming chemical industries. Tabqa itself may become a new industrial centre. This new city built for 30–40,000 people, across the river from an ancient village of a few hundreds, is completely equipped with schools, libraries, hospitals, theatres, and markets ready to serve the working forces of new industries once the dam is built. Its workshops can be transformed to new uses. Its railroads, highways, water, electricity, and other facilities, as well as its proximity to the new agricultural areas, make it an ideal future location for agricultural processing industries.

Not least of the benefits deriving from the dam is its contribution to Syria's human wealth in training the technical cadres and skilled workers the nation so badly needs. The dam constitutes a kind of school in mechanics, electricity, civil and constructional engineering.

A special centre in Aleppo trains workers for the dam. Training courses are carried on all through the project. Of the total working force—at its peak 11,000—some two-thirds will have become technicians in various specialities by the time the work is finished; they will then be available for work on other projects.

Completion of the project will bring within reach the goal of 'complete electrification of the country' and so raise living standards, especially in the villages, many of which will for the first time have electric lighting. All villages of more than 2,000 inhabitants will be lighted during the third plan. The dam, moreover, will eliminate the frequent ravages of floods in both Iraq and Syria, and regulate the flow of water.

Villages which will be swallowed up by the new lake will be rebuilt on its shores. They will, hopefully, serve as models for other settlements to be established with the expansion of cultivation and the encouragement given the beduin to settle. The government, however, has not yet projected a coherent plan to regulate inter-sectoral relations and to prepare the human, technical, administrative, and political conditions within the Euphrates basin. The institution created for this purpose is still at the very beginning. A tendency has become apparent to rely on foreign organizations and experts for elaboration and application of the plan for the Euphrates basin. This whole enterprise, moreover, is isolated from national opinion.

FINANCING

Syria's conversion into a vast and busy construction site has been made possible by foreign technical and economic assistance, sought the world over. In addition to the USSR and eastern Europe, which supply the bulk of foreign aid, China, Italy, France, Austria, Yugoslavia, Kuwait, and Algeria are also represented. Assistance from socialist countries is usually on the basis of long-term credits at low interest rates, with repayment starting only after the project is completed and sometimes made in Syrian goods.[6] A significant aspect of socialist aid is the on-the-job training it provides for Syrian engineers, technicians, and workers.

Owing to its high defence expenditures on top of the all-out development effort (more than 60 per cent of the budget is allocated to defence), the government has encountered growing difficulties in repaying its foreign creditors and in finding the means to fulfil its investment plans. Its intransigent insistence on securing higher oil-transit royalties from IPC and Aramco responded to development imperatives. Altogether in four years it had won increases in annual dues totalling about $30 million. But, a severe shortage of hard currency had developed by the second half of 1969. Since spendings had become superior to hard-currency resources, the government was unable to respect its foreign engagements and was compelled to postpone debt repayments. The pressure of the hard-currency shortage on imports created the need to seek supplementary foreign resources, again through credit facilities.

These difficulties had a dampening effect on general economic activity. Confidence in the Syrian economy was shaken. Entrepreneurs, commercial agents, and merchants began to exploit the situation. They gained very high profits by establishing monopolies in certain goods, creating artificial shortages, and raising prices, and so provoked popular discontent. On the other hand, development projects were delayed; trade, industrial, and agricultural progress was checked. Some essential articles and spare parts were not to be had. Smuggling, as well as individual and state purchases from the Lebanon, appreciably increased. Another result was the further weakening of the Syrian pound, with national sources from the parallel free (currency) market contracting and the black market becoming more active. The bigger merchants were able to tighten their hold over small shopkeepers and craftsmen. Living standards were affected. Moreover, the difficulties contributed to an increasing use of bribes and gratuities; corruption spread.

The contribution of the nationalized banks to the financing of productive projects and plans has remained unsatisfactory. The capital of the industrial and agricultural banks is well below needs. Their prerogatives in the matter of deposits and other operations are still very limited. Short-term commercial credits are very privileged in comparison with medium- and long-term credits essential for industrial and other productive activities. The Agricultural Bank's funds are often wasted because big agricultural entrepreneurs and landlords, who get a large proportion of the credits, don't always repay them. Commercial banks suffer even more from this practice. Big capitalists and merchants borrowed heavily on the eve of nationalization. They now refuse to pay their debts on the grounds that they have not received compensation for their nationalized properties. Most important, the banks continue to neglect the function of saving. The rate of local saving remains very low and wholly inadequate to the dimensions of the development effort undertaken.

Whatever the difficulties, however, the momentum of state-building will hardly be halted. What is being achieved with the construction of the dam, in conjunction with other projects, is Syria's integration as a modern state. Work on construction projects throughout the country is contributing to fusing Syria's particularisms in a new national mould.

[1] SAR: *Statistical Abstract* 1968, p. 113.

[2] 1963 amendments lowered ceilings according to the productivity of the land, the kind of crop, and proximity to the market, and so made an additional 1,372 owners and 48,767 hectares subject to the reform. As amended in 1963, the law would expropriate about 18 per cent of the cultivated land. A more radical provision relieved the beneficiary of payment for the land, requiring him instead to pay one-quarter of its price to his co-operative over a 20-year period.

[3] Dr Salah Wissan: *Al-Qita' Al-Zira'i* . . ., Damascus, 1967.

[4] ibid.

[5] With the nationalization of all IPC assets in Syria (pipeline, pumping stations, and other installations) on 1 June 1972 Syria took a further step towards oil independence. The only remaining foreign oil interest in Syria was Aramco's pipeline. The nationalization followed immediately on Baghdad's nationalization of IPC holdings in northern Iraq. It provided for compensation to the company and for retention of the services and rights of all employees. Syrian-Iraq co-operation in oil and other economic affairs is now on the order of the day.

[6] China's aid, however, is interest-free.

Chapter 12

✳ The Human Potential

SYRIA, STILL AN UNDEVELOPED COUNTRY, is already beginning to suffer the depredations of progress. Factories pollute the waters of the Orontes. A light smog occasionally appears over Damascus. The Ghuta (its green against the barren desert and naked mountains made Damascus for the Arabs one of three earthly paradises) is being invaded and diminished by ugly apartment houses and even factories. As in other parts of the world, ancient and beautiful buildings are falling to wrecking crews to make way for modern villas and offices.

Population is growing very rapidly–throughout the 1960–70 decade at an annual rate of almost 3·8 per cent. Total population–4·5 million in 1960–reached 6·2 million in 1970. Migration from the countryside contributed to a 57 per cent increase in the population of the twelve major cities during this decade. Damascus grew from 530,000 to 835,000 inhabitants.

The problem of providing housing, education, health, and other services for the overcrowded cities, and at the same time extending elementary services into the villages in the hope of stemming the rural exodus, poses a formidable challenge. The neo-Ba'th's modernist and socialist goals also demand mobilization of the people into an effective force, both to transform society and to meet the imperatives of the profound crisis facing the Arab world.

HEALTH

Health standards have gradually improved. Although health statistics are inadequate, the youthful age structure of the population suggests that both birth- and death-rates remain high. But Syria does not suffer great ravages from disease. Malaria, once widely prevalent, has been all but eradicated with the help of the World Health Organization. Tuberculosis persists at what is believed to be a 'normal' rate in third world countries. Intestinal and other diseases associated with low living standards are still common. Incidence of trachoma is limited. Relatively few cases of bilharzia have appeared. This disease is caused by a parasite that lives part of its life in water snails and part in man, penetrating liver, bladder, kidneys, even the brain,

218

to cause debilitation and ultimately death. With the completion of the Euphrates dam, however, bilharzia is expected to spread. Plans to prevent this–and to cope with other social and health problems the dam will create–are under study. Public health authorities claim that malnutrition is not a serious problem. Yet consumption of animal protein is only half the daily minimum required, while that of fresh fruits and vegetables–with the exception of the ever-present onion which is the staff of life of the poor–is very low. Lack of pure drinking water poses health hazards in both village and town. Potable water was available to only 45 per cent of village inhabitants and 58 per cent of town dwellers in 1970. The Third Five-Year Plan hopes to raise this ratio to 55 and 68 per cent respectively by 1975.

The shortage of doctors, dentists, and hospitals is almost as serious today as it was in 1945. On achieving independence, Syria had 616 doctors, or one for every 4,750 persons. By 1969 there were 5,513 Syrian doctors, but 4,000 were emigrants practising abroad. Only 1,513 doctors practised in Syria. This meant that there was one doctor for every 4,165 persons. With 1,785 hospital beds in 1945, Syria had one bed for every 1,085 persons. In 1969, with 6,156 beds, there was one for every 1,014 persons. In 1969 there was only one dentist for every 17,697 persons. Doctors, dentists, and hospitals are very badly distributed. In some Governates the number of people to one doctor is over ten thousand and the number to one hospital bed, four to five thousand.

As early as 1951, medical graduates were prohibited from practising in the five main cities for the first two years after graduation. Later, other towns were included in this prohibition, which was devised to provide rural areas with medical services. Eventually the doctor beginning practice was required to serve two years in rural areas. This obligation was effectively enforced only after the Ba'th took power. A new regulation obliges medical faculties to accept a certain percentage of students from rural areas and, if necessary, to lower entrance requirements to make this possible.

Syria has no general health insurance system, and necessary studies for applying such a system have not advanced far. Government offices and establishments in the public sector usually have their own health insurance schemes. But the great majority of people still have to pay for medical care, if they can find it. Holders of health certificates (people below a certain level of income in certain categories) get free medical care at public clinics, where they exist, and free medicine.

EDUCATION

Since independence, Syria has claimed to be of all countries in the Middle East and Africa the most eager to learn and to send its children to school. All visitors remark students reading as they stroll in country lanes or studying in the evenings clustered under street lights in the towns. In the countryside, where many villages are too small to have a school, children often walk long distances to reach the nearest school. Syrian governments of whatever complexion consistently maintained strong efforts to foster education. Since 1946 the proportion of the state budget devoted to education has ranged between 13 and 20 per cent. As a percentage of national income, public expenditures on education have grown from 2·3 in 1956 to 5·6 in 1966. When the French left Syria, education reached only 5 per cent of its population. By 1967, the proportion of the population receiving education had risen to 17·2 per cent.[1]

Since 1944, primary school (now six years) has been free and nominally compulsory. There has been an impressive increase in school attendance at all levels since independence:

	1946		1969	
	Pupils	Schools	Pupils	Schools
Primary	150,000	1,080	813,225	5,069
Intermediate and				
Secondary	12,661	73	242,947	700
University and				
Institutes	1,058	1	35,319	4

Vocational education (industrial, commercial, agricultural, domestic) also developed, but on a much smaller scale. University education grew very rapidly after the mid-1950s. The number of students in higher educational institutes of all kinds per 100,000 inhabitants was 86 in 1950 and 590 in 1966.

Syrian education appeared to have made great strides. Yet, in 1966, an official census of the employed population found 60·2 per cent illiterate, only 2·1 per cent with a secondary diploma, and a mere one per cent with a university degree. How could a working force so illiterate and unqualified transform Syria into a modern—and socialist—state? This question brought into focus the shortcomings of the educational system.

Reforms made by the first independent governments in the school system inherited from the French had given education a Syrian and Arab orientation in place of a French. But they had not discarded the French conception that the function of education was the preparation of an élite. The main emphasis of education remained general culture and theoretical knowledge; its main objective seemed to be to supply officials and employees to government bureaux.

The many private schools established by religious sects, nationality groups, and foreign missions, although gradually swamped at the primary level by the extension of public education, continued to play a major role in intermediate and secondary education. They enrolled 35 per cent of pupils at these levels in 1946 and 31 per cent in 1966. By giving their students a sectarian or particularist outlook, private schools helped to perpetuate factionalism. Yet no long-term policy of assimilating private schools into the public-school system was adopted. The 1950 Constitution, moreover, in requiring religious instruction at all levels of the public-school system gave a certain justification for the existence of sectarian schools. Private schools retained their importance in part because public schools could not accommodate all those seeking an education. In 1960, only 17 per cent of adolescents between the ages of thirteen and nineteen attended school.

The 1950 Constitution promised to eradicate illiteracy in ten years, but nothing was done to fulfil this promise. The view that extension of primary education would gradually eliminate illiteracy was widespread. This, although in 1950 a mere 35 per cent of children in the primary-school age-group attended school, and no programme was envisaged to prevent relapse into illiteracy. Education was not directed to meeting the enormous need for technically qualified people. In intermediate schools mathematics and science subjects occupied only 23 per cent of the curriculum and technical or practical subjects only 6 per cent. Technical education with a practical aim was completely divorced from general education and held in disdain. Only students who could not continue general education entered technical schools. In the period since 1945, the number of technical students has remained around 8–12 per cent of the number in general secondary schools.

University education revealed a similar distortion and did not correspond to the needs of the country. The bulk of university students specialized in the arts and humanities, law and the *Shari'a* (Islamic law). The proportion in these specializations stood, in 1969, at 5 to 2 for other specializations, although job opportunities in these fields were scant. Agriculture remains a principal source of national income and employs 60 per cent or more of the working population. Yet the number of university students specializing in agriculture still constitutes a mere 2 to 3 per cent of the total number of university students. Only 3·6 per cent of university students specialized in medicine. The proportions for science and engineering were only slightly higher.

Although the number of university students has grown rapidly, the number of graduates is relatively small—in any one year 10 per cent or less of the number of students. The official explanation is that students, especially in the theoretical faculties, frequently leave after the first year or two to work in Kuwait, Saudi Arabia, and the Gulf principalities. Many apparently do not return to finish their education.

Neo-Ba'th Reforms

In 1966, the neo-Ba'th government—acutely aware of the importance of education to modernization—began to make significant changes. An important reform was the state's assumption of full control over the private schools. Decree 127 of 9 September 1967, while leaving ownership of the private schools untouched, placed their management in the hands of the Ministry of Education and required use of the public educational system's books and programmes at every level of private education. A prolonged strike by the private schools was eventually broken by threat of confiscation; a few religious schools that refused to comply with the decree were closed. The reform should contribute to the eradication of confessionalism. Many, especially among the young, hoped it would be followed by complete secularization of the public schools, that is by the elimination of compulsory religious instruction.

Other reforms brought Syria into line with modern educational trends. Cancellation of selection examinations and of conditions defining the percentage of students accepted in the intermediate and secondary stages opened the door of these schools to all students, but there were still not enough schools, especially in rural Governates. Curricula at all levels of education were amended to strengthen mathematics, sciences, and practical subjects. Some modern mathematics was introduced into secondary schools.

Technical education received high priority. The educational motto became 'knowledge for the sake of work'. Respect for work and production was taught in the schools. Scientific courses attracted more students. Roughly 68 per cent of secondary-school graduates in 1969 had specialized in science. Intermediate institutes for various specialities, started in 1963, were steadily developed to meet the shortage of intermediate technical cadres. The number of secondary agricultural schools, admission to which was now limited to sons of peasants, grew to ten. Graduates of these schools may now take a one-year course at the Institute for Developing the Countryside, founded in 1970. This course will qualify them to work in agricultural co-operatives as assistants to engineers. The Ministry of Industry provides technical training for workers at many levels.

Facilities for higher technical and scientific study are being expanded. Five Higher Technical Institutes–including a Veterinary Institute in Hama and an Electrical and Petro-chemical Engineering Institute in Homs–will soon begin to function. A second university, with medical, science, agriculture, and other faculties, opened in Aleppo during the second plan period. A third university specializing in sciences recently opened in Latakia. The agricultural faculties at Aleppo and Damascus universities are being expanded.

In 1969, more than 23,000 Syrian students studied in foreign countries, roughly 60 per cent in the sciences, engineering, and medicine, and 40 per cent in the humanities. The biggest concentrations of students were in western Europe, the United States, and Canada, on the one hand, and in Arab countries on the other. Only 10 per cent studied in socialist countries.

Like the rest of the undeveloped world, Syria suffers a serious 'brain drain'. The annual rate of emigration of skilled manpower increased fivefold between 1956 and 1967. Roughly 10 per cent of students who go abroad to study do not return. Since the cost of training a specialist is estimated at about $20,000 (£8,400), the financial loss is substantial. A plan to halt emigration of specialists, advanced by the Supreme Council of Sciences, proposes that Syrian specialists should be treated like foreign experts and should be offered contracts on state projects at salaries comparable to those paid foreign experts. But there is a reluctance in the party and the government to make any special effort to induce graduates and specialists 'of bourgeois origin' to come home. This attitude reflects both a narrow, mechanistic conception of class origin, not infrequent in the essentially rural and militarily authoritarian regime, and the unwillingness of officials, nearly all locally formed, to face the competition of more highly educated people.

At the primary-school level progress has been slower than anticipated. In 1960, the First Five-Year Plan proposed to raise the proportion of six- to twelve-year-old children admitted to primary school from 43 to 77 per cent. But in 1971, only 63 per cent of this compulsory school age-group attended school: 80 per cent of the boys and 47 per cent of the girls; the drop-out rate was 13 per cent. The Third Five-Year Plan hopes to raise admissions to primary school to 80 per cent of this age-group.

One of the problems is the shortage of qualified teachers. The proportion of unqualified teachers in primary school was reduced from 55 per cent in 1962 to 15 per cent in 1970. But 35 per cent of intermediate and secondary-school teachers were still unqualified in 1970. Classes are overcrowded. School buildings are old. Many more are needed. In 1970, 40 per cent of the needed number of primary schools were lacking and 35 per cent of the needed intermediate and secondary schools. To supplement the efforts of the School Buildings Institute, which draws its financing from certain direct taxes, schools were also being built by 'popular work'. The 'popular work' system, inaugurated in 1963, enables a village or locality to tax itself and contribute its own volunteer labour to build needed amenities, especially schools, roads, and public services.

Illiteracy

Failure to reduce illiteracy has hampered social and economic development efforts. Sixty per cent of the population (over ten years of age) was illiterate in 1960. In the next eight years – a period during which the Ba'th regime adopted a ten-year Arab League programme to eradicate illiteracy – illiteracy decreased by only one per cent. Illiteracy among males declined from 43 to 41 per cent, but among females remained at 77 per cent, for a total illiteracy rate of 59 per cent. The highest degree of illiteracy was among rural females: 94 per cent in 1960 and 93 per cent in 1968.

This alarming lack of progress led the Ministry of Culture to decree literacy obligatory for all under forty-five and for all employed in government departments and in public and private companies. It also induced the neo-Ba'th to adopt a new policy. Basing itself on the Cuban and Chinese examples, the party decided to give the anti-illiteracy campaign a national and popular colour rather than an official and governmental one. It made the popular organizations – labour and peasant unions, youth and women's federations – responsible for carrying out the anti-illiteracy programme on a volunteer basis under the direction of the Ministry of Culture. This would reduce costs and – hopefully – spark the popular enthusiasm indispensable if two and a half million illiterates are to learn to read and write.

The results of the popular programme, which was launched in 1970, could not yet be evaluated. In that year, attendance at literacy courses reached about 15,000, and graduates of these courses numbered less than 4,000. At this rate, it would take not ten years but nearer 150 to eradicate illiteracy. The programme demands a tremendous effort from popular organizations which still lack a mass base. Since the most immediate goal is to make all industrial workers literate, concentration in the first year was on the industrial sector. The trade union and management of each factory are responsible for seeing that all its workers become literate. This is being done on a wide scale. Courses are provided in the factory. Workers must prove their literacy to be eligible for trade union committees and offices.

To reach peasants and housewives is a far more complex and difficult task. Syrian television and radio promote attendance at literacy courses: social pressures appear to be having some effect.

STATUS OF WOMEN

The high rate of illiteracy among women undermines their still inferior status. The number of females attending school and university has grown in absolute terms, but the proportion has not changed except in primary school, where girl pupils constituted 29 per cent of the total in 1946 and 34 per cent in 1969. In intermediate and secondary schools girl pupils made up 23 per cent of the total in 1946 and 24 per cent in 1969. The highest proportion of women university students—21 per cent—was attained in 1952. In 1970, the proportion was 19 per cent. Lip-service is paid to the need for women to work beside men in building society, but at the end of the 1960s only one-half of one per cent of Syrian girls were receiving technical education, compared to 10 per cent in Egypt and 2 per cent in Jordan.[2]

Women have yet to achieve the status of working and productive members of society. In Syria the ratio of the economically active to total population is very low: 29·3 per cent in 1968 compared, for example, to 47·3 per cent in the United Kingdom. The main reason lies in the exclusion of women from the working force. In 1960, only 5·4 per cent of the total female population was economically active. The ratio reached 16·5 per cent in 1968. This was due, however, entirely to a large increase in the number of women working as family workers in agriculture: in the countryside women traditionally collect animal dung, fetch water, tend flocks, and help their menfolk in the fields, leaving household chores to their daughters who, therefore, do not attend school.

At higher levels, women in small numbers are penetrating professions formerly monopolized by men. Among students in engineering, science, and medicine women constitute only a handful. But five of 200 Arab engineers working on the Euphrates dam were women; some 70 to 80 women engineers worked alongside 700 male engineers in Aleppo. In 1971, the government ordered the doors of all government bureaux opened to the employment of women. But, only four of the 173 members appointed to the People's Council that year were women.

Although the party recognized that the activation of women was necessary to social and economic advance, it did not venture to interfere with the traditional fabric of social relations, which condemns women to inferior status. It could, therefore, offer no revolutionary or even radical approaches to this problem. Labour legislation has since 1959 given women workers equal rights with men, at least on paper; maternity leave and other special protections have been widened. But women are still employed in the lowest-paying jobs and outside the public sector seldom get equal pay for equal work. Their average wage in the manufacturing industry was only two-thirds that of men in 1968. Certain legal discriminations existed even in this field. A husband, for example, received a monthly family allowance for a non-working wife, but a working wife got no allowance for a non-working husband.

Tradition still fosters distinct and separate societies for men and women. The separation of boys and girls in schools (with few exceptions) up to university level confirms these ingrained prejudices. Miniskirts and other superficial symbols of emancipation have arrived on college campuses and in some sections of upper- and middle-class society. But the patriarchal family, with its intrinsic restrictions on the rights and freedom of women, still prevails. The extreme case of the exercise of male authority, and of the conception of men as 'the guardians of women', remains the custom whereby a brother or father may kill his sister, daughter, or female relative for 'dishonouring' the family name. Instances of such murders still occur every year. The law does not actually grant the right to kill 'in defence of honour', but it provides for punishment so light in this case as to constitute an incitement to murder. The fact that a leader of the Ba'th's General Federation of Women could defend this barbaric custom as designed 'to preserve the purity of Arab women' suggests that progressive political ideas have been grafted somewhat superficially onto millennial tribal values. The man's responsibility for the 'honour' of his womenfolk, even if seldom carried to such lengths, is still the norm in village and tribal life and common in the towns. Marriages remain a family concern. Even among the upper and middle classes roughly half of all marriages are still arranged, while in the villages and among the poorer classes the proportion is much higher.

As long ago as 1944, the Arab Women's Congress in Cairo, to which seven Syrian women's groups sent delegates, demanded reform of the divorce law, equal rights of inheritance, and compulsory co-education. None of these demands has yet been met in 'revolutionary and socialist' Syria of the 1970s. To divorce his wife a husband still has only to declare 'I divorce you' three times in the presence of two witnesses. However, to discourage the husband from 'wrongful' exercise of the right of repudiation certain restraints (like the payment of financial compensation in some circumstances) have been introduced. The wife cannot oppose the divorce, nor has she any such right, although entitled to a divorce in certain cases. Polygamy is still legal, although the courts can make it difficult. A male relative still enjoys rights of control over an unmarried, divorced, or widowed woman. Inheritance laws still discriminate against women. But Syrian law, unlike the Egyptian, never incorporated the Ottoman *Bayt Al-Ta'a* ('obeying house'). This is the husband's right to enforce his wife's obedience by forbidding her to leave his house or receive anyone, even relatives. The UAR regime cancelled this right in its 1961 draft unified law. But Egypt abolished it only in 1963.

Reform of the personal status law was said to be under discussion in 1971. Any significant change in the law, however, would require removing this question from the jurisdiction of Islamic legislation. To date, no Ba'th or neo-Ba'th reform has dared to challenge the grip of this legislation which has been handed down through more than a thousand years. The religiosity of the Libyan and Egyptian governments, Syria's partners in the Federation of Arab Republics, will not make reform in this direction any easier. (The most radical reforms in this field have been made not by the 'progressive' Arab states, but by Tunisia.)

THE POPULAR ORGANIZATIONS

The neo-Ba'th's answer to the problem of women's emancipation was to establish the General Women's Federation in 1967. The federation is one of the 'popular organizations' through which the party has tried to mobilize, tightly under its control, the energies of the people and consolidate its control. The other popular organizations are the General Union of Peasants, the General Federation of Trade Unions, the General Union of Students and the Revolutionary Youth Organization.

With the exception of the General Federation of Trade Unions, all the Ba'th's popular organizations were admittedly started without a base; all their officials and ruling committees were appointed by the party. Later, the principle of elections was introduced, but elections are always of the indirect pyramid style which assures control from the top. Once the organizations had held elections, they became eligible to affiliate with international federations based in socialist countries. Friendly relations and exchanges of visits with similar organizations in Arab, third world, and socialist countries then became frequent. (From 1961 to 1965, however, owing to the conflict between Nasser and the Ba'th, the Egyptian-controlled International Confederation of Arab Trade Unions excluded the Syrian Trade Union Federation and gave to Nasserist Syrian political exiles in Cairo the right to speak for the Syrian trade union movement.)

The Women's Federation in its first four years enrolled 10,000 members. Financed by the Ba'th, it has also been given many facilities—a monthly magazine, a weekly family television programme, and a daily woman's radio programme. Its chief activities have been directed to establishing nurseries and kindergartens for the children of working women, holding courses in sewing, carpet-making, and typewriting, and conducting literacy classes. Its critics complained that it seemed more interested in teaching women to perform traditional duties efficiently than in changing the attitude of Syria's male-dominated society towards women and the attitude of women towards themselves. Yet the federation's activists undoubtedly open new horizons for the women they are able to reach; literacy classes, if sufficiently generalized, might become radical in their implications. However, for all the dedication of many of its (almost entirely middle-class) members, the federation experienced great difficulties in maintaining literacy courses even on a limited scale.

The General Union of Peasants

In 1964, in an effort to create the necessary instruments to enforce its power and to draw the peasants 'into the agricultural revolution', the Ba'th created the General Union of Peasants. Up till that time there had been only two well-organized and rooted peasant movements: that of Akram Hourani's Arab Socialist Party with its main base in central Syria and a communist movement localized in the Jazira and around Homs. The Ba'th attempt to create a nationwide peasant movement was a significant step. In 1965, on the personal initiative of the then Minister of Agrarian Reform, Colonel Abdel Kerim Jundi, representatives of the Peasants' Union were invited to participate in the various committees of the land reform. The next year this participation was made official.

The General Union's appointed leadership gave way to an elected leadership after its 1965 Congress. In 1971, with a claimed membership of 175,000, the General Union represented about 17 per cent of the agricultural working force. Thus, the union had yet to cover the whole countryside. Moreover, it had yet to play an active role in the execution of the land reform. Its leaders maintain that organization is deliberately slow: before a union can be established in a village, unity has to be created on the basis of class, not sect, tribe, or family; the poor peasant must learn that the landlord, even if a relative, is the enemy, that religion is the responsibility of God, while production and organization are that of the people. The tribal allegiances, illiteracy, religious conservatism, and political isolation of the peasantry—these realities can be rightly advanced to explain the union's minimal role; so can the fact that cadres to carry on the work have been few. Another reality – needed to complete the picture – is the union's refusal to admit politicized peasants who are not Ba'th adherents. Since independence, the peasants' movement in the Hama region has been the most active, but the regime's hostility to Akram Hourani has cut the General Union of Peasants from this important and interesting base. The peasant movement in the Jazira, where the peasants are mostly Kurds and pro-communist, has also been kept outside the Peasants' Union, and – until very recently – the land reform was not applied on any significant scale in the Jazira. Peasants who have been active in the Safita region (near Latakia) have also been isolated from the General Union because they have a pro-communist history.

Still another reality is the role relatively well-off peasants have assumed in the General Union of Peasants. The absence of a democratic mobilization of the peasantry and the very nature of the land reform have facilitated their dominance in the union. Local leaders of the Peasants' Union are often middle peasants; one had even owned enough land to be affected by the land reform.

Many city people – and not a few peasants – consider the Peasants' Union to be a puppet creation of the regime and a financial burden. But the General Union is attempting to develop peasant cadres. With the government and the party, it has established 'peasants' cultural institutes' in each Governate. In these institutes, literate peasants, who are members either of the union or a co-operative, receive one month's education in a variety of subjects. These include the problems of trade unions and co-operatives, use of agricultural machinery, 'leadership of the masses', and history of the Arab liberation movement. The best of the students take a further six-month course at a Central Peasants' Cultural Institute near Damascus. This institute's most outstanding graduates, in turn, spend six months in the German Democratic Republic, three at study and three at work in co-operatives. The numbers involved are few (up to one hundred may study at the Central Institute in any one year). Because of the literacy requirement, poor peasants are almost automatically excluded. The cultural institutes thus reinforce the dominance of well-to-do peasants in the General Union.

In 1971, the Peasants' Union, with the help of other popular organizations, launched an effort to combat illiteracy in the countryside. The union's weekly newspaper, *Nidal Al-Fellahin* (Struggle of the Peasants), tries to relate the experiences of peasant movements in other countries to the problems of Syrian peasants and to awaken a consciousness of peasant rights. The union's weekly radio and television programmes deal with agricultural and peasant questions.

The General Federation of Trade Unions

The General Federation of Trade Unions has a long history. When the Ba'th took power in 1963, the General Federation embraced workers of different political tendencies – Houranist, communist, Nasserist, and Ba'thist – although the majority of workers remained under the influence of pre-industrial and religious values. During the first three or four years of Ba'th rule, state intervention in the labour movement took openly authoritarian and repressive forms. The Ba'th government quickly replaced the federation's elected leadership as well as most of the elected officials of local unions with its own appointees. By Decree Law 31 of 25 January 1964, it then reorganized the trade unions into a pyramid structure. The novelty introduced by Decree Law 31 was that appointment replaced elections in constituting the trade union committees of the factories (the basic unit) and the Governate federations. In 1964, when an internal party *coup* reversed directions set at the sixth National Congress, the government again appointed new leaderships in the federation and many unions. These government-appointed officials prepared the trade union elections held in 1965 for such offices as remained elective. Government and party pressures at every level secured an overwhelming majority for the Ba'th.

When the neo-Ba'th took power in February 1966, government intervention in the labour movement took a more sophisticated form. The government exercised its influence through neo-Ba'th trade union leaders installed at the summit and direct pressures applied at the base on the occasion of elections. After the dismissal of the overly ambitious and notoriously corrupt neo-Ba'thist Khalid Jundi from his post as President of the General Federation in August 1967, the government followed a policy of installing weak trade union leaders whom it could be sure would not escape its control.

The neo-Ba'th strategy is permanent control of the working class but in subtle forms. In the trade union movement, unlike the other popular organizations, the party has made political concessions. Nasserist, communist, and Houranist tendencies have been tolerated and – in unions where the neo-Ba'th is weak and they are strong – even accepted so long as neo-Ba'th supremacy is assured at the national level. Political co-operation between Ba'thists and communists at a rank-and-file level often occurs when police pressures are not efficient. In general, however, the different non-Ba'th tendencies have found it easier to co-operate among themselves than with the ruling Ba'thists. The trade union movement is the most left of the 'popular organizations'. This is due to the pressure of non-Ba'th elements, especially the communists, and to the fact that the workers are closer to the problems of nationalization and the public sector.

Organized workers–as a result of the social and economic controversies of the years 1960 to 1965, the 1965 nationalizations, the continuous development of the public sector, and Ba'th indoctrination–are developing a class consciousness which has already isolated the political Right within the labour movement. Their developing consciousness, however, is continually being diluted: on the one hand, by the steady influx of workers from the countryside and, on the other, by the practice in public-sector firms of hiring (for political reasons) unnecessary workers. Overstaffing in many factories not only aggravates budget problems but also provokes dissension among workers, and lowers their morale and discipline. Overstaffing, combined with the regime's paternalist attitude to workers in the public sector, leads many workers to consider public ownership a failure. Some are convinced that the old capitalist owner has been replaced by a not less unproductive and authoritarian Ba'thist director. Among such workers, Muslim Brotherhood and bourgeois propaganda finds an audience. Yet a dynamic minority of politicized workers has at times of crisis been able to mobilize almost the entire labour movement in defence of the neo-Ba'th's left orientation–as during the 1965 nationalizations, the February 1966 *coup*, the May 1967 troubles, and the June 1967 war.

Restrictions on trade union freedoms and the appointment of trade union leaders by the government provoked great disaffection among workers. Under pressure of rising discontent, the government scrapped the January 1964 labour law which had permitted the Ba'th to name its own appointees to many union posts. Law 84 of 1968 restored the electoral principle at every level. It also emphasized the trade unions' function in developing production and assigned the labour committee in each factory a responsibility for implementing the factory's production plan.

The Ba'th goal of 'workers' self-management' in the nationalized factories, announced in 1964, has not been realized. A 1964 decree provided for management by a seven-man board of directors, four of whose members were to be chosen by the factory's Workers' Council. During a 'transitional period', however, the government was to appoint all directors. In 1965, the concept of 'workers' self-management' gave way to one of 'democratic administration' to be reached by stages. Not until 1970 did workers and employees gain the right to elect three of their number to the factory's nine-man board of directors. Workers still complained, however, that in practice the managing director remained all-powerful.

The principle of allotting a share of company profits to workers – introduced in Syria by the Nasser regime, but originally proposed in the Ba'th's 1947 platform–has not in general worked satisfactorily, at least from the worker's point of view. Some workers benefited, but many did not. The system made for great inequalities. Workers' dissatisfaction increased when, after nationalization, profits in most of the firms affected declined. Some nationalized firms did not pay out profits for several years. Among workers in the public industrial sector the most popular measure taken by the neo-Ba'th regime was its replacement of the profit share by family allowances in 1970. Family allowances–£S15 a month for a non-working wife and each child under eighteen–in some cases doubled the worker's take-home pay.

Law 91 of 1959 still governs labour and labour relations, although its modification was under study in 1971. Syria's first social security law, Law 92 of 1959, also remains on the books and is still only partially implemented. Under Law 92, industrial workers benefit from work-accident, old-age and disability, and death insurance. The necessary studies to put into effect its provisions for unemployment and health insurance have barely begun.

In 1969, the 165 unions of the General Federation claimed 145,337 members out of a total industrial labour force of nearly 300,000. The public sector, comprising most of modern industry, was almost one hundred per cent organized. Decree 250 of 1970 launched a first effort to organize artisans and craftsmen in the private sector into professional groupings in a structure similar to the General Federation's.

The General Federation devotes much effort to the problem of increasing production and productivity, since productivity is still very low and costs remain high. Many literacy, training, and technical courses are provided by the federation in co-operation with the Ministry of Industry and the United Nations. The General Federation has introduced productivity competitions, the prizes usually being the chance to join training courses in Syria or abroad. Since 1963 it has published a weekly newspaper, *Kifah Al-Ummal Al-Ishtiraki* (The Workers' Socialist Struggle), and has regular radio and television programmes three days weekly.

General Union of Students and the Revolutionary Youth Organization

The General Union of Students, although Ba'thist, has had its ups and downs with both the Ba'th and neo-Ba'th party leaderships. Soon after the Ba'th's seizure of power, the union's adoption of the leftist line of Hamoud Shufi provoked reprisals from the traditional

Ba'th leadership. After Shufi quit the party, the Students' Union became associated with the emerging neo-Ba'th trend. Yet, when the neo-Ba'th took power, it arrested certain Students' Union leaders. Eventually, however, the neo-Ba'th recognized the General Union of Students and offered it financial support. The union serves an important function in forming new cadres for the party and the regime.

The Revolutionary Youth Organization, started in 1968, has a mandate to organize youth between the ages of fourteen and twenty-seven in all sectors, including students. The question of the respective jurisdictions of the Revolutionary Youth and the Students' Union among students has yet to be sorted out.

'PEOPLE'S DEMOCRACY'

The popular organizations were intended to provide the base of a modern political infrastructure. In these institutions, ideally, the citizen would learn to overcome his particularist reflexes and so help create a modern and politically cohesive society. However, after the fall of the Jadid regime in November 1970, these organizations were revealed to have been run for the most part by Ba'th cliques playing clan and family favourites.

'People's sovereignty' is to be exercised through the popular organizations and the people's councils. The councils–to be established at every administrative level from the village up through the Governate–would culminate in a People's Council for the whole country. Candidates for the councils must be members of the popular organizations or professional associations; 60 per cent of the seats are reserved for workers, peasants, and small wage-earners. The councils are to deal not with politics, but only with day-to-day economic, social, and cultural affairs. The 1968 draft law on local administration made the councils subservient to the Ba'th's Regional Command. All stages of the structure were to have been put in place by the end of 1970.

Although this timetable was not met, a new Provisional Constitution was adopted on 1 May 1969, the seventh since independence. The new constitution made the Ba'th Party 'the leader of society and the state'; it divided the people between the Ba'th and its organizations, on the one hand, and the rest of the citizens on the other, with only the former involved in 'people's sovereignty'. Liberty is conditioned on 'social and economic liberation and the reunification of the Arab people'. Although most of its articles were copied from earlier constitutions, the 1969 Constitution omitted all reference to freedom of assembly and association; it recognized the right of the citizen to express his opinion within the limits of the law (the martial law then in force). Denial of the right to hold public meetings and to publish meant denial of the possibility of criticism and free discussion.

THE ARMY

By training and upbringing the Syrian army is a traditional and classical army constructed on the French pattern and influenced by Soviet military doctrine. The Palestine defeat of 1948 catapulted this then nascent army into political life. The permanent presence of a militarily superior enemy on Syria's south-west frontier determined the army's development both quantitatively and qualitatively, and its role in Syria's life and politics.

In a society with a great variety of social formations, a plurality of political parties, and social movements of a modern but relatively long history, the army has become both the arbiter of–and the instrument for containing–political and economic conflicts. In the past decade it has been used to settle a double conflict: first, between the city big bourgeoisie allied to the big landowners and the lower strata of the bourgeoisie pretending to speak in the name of popular movements; and secondly, the conflict within the lower strata of the bourgeoisie over the orientation to adopt. The fact that the army's officers, high and low, as well as its ranks, are largely of rural origin, predominantly middle peasants, determined the direction in which these conflicts were settled and the emergence of the rural and some-what more radical *petit bourgeoisie* in the most favourable position to rule.

The army's roots in the countryside–still disadvantaged relative to the city–preserve its sense of social mission. Yet the Ba'th claim to have created an 'indoctrinated' army (*Jaysh Al-Aqa'iidi*) is true only in the very limited sense that officers committed to Ba'th or similar ideologies established domination over the armed forces. The party's tenth Emergency National Congress in November 1970 itself admitted that there had been no 'party life' in the army for two years and that 'army loyalty to the Revolution is still practised [only] through the higher leadership and the higher ranks'.[3] Moreover, what is most characteristic of the politicized army is the complexity and rapidity with which factions appear and disappear within it, the frequency with which subjective considerations accentuate, weaken, or belie political or ideological convictions.

In giving priority to its political vocation, the army sacrificed its military vocation. Political purges, begun by Nasser in 1958 and continued periodically until 1970, eliminated, in turn, communists, Houranists, separatists of all shades, Hariri's followers, Nasserists, city

Sunnis, old-line Ba'thists, and so on. In these purges many outstanding professional officers and aviators were retired; secondary- and primary-school teachers of Ba'thist loyalties were integrated into the army to take their place.

Political purges, moreover, have contributed to the creation of a privileged social stratum with a military vocation. In order to neutralize retired officers politically President Nasser raised indemnities and pensions. Since that time, the custom has been to move the officer up a grade on retirement or dismissal, grant him a pension equal to his new rank, and allow him the privileges of an active officer. Retired officers attend the university, enter new professions, start new businesses – all while continuing to receive their pensions.

Officers have also gained many privileges. They receive higher salaries than individuals of comparable civilian status. A sub-lieutenant when he leaves the Military Academy earns as much as a secondary-school professor with five years of higher study and almost as much as a university professor at the beginning of his career. Officers also get free medical care and generous travelling allowances. Army co-operatives provide them with every conceivable article at cost price as well as duty-free foreign imports not available to the rest of the population. Interest-free loans enable them to buy houses and villas. Sometimes houses or apartments are confiscated for them under one pretext or another. Every city has its officers' club, invariably the best in town.

Careers involving social prestige and good salaries are opened to officers on a wide scale. Some move into the diplomatic service. Since 1963, many officers and ex-officers have been attached to government ministries and departments and to state economic enterprises. These posts sometimes offer additional opportunities in the form of trafficking in influence and bribes. Instances of flagrant corruption are occasionally exposed. Some officers complete their climb up the social ladder by marrying into the old aristocracy.

The army has thus become a means of social promotion. But it is not alone in being privileged. With extensive nationalizations and the expansion of the public sector, the cadres of the Ba'th Party also gained privileges. At the lowest level, they have the possibility to find work; at the higher levels they win positions of command and much money. Effective political power is exercised by this privileged stratum, military and civilian, on behalf first of all of the classes from which it comes.

TRANSCENDING PARTICULARISMS

The domination achieved in the army originally by Alawis and

Druzes together, and later by Alawis alone, stirred charges of sectarianism. This question was also sharply felt in the civil service where, since 1963, rural emigrants, many from minority sects, often replaced Sunni functionaries and employees. Urban businessmen whose properties were nationalized were also predominantly Sunnis. Sunnis, naturally, did not welcome curtailment, and even appropriation, of their traditional advantages by rurals and members of minority sects. Some, especially the Muslim Brotherhood, complained of sectarianism.

Sectarianism in Syria is not new. Always before it has worked to the advantage of the Sunni majority. What is now occurring is the entry of the religious minorities into the mainstream of Syrian life. This process is an essential step in the disappearance of sectarianism. The very fact that a non-Sunni became President of the Republic in 1971 is a significant advance. The assimilative process, however, has been the product less of a rational programme to integrate the minorities and develop backward rural areas than of individual initiatives and spontaneous reflexes, which often took the form of helping kinsfolk or pushing clan and sectarian interests. For, if Ba'th ideology has consistently rejected sectarianism, it has not always restructured the personality and orientation of its adherents sufficiently to free them of parochial loyalties and to enable them to apply its principles objectively to immediate social issues. The result is a kind of divorce between the political ideas taught and adopted and their transference in practice to the social milieu.

This contradiction has also appeared on the question of racism, but now seems to be on the way to resolution. Although the Syrian Ba'th from the beginning aligned itself with all forces in the world fighting against racism, its policies towards the Kurdish minority provoked accusations of racial persecution. When the Ba'th took power in 1963, a campaign to 'save the Jazira' from an alleged Kurdish plan to create there 'a second Israel' was already under way. A special census carried out in the Jazira in November 1962 had declared a large number of Kurds to be 'foreigners',[4] although they were in possession of Syrian identity cards. The Ba'th government expelled many of these Kurds from the area along the Turkish frontier and stripped thousands of their Syrian nationality. Moreover, it refused to apply the land reform in areas where its application would have given land to Kurdish peasants. At the same time it joined the Iraqi Ba'th's war against the Kurds. The Syrian Ba'th and neo-Ba'th governments were alone in the Arab world in opposing the cease-fires the Iraqi government concluded with the Kurds in 1964 and again in 1966.

After 1967, however, the Syrian government's pressures on the

Kurds began to ease. In 1971, a definite turn became apparent. The Syrian Ba'th's eleventh National Congress in August discussed the Kurdish problem in Iraq 'from a socialist and revolutionary' point of view. It now adopted a position similar to that taken by the Iraqi government in its March 1970 declaration, which was accepted by Kurdish leader Mulla Mustafa Barzani. The congress acknowledged that the Kurdish and Arab peoples have equal rights and that the Kurds have a right to their own nationality, although not to separation. At the end of 1971, the government for the first time distributed land-reform land to Kurdish peasants in the Jazira.

Both the Ba'th and the neo-Ba'th consistently advocated secularist principles. Neither, however, carried these principles very far. When threatened by the religious establishment, the party did not hesitate to use military force to break religion's material power (Hama 1964; troubles of spring 1967). Yet it then conceded the point to the fundamentalists—in 1967, for example, by blaming the CIA for publication of an article calling for adoption of socialist and humanist values. Even the neo-Ba'th was always careful not to challenge Islamic authority. In contrast to Tunisia which discourages observance of the month-long fast of Ramadan and requires normal hours of work during this month, the 'socialist' neo-Ba'th promotes observance of the fast and reduces government working hours for its duration from the normal six to four.

The Jadid-Z'ayyen regime did on occasion endeavour to encourage secularist attitudes. Its leaders began their public addresses simply with 'Comrades' rather than 'in the name of God'; unlike the practice in Egypt they did not open meetings with readings from the Koran. The 1969 Constitution took a few tentative steps towards secularism. The former requirement that the President of the Republic must be a Muslim was omitted. Islamic legislation remained 'the principal source' of Syrian legislation, as in earlier constitutions. But the oath taken by government officials was changed from 'I swear by All-Mighty God' to 'I swear by my honour and beliefs'. The Ba'th's reaction to the burning of the Al Aqsa Mosque in Jerusalem, as expressed in the government organ, *Al Thawra*, discouraged religious fanaticism:

Al Aqsa Mosque is not more holy than the sand of Sinai or the smallest stone of the Golan Heights, the West Bank and Palestine ... The destruction of the most humble hut should excite the indignation of mankind as much as that of the Mosque.

When General Hafez Assad came to power in November 1970, he revised the 1969 Constitution to restore the original form of oath.

Although himself an Alawi, Assad made a number of gestures towards Sunni religiosity. On the other hand, his government stubbornly defended secularism when it joined Egypt and Libya in drafting a constitution for the Federation of Arab Republics. Syria succeeded in defeating Egyptian and Libyan demands that Islam be made the state religion of the federation. The FAR's constitution is close to earlier Syrian constitutions in making Islamic legislation 'the source' of legislation. Syria did agree, however, to the federation's adoption of an educational policy aiming to create 'a believing generation'.

Neo-Ba'th endeavours to improve the wellbeing and educational standards of the people have been far from negligible. Yet the party's socialist and modernist convictions have yet to make a significant impact on traditional social relations and values which remain the formative elements of society and conditioned its backwardness in the first place. This may be explained by the fact that the neo-Ba'th revolution remained a revolution imposed from above. Its stern paternalism denied the people the right to participate in political processes and political struggle. This meant not mobilization of the human potential, but demobilization and depoliticization, hence the inability to release the popular initiatives and energies essential for social change. This was indirectly admitted when the Jadid regime was ousted in November 1970 and General Assad promised a more democratic regime.

[1] Information supplied by the Ministry of Education, 1971. Figures in this section come directly from government ministries or from annual SAR: *Statistical Abstracts* and UNESCO Annuals.
[2] Demographic Centre of Cairo: 'Report to the Arab Cultural Congress', *L'Orient*, 14 December 1970.
[3] See Proceedings of the Congress published in *Al-Rayah* (Beirut), 5 July 1971, 352/24.
[4] On the grounds that they or their parents had arrived from Turkey as refugees during the Mandate.

Chapter 13

Crossroads

THE JUNE 1967 DÉBÂCLE opened a rift between the political and military leadership of the Ba'th Party. Superficially, the conflict appeared to be a personal power-struggle between two Alawi generals, Hafez Assad and Salah Jadid. General Assad, leader of the military wing, served as Minister of Defence and Commander of the Air Force, although his simultaneous tenure of these posts violated party statutes. Retaining his military rank but no longer holding an army post, General Jadid dominated the party apparatus as its Assistant Secretary-General and directed its political wing.

The conflict has also been interpreted as the expression of a permanent opposition and rivalry between military and civilians. Yet the concept of a military-civilian duel does not adequately explain the internal crisis inherent in the neo-Ba'thist regime since 1967. It is better to speak of a continuously changing pattern of conflicts, in which two camps have confronted each other, with in each camp both civilians and officers. (This, irrespective of the relative weight the military have in face of their civilian allies and even of the decisive part played by military elements in the trials of strength engaged.)

Before June 1967, the political and military leaders of the neo-Ba'thist regime of 23 February 1966 seem to have shared the same attitudes on the Palestine-Israel issue as well as on the question of the regime's relations with the people in general and with the non-Ba'thist Left in particular. Both military and political people supported Fatah's guerrilla movement inside Israel in the belief that the time had come for decisive battle. (A few days before 5 June 1967, General Assad's partisan Colonel Mustafa Tlas appeared before some 3,000 people, mainly intellectuals and students, in Homs to announce the moment opportune to challenge Israel, which, he added, was not willing to fight.) In domestic politics, the regime was almost unanimously for a limited co-operation with the communists, while violently opposed to the recognition of any of the non-Ba'thist left parties in the country. The political and the military leaders shared a common paternalistic, if not authoritarian, approach to the people. They were as one in refusing to permit the development of any autonomous popular movement for fear of losing control of the situation.

The Israeli attack of June 1967, resulting in the occupation of the Golan, drove the Army Command towards new and distinctive attitudes. For, if the Ba'th regime was held responsible for the loss of the Golan and accused of putting its selfish interests before those of the nation, it was the army, more specifically, which was the object of the most bitter attacks from the people and from both the right and the left opposition. The most cynical claimed that the army had become no more than a party gendarmerie.

The fact that Israeli troops controlled the southern approaches to Damascus determined the Army Command to re-examine its policies. Mutual recriminations between the high commanders of the army and the political leaders over responsibility for the defeat developed into basic differences concerning the line to be pursued. General Assad accused the political leadership of having ruined the army by political purges. The political leadership attributed the 1967 defeat in large part to the exclusively classical and traditional character of Arab military action.

Divergent policies soon emerged. The Army Command demanded absolute priority for military rearmament at the expense of economic development projects and rejected all party interference in military affairs. Above all, it insisted on the primary role of the army in the confrontation with Israel. This meant army control of the party's para-military organizations and, at the least, an army veto over the activities of the Palestine commandos in order to diminish the risk of provoking Israeli retaliation. In line with its exclusive belief in a classical war, the Army Command proposed an Arab policy that would permit creation of a real Eastern Front (Syria, Jordan, Iraq), based on concrete co-ordination with Egypt. This required a modification in the style of political action in Syria.

The political leadership–General Jadid and Premier Z'ayyen supported by Head of State Nur Al-Din Atasi–dismissed as false the army-posed dilemma of a choice between military strength and economic development, holding both to be essential: 'Only by economic development can there be any preparation for liberation of our territory'. (General Assad later modified his position on this question in favour of adoption of a war economy geared to both economic development and military strength. But Mustafa Tlas, who became chief-of-staff and a general early in 1968, maintained the demand for absolute priority for military needs.)

The political leaders continued to believe in popular war, especially in the developing Palestine resistance movement. They established the party's own Palestinian commando organization, *Al-Saiqa*, continued to give assistance to Fatah and to proclaim liberty of action for the Palestinians. They also tried to assert party authority over the army,[1] insisting that the army's 'political purity' be maintained. Rejecting co-operation with 'reactionary' states like Jordan, the political leaders called for class struggle throughout the Arab world. (Like some of the Palestinians, they at times entertained hopes of bringing down the Hashemi government.)

When Egypt accepted the Security Council resolution of November 1967, that is the 'peaceful solution', the divergences between Syrian and Egyptian policies were accentuated, and Syria's isolation deepened. Egypt's decision gave the Syrian Army Command every interest to follow suit, since in a traditional war the Syrian army obviously could not stand alone against Israel, much less regain the Golan. The political leaders feared precisely that General Assad's policy would lead step by step to 'surrender solutions' and abandonment of the Palestine cause.

In their stand against capitulation and in their determination to sustain the Palestinians, the political leaders accurately translated the sentiments and will of the Syrian people. Yet the authoritarian nature of the regime made impossible the social transformations and the mobilization of popular energies indispensable to a popular war. It was, after all, the political leaders, Z'ayyen and Atasi, who during the June 1967 war rejected the pleas of their communist allies and others to arm the people and resist.

The fundamental question from the army's point of view was then this: should the party apparatus—revolutionary in its political literature and sincere in its support of the Palestinians, but incapable of creating the new conditions essential for popular mobilization—oblige the army to accept a strategy that military conditions, now much worse than before June 1967, could not justify? General Assad's answer was never in doubt. But he needed more than three years to impose his policy step by step.

The orthodox Ba'th's seizure of power in Baghdad in July 1968 aggravated dissensions. The arrival in Baghdad, soon after, of former Syrian President Amine Al-Hafez convinced the Syrian regime that the new Baghdad government was conspiring against it. Therefore General Assad's proposal that an attempt be made to compose the neo-Ba'th's differences with the old Ba'th seemed the more outrageous to the political leaders. This proposal (apparently a tactical move on General Assad's part) appeared to them to be an attempt to return to the situation before 23 February 1966, that is to deny the very basis of the neo-Ba'th.

Assad's proposal was part of a broader programme devised to move the regime out of its isolation at home and abroad and to strengthen the army. This programme involved Syria's adoption of a more moderate line on the Arab and international levels, and its participation in Arab summit conferences. On the home front, General Assad advocated enlargement of the regime's limited co-operation with the non-Ba'th Left by creation of a national Progressive Front, including not only the communists but also the Nasserists and other progressives then harshly repressed by the government. He proposed to reintegrate most, if not all, of the non-Ba'th officers purged from the army. (Since Assad's position in the party was weak and the Nasserists were to the right of the neo-Ba'th, the political leaders believed he was trying to bring in 'rightist elements' to strengthen his position.)

The party's fourth Regional Congress in September 1968 rejected Assad's programme. That Assad had taken an important step towards his goal, however, became apparent in the government reorganization that followed the congress. His principal enemies, Premier Z'ayyen and Foreign Minister Ibrahim Makhous, were dropped from the government, although both remained in the Regional Command. Head of State Nur Al-din Atasi, a supporter of the Jadid-Z'ayyen-Makhous tandem, became premier as well. Six officers named to the new government included three of Assad's immediate aides holding specially created portfolios as Deputy Defence Ministers. General Tlas became First Deputy Defence Minister. A slight opening towards non-Ba'th progressives appeared in the presence of six ministers vaguely identified with left or unionist trends.

The crisis within the party inhibited the adoption of any clear-cut policy. The party had become, in the words of one of its leaders, 'a body with two heads and two brains and so able only to march in place'. Already before the Fourth Congress, General Assad had taken the People's Army out of the party's control to bring it under the Military Command. He had also integrated into the army a number of politically purged officers, mainly pilots and technicians. After the Fourth Congress he put an end to party activity in the army. According to charges made later by the National Command,[2] he also ignored party decisions in making unauthorized contacts with Iraqi government leaders, interfered in party affairs, and arrested the entire leadership of the Latakia party branch after it decided to expel certain party members, apparently his followers.

GENERAL ASSAD'S FIRST COUP AND ITS CONSEQUENCES

On 25 February 1969, during an alert following Israeli air attacks on villages near Damascus, General Assad's tanks occupied strategic points in the capital. The general replaced the editors of the government and party dailies, *Al-Thawra* and *Al-Ba'th*, with his own men, took over the broadcasting station, and released a number of political prisoners, including Nasserist, Houranist, and former Ba'thist leaders of the Opposition Front.

The political leadership responded with a manifesto denouncing 'the army's revolt against the party'. It called on the Defence Minister to cancel these measures in order to permit an extraordinary Regional Congress to arbitrate in the conflict. Party cadres and all the popular organizations rallied to the political leadership's support. Demonstrations and local strikes against the army's interference in politics took place. Leaflets warning against 'surrender solutions' were widely distributed. The suicide of Colonel Abdel Kerim Jundi, head of the Security Services and one of the most powerful officers in the camp of the political leadership, shook the regime. Jundi, a Ba'th partisan since early youth, had long been deeply troubled by the conflict within the party. Whatever the reasons for his action, he acted when the army arrested some of his own lieutenants.

General Assad's *coup*, although technically achieved with the occupation of strategic points and troop concentrations in the capital, fell short of complete political realization. His weakness within the party, the presence of many Jadid supporters in the army, the intervention of Egypt and Algeria – these factors allowed a tactical (and temporary) compromise to be reached.

As a result, a curious situation was created in Syria. The Jadid clan controlled the regional Ba'th organization, hence nominally the government, as well as the party cadres and the popular organizations. Yet to assure the publication of its views it started a newspaper in Beirut, *Al-Rayah* (The Flag), since Military Intelligence maintained control over *Al-Ba'th*. Assad's essentially military clan applied strong pressures, constantly reinforcing its power.

The party's fourth Emergency Regional Congress met at the end of March under the shadow of the army; General Assad's views prevailed. The congress decided that new efforts should be made to establish an Eastern Command. Criticism of 'rightist' and 'agent' Arab regimes would be muted. Co-operation with other progressives in Syria would be invited. A provisional constitution would be adopted. Election of a new Regional Command gave representation to both factions. But a nine-man Politbureau composed of members from both the National and Regional Commands, including three non-Syrians, was created to act as the supreme authority in Syria. Jadid did not secure a place in the Politbureau; Assad, Tlas, and Atasi did.

A new government took office after the adoption of the Provisional

Constitution in May. It included, in addition to the communists, representatives of Sami Sufan's Socialist Unionist Movement, the Nasserist Arab Socialist Union, and the Arab Socialists (Houranists). The new government appeared to be the first step towards the more broadly-based regime advocated by General Assad.

General Assad also began to broaden his base in another direction. One of the greatest weaknesses of the Jadid regime was its isolation from the inhabitants of the cities, who constitute some 40 per cent of the total population. This, however, is not a mere question of numbers. Traditionally, urban life and preoccupations have always influenced Syrian politics and policies. Based militarily almost exclusively on rural-dwellers rejected by the city either because of their economic position or their religious-cultural affinities, the 23 February 1966 regime ignored city complaints. This neglect encouraged the lower strata of the urban bourgeoisie to turn to rightist, especially Muslim Brotherhood, and other anti-Ba'thist 'subversive' actions. As soon as the solid, essentially rural, basis of the army was undermined after 1967 by the conflict between the Jadid and Assad camps, the peasant affinity of the regime became its Achilles heel. The conflict gave the urban classes the chance to interfere to sharpen the differences between the two rural-based camps. By adopting a more understanding attitude to the problems of the city bourgeoisie, General Assad won its sympathy. His essentially more conservative programme of greater moderation at home and abroad, with its implied promise of easing the more irksome economic measures imposed by the regime, made the city bourgeoisie, big and small, his ally.

NEW POLICIES IN PRACTICE

General Assad's efforts to build the Eastern Front secured the stationing of 6,000 Iraqi troops in southern Syria; later he sent a few small artillery units to Jordan. The Eastern Command, set up under an Iraqi general headquartered in southern Syria, was placed under the overall authority of Egyptian General Mahmoud Fawzi. But it never became more than a paper construction, since none of its participants abandoned their mutual suspicions, and none took it seriously. (In summer 1970, the command was declared defunct, Iraqi troops withdrew from Syria and Syrian units from Jordan.)

Other policies proved more successful. Syria's more friendly attitudes towards other Arab regimes won it a small Kuwait development loan in what proved to be the beginning of a growing friendship. Previously hostile to the government of South Yemen because it derived from the (once Nasserist) Arab National Movement, Damascus now agreed to exchange ambassadors and offered Aden economic and technical aid. The PFLP's hijacking of a TWA airliner to Damascus late in August gave the government the opportunity to practise its more relaxed approaches. Passengers, including two Israelis, were treated with consideration; all, including two Israelis exchanged for thirteen Syrian prisoners, were released. The government invited investment of Arab capital, especially from oil-rich states, offering to guarantee private investment. Embarking on a campaign of tourist promotion, it lifted restrictions on American, British, and West German tourists. In October, Syria was elected to a two-year term on the Security Council.

The government also emphasized its commitment to the Palestine resistance movement, giving somewhat greater freedom of action to commando operations in the Golan. Serious clashes between the Lebanese army and Palestine commandos in the Lebanon in October 1969 brought Syrian support for the commandos. On 22 October, Syria, in an effort to compel Lebanon to halt its attacks, closed the Lebanese border. This action brought to a halt Lebanon's transit trade with the interior Arab countries, a factor of major importance in the Lebanese economy; it also deprived Syria itself of transit dues. This Syrian initiative may have assisted Cairo's mediation, which achieved a cease-fire in the Lebanese-Palestinian conflict in mid-November.

Syrian propaganda continued to proclaim the necessity of a popular war to liberate Palestine from Zionism and the Arab world from imperialism. Behind the scenes, however, even the political leaders began in 1969 to take a different tack. They said that, although they did not believe in an eventual political solution of the 1967 crisis, they would welcome such a solution, if it developed, and would eventually adhere to it. They told this to the Egyptians, among others.

A major reversal of earlier policy was Syria's decision to attend the Arab summit conference in Rabat in December 1969. In deference to strong opposition to this decision within the party, the government sent to the Summit, not the Head of State, but a low-level delegation led by the Interior Minister. The Syrian delegation did not find the opportunity to make a request for financial aid, the principal reason for its participation. The Summit's failure to concert Arab efforts against Israel had important consequences.

Arab mobilization efforts shifted to the 'front line' states – Egypt, Syria, Jordan, and Iraq, backed by the Sudan and Libya. A meeting of these states in Cairo in February 1970 coincided with a sudden activation of the Syrian front which had been dormant for the two and a half years since the war. Air battles and ground action erupted periodically on the Syrian front throughout the first half of 1970.

General Assad appeared to be trying to relieve pressures on Egypt, then under punishing attack. In May, Syrian tanks, planes, and artillery went into action against Israeli forces engaged in a large-scale assault on Palestinian guerrillas in the Arkoub area in southern Lebanon.

At the conclusion of the Rabat Summit, President Nasser met in Tripoli with General Numeiri and Colonel Mo'ammer Qadafi who had seized power in the Sudan and Libya respectively in pro-Nasserist *coups* in 1969. The three leaders concluded the Tripoli Charter, forming a 'revolutionary front' to co-operate in defence and foreign policy and economic development. President Nasser did not envisage union of the three states in any near future; he explicitly cautioned against precipitous union during a visit to Khartum in May.

Colonel Qadafi, however, pursued a vision of early and all-embracing Arab unity to rid the Arab nation of imperialism, Zionism, and communism. His peregrinations throughout the Arab world to promote this idea took him to Damascus in June. There, he appeared on Damascus Radio (controlled by Military Intelligence) to attack the Syrian regime's strategy of popular liberation war: 'for 100 million Arabs to fight a guerrilla war against two million Israelis is wrong . . . The confrontation must be between regular armies'. The Palestine commando movement, to which he assigned a secondary role, must rid itself of 'ideologies' and operate only according to a strategy laid down by Arab governments. Qadafi thus stood squarely behind the policies advocated by General Assad at a time when these questions were becoming urgent.

THE ROGERS 'PEACE' PROPOSALS

Early in June 1970, Egypt and Jordan responded positively to American Secretary of State Rogers's indication that a new American initiative 'to get negotiations started' was imminent. His proposals, presented on 25 June, apparently spoke of Israeli withdrawal from Sinai and the West Bank, but made no mention of the Golan Heights. For President Nasser, in reply, insisted that Syria's interests 'take precedence over Egypt's' and that Egypt would not make a separate peace at Syria's expense. With this reservation, he accepted the proposals on 23 July. A week later, Syria rejected them. On 7 August, a three-month cease-fire began on the Suez Canal and was later renewed.

Egypt's agreement to negotiations and their presumed imminence brought closer the moment of decision for the Syrian Army Command. Participation of a Syrian delegation—led by Army Chief-of-Staff Tlas—in a conference, held in Tripoli in August, to discuss questions relating to the American proposals suggested that Syria's rejection might not be as firm as claimed; it also inspired reports of a tacit understanding between Cairo and Damascus on this question. After this conference, the Syrian Army Command closed all branches of *Saiqa* outside Damascus. This move was aimed against the political leadership, of which the army considered *Saiqa* to be a tool.

THE JORDANIAN CIVIL WAR

Serious confrontations had taken place in February and again in June 1970 between King Husain and the Palestine resistance movement. For the king was determined to assert his control and remove the Palestinian obstacle to his efforts to reach a settlement with Israel. His weakened position as a result of the June fighting was one of the factors prompting the American peace initiative. The American proposals, in turn, reinforced the king's determination to crush the Palestinian commandos. The PFLP's hijacking of four commercial jet airplanes on 7 and 9 September gave the king the pretext to make a full-scale assault on the Palestinians, civilian as well as military. In a savage week-long civil war the Jordanian army's artillery and tank units spread death and devastation in Amman.

Syria alone came to the aid of the Palestinians. On 17 September, the day the king launched his offensive, the Syrian Regional Command, of which both Assad and Tlas were members, decided to intervene. The action was planned by the Regional Command in agreement with the leadership of PLA (Palestine Liberation Army), units of which were stationed in Syria. On the 20th, PLA tank units – assisted by the Syrian army and under the direction of General Assad from headquarters in Deraa near the Jordanian frontier – entered north Jordan. These units virtually destroyed Jordan's crack 40th Brigade. Many of its soldiers and some of its officers defected to the commandos. The Syrian-directed PLA intervention constituted the backbone of the Palestine resistance battle in the north. Moreover, it enabled the hard-pressed commandos to save far more of their effectives than they could otherwise have done.

From the beginning the intervention had a clearly defined geographical limit: it was to be confined to north Jordan. The Palestinian objective was to try to hold there a 'liberated zone'. A threat of American intervention, reinforced by menacing movements of American military forces in the area, induced General Assad to order withdrawal of the Syrian-directed units from Jordan. Since these units had no air cover, their losses during the withdrawal were relatively heavy. Although General Assad was reported to have opposed the entire intervention and therefore to have denied it air support, it is worth noting that he later called it 'a victory which raised the party's name higher and higher among the Arab masses'.[3]

The Syrian intervention provoked a storm of world denunciation. Pressures were applied not only by the Americans, seconded by the Israelis, but also by the Soviet ambassador and President Nasser. Palestinians, however, paid tribute to the neo-Ba'th regime as the only Arab government that had lived up to its words. At a popular level the prestige of the neo-Ba'th was enhanced, the more so because of the growing ambiguities apparent in the attitudes of other Arab governments towards the Palestine resistance movement. These governments took a 'neutral' position in the Jordanian civil war, putting both sides on the same footing. Their mediation halted the massacres, but only at the price of many new and severe restrictions on the Palestinians. Syria rejected the Cairo Agreement for settlement of the conflict, concluded under President Nasser's auspices, terming it a 'sell-out'.

GENERAL ASSAD'S SECOND COUP, 13 NOVEMBER 1970

President Nasser's death on 28 September contributed, indirectly, to General Assad's decision to end the duality of power in Syria. Egypt's new President, Anwar Sadat, did not share Nasser's caution about Arab union projects. Barely a month after Nasser's death, Egypt, Libya, and the Sudan announced their decision to conclude a union. For the Ba'th, always the spearhead of pan-Arab unity movements, Syria's participation in the union became an immediate issue. Since General Assad's views on major problems were in accord with those of the Tripoli Charter governments, his position was reinforced. Dr Atasi's resignation as premier and Head of State on 18 October reflected the sharpening internal crisis and led to the convocation of an Emergency National Congress of the party.

On the eve of the tenth Emergency National Congress (30 October –12 November), General Assad began to transfer officers loyal to the political leadership. The congress opened with his rejection of a plea to halt the army transfers for its duration. Congress proceedings reveal that Assad and Tlas were completely isolated. The main charges against the two military leaders were that they had created a 'duality of power' by violating party discipline, preventing the carrying-out of party decisions, even arresting party members, and censoring party mail. The most serious accusation was that General Assad sought to introduce a 'defeatist reactionary line'.

Congress decisions reaffirmed the party's revolutionary strategy and its rejection of 'surrender' solutions. A decree was announced removing Assad and Tlas from their posts in the government and the army. The prerogative to take this decision, however, belonged, not to the National Congress, but to the Regional Command. Assad at once ordered army units to occupy the offices of the party and the popular organizations, arrested a number of officers, and jailed the top political leaders. This action, he later explained,[4] was not a *coup d'état*, but 'a normal development in our party'. There was in fact no bloodshed. Army units were not much in evidence. Many congress members who fled to the Lebanon soon returned.

On the morrow of the *coup*, Colonel Qadafi arrived in Damascus to give the new master of Syria the backing of the nascent Tripoli Federation–Libya, Egypt, and the Sudan. This intervention came at a crucial moment when Assad was seeking acclaim from a largely apathetic public. Championed by the federation, he could count on the Nasserist current in Syria and a more favourable attitude from many party cadres. He announced that Syria would take its 'natural place' within the federation.

A veteran party member, General Assad did not want to cut his lines to the Ba'th, but he also intended to broaden his base. Accordingly he set up a Provisional Regional Ba'th Command as the nominal governing authority, while also calling for a 'national Progressive Front' embracing Nasserists and former Ba'thists as well as communists. The Communist Party, a consistent supporter of the political leadership in its conflict with the general, had at first condemned his *coup*; it switched sides when the general announced his Progressive Front programme. Assad also implemented the front concept in the army by gradually reintegrating many politically purged officers, including even most of the left Palestinians ousted by Nasser in 1958.

In his first policy statement after the *coup*, Assad made no mention of 'popular liberation war' or Security Council Resolution 242; otherwise he endorsed the main themes of the former regime. He attacked the American peace proposals as 'defeatist', the Iraqi government as 'rightist', and the Jordanian regime as one of 'lackey reaction'. He promised full support for the Palestine resistance and pledged friendly relations with the USSR. Syrian opinion, especially the convictions of the party bases, made any other line impossible.

NEW POLITICAL INSTITUTIONS

General Assad promised to establish 'popular democracy' through the Progressive Front and the People's Council. His government for the first time included non-Ba'th progressives as representatives of recognized political parties. These parties were, in addition to the

Ba'th and the Communist Party, the Nasserist Arab Socialist Union, the Socialist Unionist Movement of former Ba'thists, and the Arab Socialists. (The Arab Socialists called themselves Houranists because they wanted to profit from Akram Hourani's following in Syria. But Hourani, a political exile in Beirut, did not endorse the policy of co-operation with the regime adopted by his erstwhile followers.)

A People's Council came into being on 17 February 1971. The Ba'th's Provisional Regional Command appointed every one of its 173 members. The council did, however, at least include representatives of all the recognized parties and the popular organizations. During its two-year term it was to act as a kind of legislature and would draft a permanent constitution. The next council, Assad promised, would be elected. The council had no real authority. Its decisions remained without validity unless approved by the President of the Republic who could also dissolve it at will.

The council's first act was to endorse Assad's nomination for the Presidency. A referendum on 12 March made Assad President by a 99·2 per cent vote. He also became Commander-in-Chief of the Army. He established a presidential system with power concentrated in his own hands and those of a few key officers. Al-Thawra commented that formation of the People's Council and the election of the President had 'established democracy in its fullest sense'. Adoption of the long-delayed Local Administration Law permitted elections to be held early in 1972 for the People's Councils in the Governates.[5] These non-political councils are mainly supervisory.

A crucial question was the form to be taken by the Progressive Front. The federation governments (Egypt, Sudan, Libya) had agreed that the political structure of each member state should be modelled on that of Egypt. This required the dissolution of political parties and formation of a *parti unique*. General Assad himself announced that the front would follow this formula. The parties in the front, Nasserists excepted, had other ideas. Their insistence that the front should be formed on the basis of an alliance of political parties, and not their dissolution, carried the day. In this alliance the other parties agreed to accept 'the leadership of the Ba'th'.

Another critical question concerned the inclusion of the communists in the front. (Egypt, Libya, and the Sudan ban the Communist Party.) The question was dramatically posed in July 1971 when Egypt and Libya intervened to crush a pro-communist *coup* in the Sudan and General Numeiri executed many communists and pro-communists. Assad rejected a demand, made at this time by Colonel Qadafi, that he oust the Communist Party from the front and the government. To the Ba'th's eleventh National Congress held in August, the Regional Command, however, presented a draft resolution qualifying the executed Sudanese communists and pro-communists as 'Qasimites, regionalists and false progressives'. The congress rejected this resolution by a large majority. Instead, it adopted another resolution. This resolution upheld the national Progressive Front as the only workable formula of political action and demanded its extension to all Arab countries. The resolution thus directly challenged the policies of Egypt and Libya.

Negotiations on the terms of the Progressive Front continued from May 1971 to March 1972. The agreed charter confirmed Ba'th domination,[6] but at least gave the other parties a political function however limited. Assad's goal remains the dissolution of the front's parties in a *parti unique*. Owing to strong opposition to this idea, not only from the communists[7] but also from many Ba'thists, this 'next stage' did not yet appear imminent. Is the front to be a mere façade for authoritarian rule or an opening towards democratization? This basic issue has perhaps yet to be definitively settled. So far not much has changed.

LIBERALIZATION

Many of the measures enacted by Assad's regime were devised to assure city people that he understood their problems and had their interests at heart. Assad hoped not only to rally the urban middle and lower-middle classes behind his rule, but also to identify these classes with the construction effort. He eased travel restrictions, especially restrictions on travel to the Lebanon, decreed price reductions on many essential foodstuffs, and increased family allowances. A more or less general amnesty allowed many citizens to return to public life. Martial law was lifted. Arbitrary arrests were prohibited. The political police, if still present in strength, were not so much in evidence. Assad's decision to permit the entry of Lebanese newspapers not hostile to his regime was warmly welcomed by the city intelligentsia.

Restrictions on foreign trade were relaxed. Syrian importers were given the right to import foreign products on their own account and directly from exporters. Previously, Simex, the government trading corporation, had handled 75 per cent of foreign trade. Under the new measures every Syrian was allowed to import raw materials, industrial and agricultural equipment, and spare parts provided he paid for them with his own foreign currency held abroad. The private sector was also allowed to import luxury goods (cosmetics, watches, cameras, etc.) under similar terms. Free trade zones were set up in different parts of Syria to enhance private-sector trade.

In the hope of replenishing diminishing foreign exchange reserves, Assad offered inducements for emigrants to repatriate their capital.

He appealed to exiled businessmen to come home, promising them immunity from punishment for smuggling out their capital, special facilities, and attractive investment opportunities. He personally invited a number of former public figures to come back to contribute to the construction effort. To technically qualified young men who had left Syria to avoid military conscription, he promised immunity from punishment and alternative public service. (The three-year term of military service and the fact that the army could retain the conscript indefinitely, if it needed his services, however, still led many young men to try to get away.)

These measures evoked a cautious response. Syrian emigrants and other Arabs invested £S60 million ($13·5 million) in Syria during Assad's first year in power. And, if very few of the thousands of emigrant businessmen returned permanently to Syria, a good many came back for exploratory temporary visits. (The domains open to private investment were construction, transport, and tourism. Investment in industry required special authorization.)[8]

ARAB POLICY

Assad considered amelioration of relations with non-progressive Arab states to be necessary to realize a minimum of political and diplomatic co-operation in the confrontation with Israel. He therefore restored diplomatic relations with Morocco and Tunisia.[9] Relations with Jordan eased somewhat when Crown Prince Hassan paid an official visit to Damascus. Syrian-Lebanese relations entered a 'honeymoon era' with a big increase in trade and heavy purchases by Syrian visitors in the Lebanon. Assad's government cancelled the support given by the Jadid regime to an anti-feudalist peasant movement in Lebanon's Akkar plain.

The sharpest turn came in relations with Saudi Arabia. These had reached a near breaking-point following accidental rupture of Aramco's Tapline (trans-Syrian pipeline) in May 1970. The Jadid regime had then refused to permit its repair until the company agreed to resume negotiations over Syria's 1967 demands for higher oil-transit fees. Assad allowed the necessary repairs, won a substantial increase in oil royalties, and removed restrictions on Saudi trade and Saudi overflights. He also closed down Damascus Radio's *Voice of the Arabian Peninsula*, which under the Jadid regime had encouraged liberation movements in Saudi Arabia and throughout the peninsula. Assad also endorsed King Faisal's project for a federation of Gulf principalities, which the Jadid regime had opposed as an imperialist plot. The Syrian-Saudi *rapprochement* found its parallel in a new warmth in Saudi-Egyptian relations and in an agreement between

King Faisal and President Sadat to abandon the distinction between 'reactionary' and 'progressive' states, and adopt a common policy towards the Palestine resistance.

The distinction between 'reactionary' and 'progressive' regimes had been fundamental to the concept of Arab nationalism being developed by the neo-Ba'th. Assad's policy in actions, if not in words, went along with the cancellation of this distinction, a reversion to traditional Arab nationalism. He also gradually moved towards the 'common approach' to the Palestine resistance of Arab regimes which feared it as a threat to the *status quo*. On these questions the Assad regime continued to parade the slogans of the Jadid regime. Pressures from bases in the party and the army, as well as the Ba'th's preoccupation with its popularity among the Arab masses, assured continuation of these slogans. The fervour of official Syrian support for the Palestinians, however, appreciably declined.

Soon after assuming power, Assad carried out a sweeping purge of the Ba'th Palestinian commando organization, *Saiqa*, arrested its three most respected leaders, drastically reduced its numbers, and brought it under army control. General Assad considered *Saiqa* a tool of the political leadership, but there was a further reason for his action. During the September 1970 fighting in Jordan the bases of the various commando movements gained a new unity and began to pressure their leaders to make a united movement. *Saiqa* pushed this line in Syria, proposing closer links with Fatah. Those arrested were the leaders of this trend. For Assad would not tolerate a Palestinian movement independent of his control.

The change in Syrian policy became dramatically clear in June 1971 when King Husain set out to liquidate the now weakened Palestine resistance. On the eve of his new, and predicted, assault, the Assad government seized in Latakia harbour an Algerian shipment of arms destined for the commandos. To President Boumeddiene's urgent pleas to release the arms, conveyed to Damascus by special courier, the government paid no heed.

King Husain's military operations against the commandos in northern Jordan in July evoked from Syria passionate verbal denunciation but, in deeds, only a telephone call from Chief-of-Staff Tlas to his counterpart in Amman and dispatch of a Syrian delegation to Jordan to mediate. Rebuffed by Jordan, the delegation withdrew, having accomplished nothing.

Yet Syria did shelter commandos fleeing the massacres in Jordan. Commando organizations retained their Syrian bases, at least for the time being, though subjected to strict restrictions. In face of popular outrage over the massacres and strong pressures from the party and army ranks, the government could do no less. Moreover, the government itself was angered by the Jordanian rejection of its mediation efforts and by the massacres. Jordanian-Syrian hostility erupted in military clashes along the border in August. Syria then broke diplomatic relations with Jordan, closed the border, and barred its air-space to Jordanian planes. The border closure caused the Jordanian economy heavy losses; it also imposed sacrifices on Syria. At the same time, the Assad government associated itself with the Saudi-Egyptian effort to find a new basis for 'compromise' between the king and the Palestinians on terms that would subordinate the resistance movement to Arab governments.

Officially Syria still opposed the Security Council resolution and recognition of Israel's existence. Yet it seemed clear that the Assad regime had already decided to consider liberation of the territories occupied in 1967 as an immediate goal separated from the ultimate goal of the de-zionization (not de-judaization) of Palestine. In this Syria joined Egyptian and Soviet policy.

FEDERATION OF ARAB REPUBLICS

The central conception of Assad's Arab policy was his belief in the imperative of military and political co-ordination with Egypt. His decision to make Syria a part of the Federation of Arab Republics (FAR) responded to this imperative. Syrian co-ordination with Egypt had been urged on Syria by the USSR since the June 1967 defeat. A not less important motive for entering the FAR was the regime's desire to command the support of the fairly numerous but heterogeneous and badly organized Syrian Nasserists.

The FAR was proclaimed on 17 April 1971 by Presidents Assad and Sadat, and Colonel Qadafi, General Numeiri having postponed the Sudan's participation owing to powerful opposition at home. Syria's unhappy experience in the union with Egypt imposed a very loose frame on the new union. Each member state retained control of its internal affairs and direct command of its armed forces, maintained its own diplomatic service and seats in Arab and international bodies. Moreover, existing divergences in the attitudes and interests of the member states – especially between Syria and Libya – suggested that the constitutional provision for common foreign and defence policies and common teaching and information programmes may not be very meaningful.

The economies of the member states are in certain respects complementary: Libya possessing oil wealth; Egypt, manpower and technical cadres; the Sudan and Syria, natural resources and vast expanses of cultivable land. The integration of these economies will surely require a very long-term effort. Syria's trade with Libya,

Egypt, and the Sudan makes up less than 5 per cent of its total trade. Development of trade within the federation demands construction of an entire transport and communications network with auxiliary services. The FAR's very limited internal market must be expanded if industry is to develop. At the end of the 1960s, *per capita* income in Syria was only $210, in Egypt $170, in the Sudan $103, and in Libya, with a population of less than 2 million, $1,020.

The FAR, if the Sudan is included, brings together 57 million people, more than half the total population of the Arab world, in an area a little more than half the size of China. Formation of the FAR, however, did not arouse the popular enthusiasm for which its sponsors had hoped. Plebiscites on 1 September 1971 automatically approved the federation by 96·4 per cent in Syria, 99·9 per cent in Egypt, and 98 per cent in Libya. (In Syria, 10 per cent of eligible voters abstained from voting.) The prevailing reaction was one of apathy. This could not be separated from the fact that none of the regimes involved had succeeded in resolving the crisis of the Israeli occupation. Nor could it be divorced from the hollow ring of the federation's affirmation of 'no compromise' on the Palestine cause when placed beside the policies of these governments towards the Palestine resistance and beside Egypt's agreement to sign a peace treaty with Israel. Many believed the FAR was created to facilitate acceptance of 'surrender solutions' by Arab governments, especially the Syrian government.

The bloody suppression of the pro-communist *coup* in the Sudan in July by Egypt and Libya provoked profound cynicism. The spectacle of Arab governments killing Arabs – massacres in Jordan followed closely by massacres in the Sudan – while doing nothing about the Israeli occupation deepened the growing alienation of the Arab peoples from their governments. Egyptian and Libyan intervention in the Sudan was made under a clause in the FAR Constitution providing for the FAR's intervention to crush internal troubles in any member state 'even if the government is not in a position to appeal for help'. To many, therefore, the FAR appeared not as a front of revolutionary Arab states, but as a holy alliance designed to preserve power and the *status quo* at any price.

During this crisis Syria's attitude was both contradictory and ambiguous. The government officially supported General Numeiri and sent its Vice-President to congratulate him on his return to power. On the other hand, the General Federation of Trade Unions denounced the anti-communist repression both at national and local levels. The General Federation's national leadership threatened to resign collectively if it was not allowed to send a message condemning the executions to the pro-communist Workers' Federation; in the end the message was sent. The trade union newspaper published an editorial in the same sense. All the Arab sections of the General Union of Students in Damascus issued a joint communiqué denouncing the executions. General Assad himself, whatever his real thoughts, told a delegation of the communist leadership that he did not support the anti-communist actions in the Sudan. And, as we have noted, the Ba'th's National Congress called for the extension of the national Progressive Front to all Arab countries.

These reactions suggested that Syrians are trying to overcome the political sterility engendered by successive authoritarian regimes. From the 1930s, and especially from the 1940s, Syria inherited a richly diversified political life. Nasser's attempts to domesticate Syria's political life and force it into a uniform mould did not succeed. Ba'th regimes made similar efforts; yet the Ba'th has been obliged to coexist in one way or another, however unequal the terms, first with the Communist Party and then with other forces of pressure. The social structure of Syria, the survival of its political traditions, and the multitude of its component regions and social groups make it impossible to expect an early disappearance of political groups or even stability within the Ba'th or the army. The national Progressive Front, if it could be made meaningful, might provide a formula for the realistic coexistence in democratic competition of the various social and political forces in Syria. But the enterprise is conditioned on the willingness of the regime to allow these forces real and concrete liberties of expression, organization, action, and – above all – criticism.

Democratization is, in fact, a pre-condition for the solution of the problems Syria faces. If agriculture is to be reorganized to sustain industrialization, the peasant must acquire a self-interest in his own future, become literate, and learn new techniques. Fulfilment of these tasks requires democratic conditions, as the failure of authoritarian regimes to achieve them has shown. Trade union democracy constitutes a double necessity – for satisfactory economic development, especially of the public sector, and for political stability. Syria has lost a high proportion of its human resources – intellectuals, technicians, scientists, professional people – owing, above all, to the exclusion of the intelligentsia from constructive work by enforcement of political conformism.

Since the 1967 defeat workers have become more active in trying to extend trade union and political liberties. A certain political animation has appeared among the peasantry. General Assad's efforts to broaden the base of his regime are significant in the sense that they responded to a political imperative. Yet the critical examination of hitherto sacrosanct political concepts – Arab unity, Arab socialism, etc.—inspired among the intelligentsia by the 1967 débâcle has been suffocated. Since 1969 continuing frustration and lack of freedom of criticism have reinforced the taboos around these questions. Syria's goal is officially still socialism. Here it stands at the very beginning of the road. The old ruling class of big capitalists and semi-feudalists has been swept away. Its place has been taken by advancing capitalist middle and lower-middle classes in city and countryside. These classes are omnipresent in agriculture, medium and small industry, and internal commerce. They control both the state apparatus and the army and dominate the ideological domain.

Yet the experiences of the past decade, and the Ba'th's socialist indoctrination itself, have created greater expectations, both economic and political, among the poorer classes than the gains these classes have won. In this way the ground has been laid for more radical changes. Thus, the question is posed whether Syria will move forward along the difficult path of 'socialist transformation' or whether a renewed bourgeois development will issue from the state-building already achieved. The answer will, of course, be influenced by the social struggles that seem implicit in present contrasts. Pertinent also is the degree, if any, to which social and political forces find a way to face up to governmental power embodied in the institution of organized violence, itself the version of one social group.

Of all Arab states, Syria has been among the most deeply influenced by the creation and existence of Israel. The Palestine defeat of 1948 put the army on the road to its dominating role in Syrian life and politics. Whether it likes it or not, Syria's evolution remains a function of continuing Israeli pressure and the permanence of the Palestine tragedy. Since 1967 the Palestine tragedy has become more than ever central to Syrian politics. The cruel imbalance resulting from the 1967 occupation put the Arab states, and especially Syria, in an impasse. The question of how to recover the occupied territories and how to resolve the Palestine question will inevitably dominate Syria's future and exert powerful pressure on the *status quo*.

---

[1] Soon after the ninth National Congress in September 1967, the party apparently tried to remove Assad from the Defence Ministry, but he refused. See Atasi's statement to the tenth Emergency National Congress, *Al-Rayah*, Beirut (352/24), 3 July 1971.
[2] See Proceedings of the tenth Emergency National Congress held in Damascus, 30 October to 12 November 1970, published in *Al-Rayah* (Beirut), 24 May 1971 (346/18–19 July 1971 (354/26)). Publication of the text of the proceedings was broken off after an armed attack on those responsible for the paper, members of the ousted Jadid faction of the party.
[3] During the party's tenth Emergency National Congress in November. *Rayah*, op. cit.
[4] *Jaysh Al-Sha'b* (The People's Army), 25 November 1970.

⁵ Roughly 50 per cent of those eligible were said to have voted. The political parties of the Progressive Front campaigned as a front since, although not yet officially constituted, the front had existed since early 1971. In general, front candidates won, but 'reactionaries' and 'religious elements' were reported victorious in some localities.

⁶ Of the front's 18-member Central Leadership, ten, including President Assad, its head, are Ba'thists, the other parties being represented by two members each. The President is the front's spokesman and must sign its resolutions. Ba'th congress resolutions are to provide the front's guidelines. Only the Ba'th is allowed to work politically in the army and among students. The Ba'th alone, moreover, continued to conduct all relations with the Arab Socialist Unions of Egypt and Libya and with foreign socialist and communist parties. The front, however, was promised a newspaper of its own. It will also have a role in the popular organizations.

⁷ By this time the Communist Party was torn by an internal conflict. One of the issues in the dispute between the two factions was the question of the degree and nature of the party's co-operation with the regime.

⁸ Later, the government set out to encourage development of a mixed sector. Minimum state participation in mixed-sector companies would be 40 per cent; the state would not interfere in the private sector's choice of directors in these firms.

⁹ Relations with Morocco had been broken in 1965 over the Moroccan government's implication in the murder of Moroccan opposition leader Mahdi Ben Barka. Tunisia severed relations with Syria in 1968 on the grounds that Syrian diplomats had been involved in a Ba'th plot to overthrow the Bourguiba regime.

Bibliography

Periodicals and Reports

Arab Report & Record, from 1967, London.
Arab World (daily digest of the Arab press), Beirut.
BBC *Summary of World Broadcasts*, Part IV, The Middle East and North Africa.
Cahiers de l'Orient Contemporaine (COC) 1946–69, Paris.
Étude mensuelle sur l'économie et les finances de la Syrie et des pays arabes (EFSPA) 1958-August 1966; *Étude mensuelle sur l'économie et les finances des pays arabes* (EFPA) September 1966–March 1971; *L'Économie des pays arabes*, from April 1971, Damascus and Beirut.
France Ministère des affaires étrangères: *Rapport à la Société des Nations sur la situation de la Syrie et du Liban*, annual 1924–38.
Middle Eastern Affairs, 1950–63, New York.
Middle East Economic Papers, from 1954, Beirut.
Middle East Forum, from 1916, Beirut.
Middle East Journal, from 1947, Washington.
Office Arabe de Presse et de Documentation (Damascus): *Syrie & Monde Arabe* (monthly). Earlier titles: *Étude mensuelle sur l'économie et les marches arabes* (1959–64): *Étude mensuelle sur la vie économique et financière de la RAU et des pays arabes* (1965): *Études économiques sur la Syrie et les pays arabes* (1966).
L'Agriculture syrienne, 1970.
Alimentation & Budget Alimentaire en RAS, 1970.
Le Commerce Interieur Syrien, 1971.
Les Cooperatives en RAS, 1968.
L'Industrie Syrienne 1969–1970, 1970.
La Planification économique & sociale en RAS 1960–1970.
Rapport sur l'économie Syrienne 1970–1971.
Socialist Transformations in the Financial and Banking Sectors, 1970.
Orient, 1957–68, Paris.
Proche-Orient études économiques, from 1967, Beirut.
Proceedings of the Permanent Mandates Commission of the League of Nations.
Syria, Ministry of Planning:
  The First Five Year Plan 1960–1965.

Second Annual Report on the Economic and Social Development Plan of Syria 1961–1962.

Implementation Report of the 4th stage of the Plan January–December 1964.

The Second Five Year Plan 1966–1970.

The Third Five Year Plan 1971–1975.

Ministry of Planning (1968 and after Central Bureau of Statistics):
Statistical Abstracts (annual).

Books

* Arabic

* Abbas, Abdel Hadi: *Al-Ard Wal-Islah Al-Zira'i Fi Suriyyah* (The Land Reform in Syria), Damascus, 1962.

* Abdel Kerim, Ahmed: *Adwa' Ala Tajribat Al-Widah* (Lights on the Unity Experience), Damascus, 1962.

Abouchdid, E. E.: *Thirty Years of Lebanon and Syria 1917–1947*, Beirut, 1948.

Abu Jaber, Kamel S.: *The Arab Ba'th Socialist Party, History, Ideology, and Organization*, Syracuse, N.Y., 1966.

Abu-Lughod, Ibrahim: *Arab Rediscovery of Europe, A Study in Cultural Encounters*, Princeton, N.J., 1963.

Ahmad, Djemal Pasha: *Memoirs of a Turkish Statesman 1913–1919*, London, 1922.

Amine, Mustafa: *Le Développement des partis politiques en Syrie entre 1936 et 1947*, unpublished thesis, University of Paris, 1950.

Andrea, C. J. E., General: *La Révolte druze et l'insurrection de Damas 1925–1926*, Paris, 1937.

Antonius, George: *The Arab Awakening*, London, 1938.

Asfour, Edmond Y.: *Syria: Development and Monetary Policy*, Cambridge, Mass., 1959.

Azmeh, Abdullah: *L'Évolution de la banque commerciale dans le cadre économique de la Syrie 1920–1957*, Lausanne, 1961.

Banque de Syrie et du Grand Liban: *15 Ans de Mandat*, Beirut, 1936.

Barbour, Neville: *Nisi Dominus*, Beirut, 1969 (Reprint).

Beauplan, Robert de: *Ou va la Syrie? le mandat sous les cedres*, Paris, 1929.

Be'eri, Eliezer: *Army Officers in Arab Politics and Society*, New York, 1970.

* Al-Bizri, Afif: *Al-Nasiriyah Fi Jomlat Al-Isti'mar Al-Hadith* (Nasserism A Part of the New Imperialism), Damascus, 1962.

Bonardi, Pierre: *L'Imbroglio syrien*, Paris, 1927.

Bottéro, Jean, Cassin, Elena, & Vercoutter, Jean: *The Near East, The Early Civilizations*, New York, 1967.

Bowering, John: *Report on the Commercial Statistics of Syria*, London, 1840.

Brice, William C.: *South-West Asia, A Systematic Regional Geography*, London, 1966.

Burns, Norman: *The Tariff of Syria 1919–1932*, Beirut, 1933.

Cahen, Claude: *Syrie au nord à l'époque des croisades et la principauté franque d'Antioche*, Paris, 1940.

Classicisme et déclin culturel dans l'histoire de l'Islam, Symposium Intl d'histoire de la civilisation musulman, Bordeaux, 1956, organisé par Brunschvig, R., et von Grunebaum, G. E., Paris, 1957.

Cook, M. A.: *Studies in the Economic History of the Middle East*, London, 1970.

Copeland, Miles: *The Game of Nations*, London, 1969.

Cuinet, V.: *Syrie, Liban et Palestine*, Paris, 1896.

David, Philippe: *Un Gouvernement Arabe à Damas, le congrès Syrien*, Paris, 1923.

Dubertret, L. & Weulersse, J.: *Manuel de géographie, Syrie, Liban et Proche Orient*, Beirut, 1940.

Dunand, Maurice: *De L'Ammanus au Sinai*, Beirut, 1953.

Dussaud, René: *Topographie Historique de la Syrie antique et médievale*, Paris, 1927.

— *La Pénétration des Arabes en Syrie avant l'Islam*, Paris, 1955.

FAO Mediterranean Development Project: *United Arab Republic (Syrian Region)* Country Report, Food and Agricultural Organization of the United Nations, Rome, 1959.

Faris, N. A. & Husayn, M. T.: *The Crescent in Crisis*, Lawrence, Kansas, 1955.

Fisher, W. B.: *The Middle East, A Physical, Social and Regional Geography*, London, 4th ed., 1961.

Fisher, S. N.: *The Middle East, A History*, New York, 1959.

Gibb, Sir Alexander & Partners: *The Economic Development of Syria*, London, 1947.

Gontaut-Biron: *Comment la France s'est installée en Syrie 1918–1919*, Paris, 1922.

Grant, Christina P.: *The Syrian Desert*, London, 1937.

Haddad, George: *Fifty Years of Modern Syria and Lebanon*, Beirut, 1950.

Al-Hafez, M. A.: *La Structure et la politique économique en Syrie et au Liban*, Beirut, 1953.

Halpern, Manfred: *The Politics of Social Change in the Middle East and North Africa*, Princeton, N.J., 1963.

— 'The Middle East and North Africa', in Black & Thornton: *Communism and Revolution*, Princeton, N.J., 1964.

* Haykal, Muhammad Hassaneen: *Ma Illadhi Jara Fi Suriyyah* (What Happened in Syria), Cairo, 1962.

Helbaoui, Yussef: *La Syrie mise en valeur d'un pays sous développé*, Paris, 1956.

Hilan, Rizkallah: *Culture et développement en Syrie et dans les pays retardés*, Paris, 1969.

Himadeh, S. B., ed.: *Economic Organization of Syria*, Beirut, 1936.

Hitti, Philip K.: *History of Syria*, London, 1951.

Hocking, W. E.: *The Spirit of World Politics with Special Studies of the Near East*, New York, 1932.

Hourani, Albert: *Arabic Thought in the Liberal Age 1798–1939*, London, 1962.

— *Syria and Lebanon*, London, 1946.

* Al-Husri, Sati: *Yawm Maysaloun* (Day of Maysaloun), Beirut, 1947.

International Bank for Reconstruction & Development: *The Economic Development of Syria*, Baltimore, 1955.

Issawi, Charles, ed.: *The Economic History of the Middle East 1800–1914*, Chicago, 1966.

* Jundi, Sami: *Al-Ba'th* (The Ba'th), Beirut, 1969.

* Kallas, Khalil: *Aradnaha Wihda Wa Araduha Mazra'a* (We Wanted Union, They Wanted a Plantation), Damascus, 1962.

* Kallas, Khalil, *et al*: *Suriyyah Al-Muhattima lil Isti'mar w'al-Diktaturiyya* (Syria Crusher of Imperialism and Dictatorship), Damascus, 1962.

Kerr, Malcolm: *The Arab Cold War 1958–1967*, London, 1967.

Khairallah, K. T.: *La Syrie*, Paris, 1912.

Khalil, Muhammad: *The Arab States and the Arab League, A Documentary Record*, 2 vols., Beirut, 1962.

Khouri, Fred J.: *The Arab Israeli Dilemma*, Syracuse, N.Y., 1968.

Kirk, George: *Contemporary Arab Politics*, New York, 1961.

Kodsy, Ahmad & Lobel, Eli: *The Arab World and Israel*, New York, 1970.

Lammens, H.: *La Syrie et sa mission historique*, Cairo, 1915.

— *La Syrie Précis Historique*, 2 vols., Beirut, 1921.

Lapidus, Ira: *Muslim Cities in the Late Middle Ages*, Cambridge, Mass., 1967.

Latron, A.: *La Vie rurale en Syrie et au Liban*, Beirut, 1936.

Lewis, Bernard: *The Arabs in History*, London, 1958.

— *The Assassins: A Radical Sect in Islam*, London, 1967.

Longrigg, S.N.: *Syria and Lebanon Under French Mandate*, London, 1958.

Love, Kennett: *Suez The Twice-Fought War*, New York, 1969.

MacCallum, E. P.: *The Nationalist Crusade in Syria*, New York, 1928.

* *Mahadir jalsat mubahathat al-wihda* (Minutes of the Unity Talks), Cairo, 1963.

Ma'oz, Moshe: *Ottoman Reform in Syria and Palestine 1840–1861*, London, 1968.

Marlowe, John: *Arab Nationalism and British Imperialism*, London, 1961.

La Mazière, Pierre: *Partant pour la Syrie*, Paris, 1926.

Mellaart, James: *Earliest Civilizations of the Near East*, London, 1965.

Memoirs of Muhammad Kurd 'Ali, A Selection, trans. by Khalil Totah, Washington D.C., 1954.

Moscati, Sabatino: *The Semites in Ancient History*, Cardiff, 1959.

Mundy, Angus: *The Arab Government in Syria from the Capture of Damascus to the Battle of Meisalun (30 September 1918–24 July 1920)*, unpublished AUB thesis, 1965.

Nevakivi, Jukka: *Britain, France and the Arab Middle East 1914–1920*, London, 1969.

Nicholson, R. A.: *A Literary History of the Arabs*, London, 1907.

Nishabi, Hisham: *The Political Parties in Syria 1918–1933*, unpublished AUB thesis, 1952.

O'Leary, De Lacey: *How Greek Science Passed to the Arabs*, London, 1948.

Orgels, Bernard: *Contribution à l'étude des problèmes agricoles de la Syrie*, Brussels, 1962.

Patai, Raphael, ed.: *The Republic of Syria*, Human Relations Area Files, Inc., New Haven, Conn., 2 vols., 1956.

Pearse, Richard: *Three Years in the Levant*, London, 1949.

Perrier, Ferdinand: *La Syrie sous le gouvernement de Méhémet Ali jusqu'en 1840*, Paris, 1842.

Poliak, A. N.: *Feudalism in Egypt, Syria, Palestine and the Lebanon 1250–1900*, London, 1939.

Polk, W. R. & Chambers, R. L.: *Beginnings of Modernization in the Middle East*, Chicago, 1968.

Porter, Rev. J. L.: *Five Years in Damascus*, 2 vols., London, 1855.

Poulleau, Alice: *Damas sous les bombes*, Paris, 1928.

Rabbath, E.: *Unité Syrienne et devenir Arabe*, Paris, 1937.

— *L'Évolution politique de la Syrie sous mandat*, Paris, 1928.

— *Les 'états-unis de Syrie'*, Aleppo, 1925.

* Al-Razzaz, Munif: *Al-Tajriba Al-Murra* (The Bitter Experience), Beirut, 1967.

Saab, Dr Hassan: *The Arab Federalists of the Ottoman Empire*, Amsterdam, 1958.

* Al-Safadi, Muta': *Al-Hizb Al-Ba'th* (The Ba'th Party), Beirut, 1964.

Saint-Point, V. de (pseud.): *La Vérité sur la Syrie*, Paris, 1929.

Sauvaget, Jean: *Esquisse d'une histoire de la ville de Damas*, Paris, 1935.

— *Alep: essai sur le développement d'une grande ville syrienne*, Paris, 1971.

Seale, Patrick: *The Struggle for Syria*, London, 1965.

* Al-Sebai, Badr: *Al-Iqtissad Al-Suriyyah 1850–1958* (Syrian Economy 1850–1958), Damascus, 1970.

Sharabi, Hisham: *Arab Intellectuals and the West: The Formative Years, 1875–1914*, Baltimore, 1970.
— *Nationalism and Revolution in the Arab World*, Princeton, 1966.
Smith, George Adam: *The Historical Geography of the Holy Land*, 4th ed., London, 1897.
Le Strange, Guy: *Palestine Under the Moslems 650–1500*, Beirut, 1965 (Reprint).
Stripling, G. W. F.: *Ottoman Turks and Arabs*, Chicago, 1942.
Thoumin, R.: *Histoire de Syrie*, Paris, 1929.
Tibawi, A. L.: *A Modern History of Syria*, London, 1969.
Torrey, Gordon H.: *Syrian Politics and the Military*, Columbus, Ohio, 1964.
Tower, James Allen: *The Oasis of Damascus*, Beirut, 1935.
U.S. Army: *Area Handbook for Syria*, Dept. of the Army Pamphlet, No. 550–49, July 1965, Washington D.C.
*Umran, Muhammad: *Tajribati Fil Thawra* (My Experience in the Revolution), Beirut, n.d.
Vernier, Bernard: *Armée et Politique au Moyen-Orient*, Paris, 1966.
Volney, G. F. C.: *Travels Through Syria and Egypt*, 2 vols., London, 1787.
Warriner, Doreen: *Land and Poverty in the Middle East*, London, 1948.
— *Land Reform and Development in the Middle East*, London, 1957.
Waters, Robert T.: *A Social-Political Analysis of Syria 1943–1958*, unpublished AUB thesis, 1962.
* *Watha'iq Mou'tamar Shoutura* (Documents of the Chtaura Conference), Syrian Government Publishing House, Damascus, 1962.
Wellhausen, J.: *The Arab Kingdom and Its Fall*, Beirut, 1963 (Reprint).
Weulersse, J.: *Paysans de Syrie et du Proche Orient*, Paris, 1946.
— *Les Pays des Alaouites*, 2 vols., Tours, 1940.
*Wissan, Dr Salah: *Al-Qita' Al-Zira'i: Min Al-Takhalluf ila al-Numu Al-Ishtiraki* (The Agricultural Sector: From Underdevelopment to Socialist Development), Damascus, 1967.
Yamak, Labib Zuwiyya: *The Syrian Social Nationalist Party*, Cambridge, Mass., 1966.
* Zahreddine, Abdel Kerim: *Mudhakkirat* (Memoirs), Beirut, 1968.
Zeine, Zeine N.: *The Struggle for Arab Independence*, Beirut, 1960.
— *Arab-Turkish Relations and the Emergence of Arab Nationalism*, Beirut, 1958.
Ziyadeh, N. A.: *Syria and Lebanon*, London, 1957.

Articles

?Al-Azm, Khalid: *Mudhakkirat* (Memoirs), excerpts published in *Al Nahar* (Beirut), 20 June–1 July 1972.

Ben-Tzur, Avraham: 'The Neo-Ba'th Party of Syria', *Journal of Contemporary History*, Vol. 3, No. 3, July 1968.

Cahen, Claude: 'Réflexions sur l'usage du mot de "Féodalité" ', *Journal of the Economic and Social History of the Orient*, III, 1960.

— 'IKTA', *Encyclopedia of Islam*, London, 1970.

Chevalier, François: 'Forces en présence dans la Syrie d'aujourd'hui', *Orient*, No. 4, 1957.

Colombe, Marcel: 'La nouvelle politique arabe de la République Arabe Unie', *Orient*, No. 11, 1959.

— 'La seconde RAU sera-t-elle proclamée?', *Orient*, No. 26, 1963.

— 'Remarques sur le Ba'th et les institutions de la Syrie d'aujourd'-hui', *Orient*, No. 37, 1966.

Dawn, Ernest C.: 'The Rise of Arabism in Syria', *MEJ*, 16/2, 1962.

Gotein, S. D.: 'The Rise of the Near Eastern Bourgeoisie in Early Islamic Times', *Journal of World History*, No. 3, 1956.

Jargy, Simon: 'Déclin d'un parti', *Orient*, No. 11, 1959.

— 'La Syrie province de la RAU', *Orient*, No. 8, 1958.

Rondot, Pierre: 'Quelques remarques sur le Ba'th', *Orient*, No. 31, 1964.

— 'Tendances particularistes et tendances unitaires en Syrie', *Orient*, No. 5, 1958.

Viennot, Jean-Pierre: 'Le Ba'th entre la théorie et la pratique', *Orient*, No. 30, 1964.

— 'Le Rôle du Ba'th dans la genèse du nationalisme arabe', *ibid.*, No. 35, 1965.

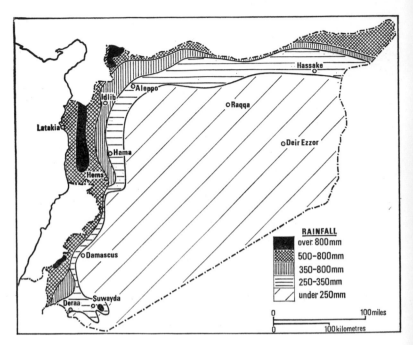

RAINFALL
over 800mm
500–800mm
350–800mm
250–350mm
under 250mm

0   100 miles

0   100 kilometres

Hassake
Aleppo
Idlib
Raqqa
Latakia
Hama
Deir Ezzor
Hems
Damascus
Suwayda
Deraa

1   Syria Rainfall

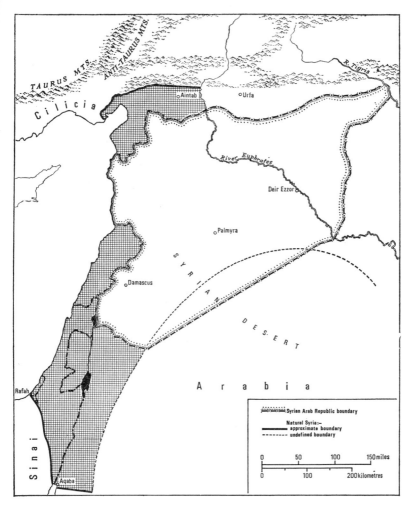

2 Natural Syria, an area which has never been precisely defined, stretched from the southern slopes of the Taurus mountains to the Sinai desert and from the Mediterranean to the Arabian and Syrian deserts. The Jazira, though not geographically part of natural Syria, was culturally Syrian and part of it was included in the Syrian administrative divisions of the Ottoman Empire in the nineteenth century

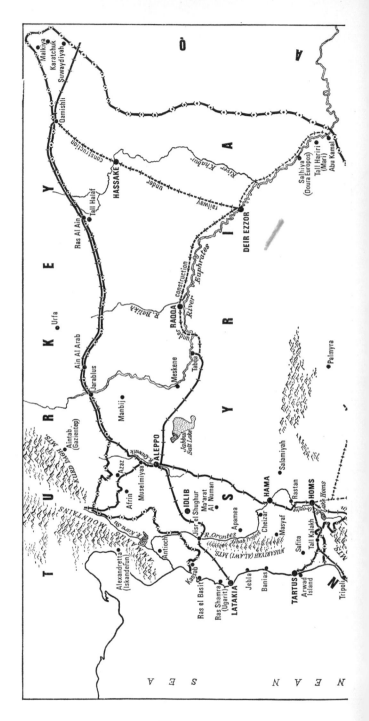

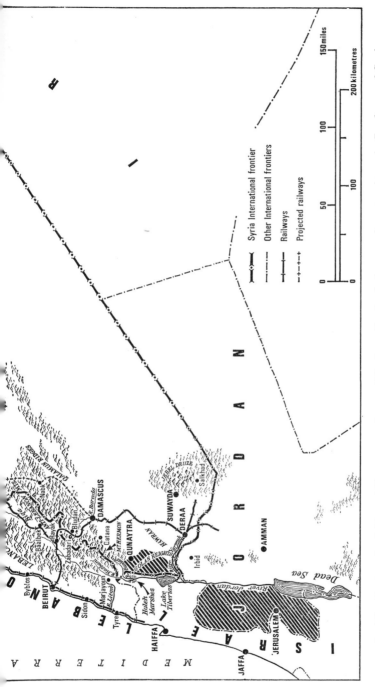

3 The Syrian Arab Republic—general map. The heavily shaded areas show territory in Jordan and Syria occupied by Israel since the June War of 1967

Syria International frontier
Other International frontiers
Railways
Projected railways

150 miles
100
50
0

200 kilometres
100
0

Index

Printed in Great Britain
by W & J Mackay Limited, Chatham

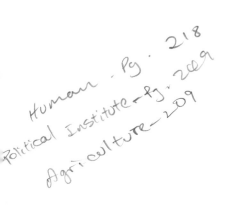

Human . Pg . 218
Political Institute — Pg . 209
Agriculture — 209